THE ILLUSTRATED DIRECTORY OF

American Cars

THE ILLUSTRATED DIRECTORY OF
American
Cars

ANDREW MONTGOMERY

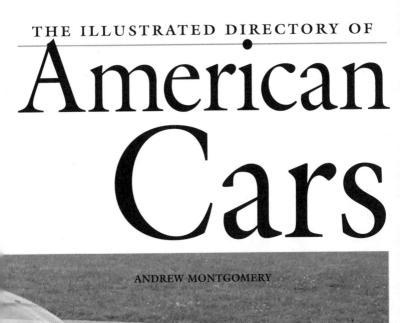

SALAMANDER

A SALAMANDER BOOK

Published by Salamander Books Ltd.
The Chrysalis Building
Bramley Road
London W10 6SP

© Salamander Books Ltd., 2003

An imprint of **Chrysalis** Books Group plc

ISBN 1-84065-534-8

CREDITS

Project Manager: Ray Bonds
Designers: Q2A Solutions
Reproduction: Anorax Imaging Ltd
Printed and bound in: Italy

CONTENTS

INTRODUCTION

The past is a foreign country;
they do things differently there.
L. P. Hartley (1895-1972)
The Go-Between

It's true. Even when we recognize the places or the faces in these pages, we know that we can never visit them or speak to them because they're then and we're now - like it or not. Some who read this book may remember, most may only imagine, what it was like to drive down a dirt road in a Model T Ford, pursued by a plume of dust and a troupe of laughing kids, or to emerge from the Met, in top hat, white tie and tails, to be whisked to a party at the Plaza in the back of a sixteen cylinder Duesenberg, or to put the pedal to the metal in a GTO and see the blacktop blur as the hood-mounted tacho hit the red zone. Remembered or imagined or merely dreamed about, American automobiles have woven themselves into the pattern of the nation's past more strongly and securely than those of any other country on Earth.

The United States is a big place. Unlike any other country, and with due respect to its indigenous peoples, the vast majority of its population is descended from adventurers: those who had set out from the Old World and crossed an ocean before setting out to traverse a continent and create a nation. If we accept the beginning of the twentieth century as coinciding with the birth of the automobile, it is worth noting that, whereas in Europe and the rest of the world, few people ever traveled more than a few miles from the place where they were born, most Americans had come a long way already. Maybe it would be stretching a point to suggest that the covered wagon was the father of the Cadillac or that the

Pontiac descends directly from the prairie schooner, but the spirit of the pioneer, the desire - the need - to know what's beyond the horizon has surely inspired those who have designed and built and driven and fallen in love with (if not actually in) America's automobiles.

Those who came to America abandoned the Old World not only geographically, but also socially and spiritually as well. The Spirit of '76 was an inspiration to the world and offered a promise of unimaginable freedom to millions. The world that they left behind was static: it was a world where physical mobility was as restricted as social mobility, where what mattered most was blood and borders and staying within the boundaries of both. In that world, the automobile, like the horse-drawn carriage, was, from the beginning, a symbol of rank and privilege; as with the carriage, the owner didn't drive it but was driven. After all, poor people had nowhere to go, did they? In the New World, however, all of the people were on the move, all of the time, and were as happy to be behind the wheel as they'd been to hold the reins. Even today, this division in attitude between America and Europe is discernible and certain European manufacturers still retain an aura of aristocracy. Not surprisingly, the concept of class-distinction by car is most noticeable in British marques. Names like Rolls Royce, Bentley, Aston-Martin and Daimler still conjure up images of ancestral castles and liveried chauffeurs, although each of these companies is now German or American owned!

To drive one of those cars without being, as Shakespeare (who else?) put it "to the manner born" is still regarded by many as like wearing an old school tie when you didn't go to the old school. To an American, this doesn't make a whole lot of sense because - it doesn't make a whole lot of sense. In America, if you can earn enough for an Eldorado, you have as much right as anybody to drive one. Let it ever be so.

Because automobiles are and have ever been accessible in the United States, their place in popular culture is unique. No other country has ever celebrated

Above: With their plated and polished engine bays, the magnificent, V16 Cadillacs of 1931 were as perfectly presented under the hood as they were to the envious, outside world.

cars in song as America has, from the Cadillacs, all shiny and new, to the T-Bird that Daddy took away and the Chevy that drove to the levy to... you can pick it up from here!

Andrew Montgomery
2002

THE EARLY YEARS

SPECIFICATIONS

SIMPLEX 1907

Engine:
Cast iron – 4 cylinders in line

Displacement:
598 cu. ins.

Bore and stroke:
5 3/4 x 5 3/4 ins.

Horsepower:
50

Body styles:
Various, from prestigious coachbuilders

No. of seats:
2-5

Weight (lbs):
c. 3,750 lbs

Price:
$4,500 for the chassis alone

Produced:

The oldest make of American auto still in production is easy to remember – it's the Oldsmobile. Ransom Eli Olds started experimenting with various kinds of self-propelled buggies in the late eighteen-eighties, in Lansing, Michigan, preferring steam power to begin with. In the mid eighteen-nineties he came up with a gasoline powered rig with a 5hp, single cylinder motor mounted under its buckboard body. Unlike many of his earlier experiments, it worked, and it sold. Olds was able to raise sufficient capital to set up the Olds Motor Vehicle Company but his initial efforts at volume production failed to produce any volume. At the turn of the century the company received a massive injection of capital and Olds went back to experimenting, this time with electrically powered cars. The fate of the embryo firm was finally fixed by fire. In 1901 the new Detroit factory burned down and the only automobile to be rescued from the flames was a gasoline-powered runabout. The company's survival depended entirely on the success of what came to be known as the curved dash Oldsmobile. Happily, it was a great car and a great success; by 1905 production exceeded five and a half thousand units, making it America's first "volume production" automobile and paving the way for an army of manufacturers to enter this burgeoning and potentially lucrative market.

Just how many took the plunge we will probably never know; for some it turned out to be a long, hot bath, for others it was a distinctly cold shower. In the years before World War I, there were, as now, plenty of people out to make a quick buck from new technology stocks and a lot of investors on hand to make or lose fortunes. Numerous auto companies raised millions of dollars in backing and never built a single car, while Henry Ford tested his first engine in his wife's kitchen. The roll call of freaks and flops and also-rans is very, very long. I suspect that some, especially some of those eye-catching eccentricities driven by springs or compressed air or farmyard manure, have been invented by the compilers and publishers of books

Above: *As suggested by its name, the Simplex was mechanically simple, but sold for a very grand price. This 50hp model was built in 1909 - the later 75hp car was even faster and more massive.*

like this just to check if someone else is plagiarizing their work. To the best of our knowledge and belief, all the automobiles listed, described and illustrated in the following pages actually existed and many of them exist today! Sadly, many didn't make it, so today we can't go out and buy a Biddle or a Carter or a Heseltine or any of the hundreds of pioneer marques that came, and went, before 1919. Even so, the fact that today we can drive safely and speedily, comfortably and economically is due to their efforts as much as to those of the survivors. The men who dreamed of fame and fortune built on the success of the Friction Drive contributed to the dynamism and vitality of the American automobile industry simply by providing their know-how at a time when nobody knew anything.

It's easy to smile at their efforts, but who knows what might have happened if Olds hadn't managed to pull his gasoline-engined prototype out of that fire? He might have ended up with no more than an insurance payoff and we might all be driving steamers. Stanleys and Dobles would be quietly cruising the highways, nobody would be worried about OPEC and Texas would have more room for raising beef. Would that be so bad?

As it is, America can't claim to have invented the automobile. The work of German engineers, from around the 1870s, produced the Otto four-stroke engine and the Daimler-Benz horseless carriages of the early 1880s. The effect that these developments had, on men like Henry Ford, Ransom Olds, John and Horace Dodge and David Buick, was phenomenal. Within a few years America had taken a European idea and created an industry out of it.

Among the illustrious names of the early days, that of Henry Leland is particularly worthy of mention and especially worthy of respect. Leland was born in 1843; at the outbreak of the civil war he was a passionate supporter of the Union cause but his Quaker principles prevented him from fighting. Instead, he volunteered for work in the Colt factory in Connecticut. Samuel Colt had pioneered techniques of precision engineering on an industrial scale, managing to work to tolerances of a thousandth of an inch on hand lathes. This allowed him to produce standardized parts, so that, in the event of failure or damage in away in the field,

SPECIFICATIONS

CADILLAC 1908

Engine:
Cast iron – 4 cylinders
in line

Displacement:
176.7 cu. ins.

Bore and stroke:
3 3/4 x 4 ins.

Horsepower:
22

Body styles:
Tourer; Coupe;
Runabout; Laundalet;
Town Car

No. of seats:
2-5

Weight (lbs)
c. 1,200 lbs

Price:
$850 - $1,000

Produced:
11,145

a replacement could be immediately fitted - and would fit! The advantage of this approach over traditional "bespoke" production techniques is obvious and the young Leland was quick to recognize its potential in the building of automobiles. Whatever romantic notions we may harbor about owning an Aston Martin with a little polished plate mounted on the engine block, bearing the name of the craftsman who lovingly assembled it on a bench in Newport Pagnell, the prospect of being stranded with it in Seattle, with a seized motor, tends to take the gloss off.

Leland entered the auto business in 1902, a year after the fire at Olds' factory. Some of Henry Ford's original backers were getting cold feet over the fact

that Ford only seemed interested in building racing cars. Leland, who already had a reputation as a precision engineer and toolmaker, was called in to value the premises and equipment that had been purchased for producing saleable cars so that it could be sold to recover the investment. Instead, he offered them an improved engine design that had been turned down by Olds and thus was created what has become perhaps the most famous and respected name in the American automobile industry and a by-word for glamour: Cadillac.

The company was named after the aristocratic French explorer who founded the city of Detroit, Antoine de la Mothe Cadillac. From the very beginning the Cadillac was an object of desire. In January 1903, just a few months after its initial test drive, a ten horsepower, Model "A" car was exhibited at the New York Automobile

Below: In 1908 Cadillac added a limousine to its model G range, powered by a 25 horsepower, as measured by the new ALAM rating system.

SPECIFICATIONS

STUTZ BEARCAT 1912

Engine:
Cast iron – 4 cylinders in line

Displacement:
389 cu. ins.

Bore and stroke
-

Horsepower
60

Body styles:
Sports/competition roadster

No. of seats:
2

Weight (lbs):
-

Price:
$2,000

Produced:
266 (all models)

Above Right: Detail of a 1912 Stutz Bearcat. The forerunner of this legendary car had been built in little over a month and taken to Indianapolis the day after it was completed to run in the inaugural "500" where it managed to finish, in 11th place, and lay the foundation of one of America's first automotive legends.

show and within a week orders for more than twenty-two hundred had been secured. The Cadillac was a sensation - and a sell-out. Under Leland's stewardship, Cadillac achieved honor and distinction through superior engineering and innovative design. Most famously, in 1912, Cadillac became the first car to relieve its driver of the task of cranking it up by hand - surely one of the most welcome advances in technology in the whole history of the automobile. To this day, the lavishly produced quarterly magazine, distributed to members of the Cadillac /La Salle Owners Club, bears the proud title *The Self Starter*. Even before this, in 1908, Leland had demonstrated the excellence of his engineering by taking three, single-cylinder cars to England to compete in endurance trials. There, at the famous Brooklands

track, under the supervision of the Royal Automobile Club, the three cars were completely stripped down and their components scrambled. Three cars were then assembled from the pile of parts, started, and ran. At the time, such accuracy in the machining of parts to render them interchangeable in this way was regarded as little short of miraculous. Cadillac won the prestigious Dewar Trophy, the first time this had been awarded to any American manufacturer.

Sadly, in 1917, Leland parted company with Cadillac and with the General Motors Corporation of which it had become part. It was war work that

had first inspired him and, ironically, it was war work - or rather the reluctance of William Durant, the then head of General Motors, to switch Cadillac over to war work - that caused him to abandon the company that he had inspired. Though now in his seventies, Leland was still driven by the desire to build better. He founded a new company and named it after the president who he had so admired in his youth: Lincoln.

As with the Cadillac, the Lincoln was a prestige automobile, precision built and held in high esteem today. There was, however, one final twist in Henry Leland's tale... In the early 1920s, largely due to Leland's insistence on

Engine:
Cast iron – V8 with
alloy crankcase

Displacement:
314 cu. ins.

Bore and stroke:
3 1/8 x 5 1/8

Horsepower:
70

Body styles:
Numerous

No. of seats:
2 - 7

Weight (lbs):
c. 4,000 lbs

Price:
$3,600

Produced:
c. 13,000

Above Right: The first left-drive Cadillacs were produced in 1915, but right-drive remained available as an option. Power came from a 315 cu. in. V8 that produced over 60 horsepower. The following year "Cannonball" Baker and William Sturm would drive a V8 Cadillac from Los Angeles to New York in seven and a half days, beating the previous record by almost four days!

engineering perfection, production fell way below projections and the company was forced into receivership. Who was it who came along and bought Lincoln out? The very man whose factory Leland had acquired some twenty years earlier to create the Cadillac: Henry Ford. As the Irish say, what goes around comes around; Ford was now the largest manufacturer of automobiles in the world. In 1914, the company had produced over 300,000 Model T's; in that same year, the whole of the rest of the American auto industry put together produced less than 200,000 cars.

So the father of the cars that still transport the presidents of the United States passed into history.

No car bears his name, but it is, without doubt, one of the most illustrious in the history of automobile manufacture.

Cadillac once produced an unusual advertisement under the heading *The Penalty of Leadership*. The words may applied as well to Henry Leland as to the car he created: "That which is good or great makes itself known, no matter how loud the clamor of denial. That which deserves to live - lives." In the words of one of his engineers, "He was a great mechanic. He understood quality."

The Lincoln Motor Company was founded to produce Liberty aero engines, with not only Leland's son, Wilfrid, leaving Cadillac with his father, but a considerable number of engineers, executives and production-line workers as well.

Shortly afterwards, Durant was forced to begin Liberty engine production and implored the Lelands to return to supervize the transition but they were already committed to their new venture.

The Cadillac auto division, now

SPECIFICATIONS

CADILLAC
TYPE 55 1917

Engine:
V8 - Cast iron blocks
on alloy crankcase

Displacement:
314.5 cu. ins.

Bore and stroke:
3 1/8 x 5 1/8

Horsepower:
31.25

Body styles:
Roadster; Tourer;
Phaeton; Limousine;
Hearse; Police Patrol;
Military

No. of seats:
2 - 7

Weight (lbs):
c. 4,000 lbs

Price:
c. $3,600

Produced:
c. 18,000

Above Right: After extensive tests in 1917, the Cadillac car was adapted as a standard model for war use. Here is a Cadillac that is believed to be one of the first armored vehicles.

Trucks, Liberty aircraft engines and field kitchen trailers were among the many products manufactured by General Motors during World War I

under new management, continued to supply America's troops - and those of her allies in Europe - with the world's first fully armored cars, as well as staff cars, communications vehicles, field ambulances balloon winches and even artillery tractors, powered by the new V8 engine. The marque gained great distinction during the conflict. A Cadillac was the first Allied car across the Rhine and President Wilson had a convoy of fifty Cadillacs supplied for his visit to Paris. It was even suggested that General Pershing might nominate the Cadillac for the D.F.C.

The army had taken the Cadillac Touring Car exactly as it was, adding only an additional fuel tank, tire chains and olive drab paint. It performed impeccably and won the hearts of many, doubtless influencing many ex-servicemen's post-war purchase choices along the way. As an example of this, Colonel Hall, who had been involved with the design of the Liberty engine, is quoted as saying, "I believe these cars from my observations gave better service than any other make of car in France. I used Cadillac cars from fourteen to sixteen hours a day and most of the driving was done around an average of forty miles an hour. I was never tied up with car trouble at any time. Furthermore, I never saw a Cadillac tied up for trouble of any kind. Many officers would delay their trips until they could get Cadillacs... One of the first things I did on my arrival home was to purchase one for my own use."

SPECIFICATIONS

FORD MODEL T

Engine:
Cast iron - 4 Cylinders
in line

Displacement:
176.5 cu. ins.

Bore and stroke:
3 3/4 x 4 ins.

Horsepower:
20

Body styles:
Tourer; Coupe;
Runabout; Sedan

Number of seats:
2-5

Weight (lbs):
c. 1,500 lbs

Price;
$474 - $875

Number Produced:
350,000

Above Right: At just $500, the two-seat Runabout was the cheapest Model T on offer in 1919 and yet it was acceptable for use even on formal occasions. By this time Ford only offered cars in any color as long as it was black, but prior to 1914 Model Ts were painted in a number of hues.

World War One had ended in November 1918, the economy was experiencing a post-war mini-boom based on the euphoria of victory, and the population of Detroit was nearly four times what it had been at the start of the century, thanks to the burgeoning business of building automobiles. At the heart of the Motor City's prosperity was the incredible and ever-expanding empire of Henry Ford, based on the corner-stone of just one model – the Model T.

Arriving in October 1908, the Model T Ford was to revolutionize the automobile industry and help establish a freedom of movement for Americans – the car would come within reach of almost anyone. Eleven years on, the Model T was going strong and, if altered in appearance (it had a major facelift in 1917), no backwoods mechanic could fail to recognize the car or its components and

know exactly how to fix whatever went wrong.

Mass production was the main key to its phenomenal success, but what was equally important was Ford's insistence on reducing the price whenever possible, stimulating demand even more and creating further profits. When introduced, the Model T sold at $850, but by 1919 the 2-door Runabout was only $500. And while the first full year of production saw 17,771 put together, with the coming of the moving assembly line and its refinement of operation, in 1919 an amazing 820,455 cars bearing the Ford name were manufactured – almost double the previous year's output and nearly half the total for the whole US auto industry. A further milestone reached in this year was the production of the three millionth Model T.

It is widely assumed that Ford could keep the price of the Model T so low because it was churned out, year after year, without any alterations. This isn't so. Changes were made all the time – models came and went, different suppliers were often used and components were modified, either to cure problems or to provide a cheaper method of production.

But the original concept of a car for the masses remained and the specification was more or less constant. The engine was a four cylinder L-head of 176.7 cu.in. developing 20 horsepower,

Above: The Dodge's sound design and rugged construction allowed many of their cars to perform active service in World War I. By 1919 their reputation was firmly established and cars like this were being produced at a rate of over 500 a day. The Dodge brothers, Horace and John, had been in the auto parts business since 1901, supplying engine and transmission components to both Henry Ford and Ransom Olds. Their own cars first went into production in 1915.

cooled by thermo-syphon action, coupled to a unique planetary transmission with two forward speeds and reverse and a multiple disc clutch, while a torque tube drive connected this to the rear axle. The wheelbase was 100 inches, wooden spoked wheels were 30 inches and suspension was by transverse semi-elliptic leaf springs.

Within that framework the Model T evolved bit by bit, and 1919 saw an electric starter and battery as standard on closed models and offered as an option on open cars. This in turn led to an instrument panel being fitted with a single gauge (an ammeter), ignition/light switch and choke knob – speedometers were installed by dealers or owners. Demountable rim wheels were also available for the first time to make tire changing easier.

The Model T became forever enshrined in American folklore for being virtually indestructible and, in spite of its quirky features, utterly reliable. Cheerfully used and savagely abused, it was a target of derision and affection in like amounts, at home on the remotest farm or in the teeming city, and it captured the heart of the nation in a

our view of it - might be, had Henry Ford's views and attitudes to production prevailed. He believed that the automobile was the means by which the population might be made mobile; it was an engine of social change and, as such, of primarily practical significance, just like electric light or refrigeration. He didn't see why the car should have any more romance attached to it than the horse and buggy or the bicycle; it was simply a device for transporting persons from A to B. So long as the car enabled the doctor to get to the patient and the farmer to market, what did it matter what color it was painted? In truth, the automobile simply provides mobility - and clothes simply keep out the cold. In reality, these things are the means by which we inform the world at large of who and what we are, or at least would like to be.

manner that no other automobile in history – before or since – has come close to equaling.

It is interesting to speculate as to how different the modern automobile - and

Below: Prior to 1919, Willys-Overland was second to Ford in production, but a factory strike delayed a new model intended to combat the Model T. When it did arrive, it was priced at over $800 – way above the Ford – and could no longer compete. To generate publicity, Overland were involved in several automobile events, including a seven day, non-stop run in high gear.

SPECIFICATIONS

PACKARD TWIN SIX

Engine:
Cast iron - 60 degree
V12

Displacement:
424 cu. ins.

Bore and stroke:
3 x 5 ins.

Horsepower:
90

Body styles:
Runabout;
Tourer; Phaeton;
Coupe; Sedan;
Limousine

Number of seats:
4-7

Weight (lbs):
-

Price:
$5,500 - $8,000

**Number
Produced:**
5,200

*Right: The 1920
Packard Twin Six. This
was the world's first 12
cylinder car
manufactured in series
quantity with over
35,000 built between
1916 and 1923. Its 60°
L-head V12 of 424
cu.in engine produced
90bhp.*

Choosing a suitable name for a new car company must have been a vexing task for the hundreds of so-called entrepreneurs in the Twenties, as proposing to set up an automobile producing business had been a lucrative method of selling stock and raising millions of dollars to fund the business since the turn of the century. Spurred on by the successes of people like Ransom E. Olds (Oldsmobile and Reo), William C. Durant (Buick, Chevrolet and General Motors), Henry Ford and many others in making personal fortunes out of the fledgling auto industry, the crooked speculators took full advantage of the boom, and the naiveté of investors. During this frantic time, almost every name that would look good at the head of a certificate had been used (some more than once) and the names of US automobile companies registered run the whole gamut of the alphabet, from Abbott-Akin to Zip (both of whom, coincidentally, didn't survive 1914).

Prospective manufacturers named cars after themselves: Hupmobile, Cord, Duesenberg, Maxwell, Nash etc., etc. Cars were called after the places they were made: Auburn, Michigan, Detroit, Muskegon and many others, and after figures from history, myth and legend, as with Pontiac, Lincoln, Cadillac and Mercury. Sometimes the names simply reflected certain qualities that the maker wished to be associated with his product: Peerless, Inter-State, Endurance and Flyer are good examples. This practice was carried over into model delineations and remains with us to this day, providing some of the most striking examples of the marketing strategist's art with titles such as ElDorado, Thunderbird, Voyager, Pacer and Mustang. Human nature being what it is, however, the most common practice was for a car maker to call his car after himself. so it was with James Ward Packard.

Packard had purchased a Winton Waggon in the closing years of the nineteenth century - and he was not happy with it. Mr. Winton was unwilling to make the alterations that Mr. Packard suggested might improve matters and so Packard decided to build a better car himself - and he did. The first Packard had a single-cylinder, 7hp motor, two speed transmission and chain drive, with some novel features including an automatic ignition advance system. In 1900 some fifty cars were produced, and in the Fall of that year the company was incorporated, two employees of the Winton Waggon company having defected to join!

Early customers included William D.

Rockefeller - another defector from Winton's - and the company's slogan "Ask the man who owns one," reflected the confidence they had in their product. New models followed thick and fast, always featuring technical improvements and always selling well. The marque enjoyed success in speed trials, and on the race track, and Packard's stock soared in value. During World War I the company produced the Liberty aero engine which was widely regarded as the finest aircraft engine yet produced. By 1916 their first twelve-cylinder model had arrived - the first in

volume production anywhere in the world. Priced initially at a base of $2,600, the Twin-Six would remain in production until 1923, by which point better than 35,000 would have been sold. In 1924 a straight-eight replaced the Twin-Six and sales continued to improve - to the point that Packard's lawyers had to deal with a number of cases of breach-of-copyright relating to registered Packard features. By the time old Mr. Packard died, in 1928, the company was one of America's leading prestige auto manufacturers and the Packard family crest was adopted as the badge as

a mark of respect for departed merit.

All Packards were now straight-eights but the threat of the forthcoming V16 engine from Cadillac prompted the return of the twelve-cylinder engine in a new and improved form and producing 160hp, complemented, in 1932, by a 110hp Light Eight that lasted only a

Below: J. Dallas Dort was a carriage builder who became an automobile manufacturer in 1915. He produced a first rate car, living up to his motto, "Quality Goes Through." nfortunately the Dort Company only survived until 1924

year. Packard's sales had collapsed during the disastrous period of the early' thirties; at the time that they were producing what many consider to be their finest automobiles. By 1935, Packard had produced a range of lower-priced automobiles that was to prove its (temporary) salvation. These "Junior" Packards pushed sales over the 100,000 mark in 1937 but some consider them to have damaged Packard's up-market image. It is certainly true that, as sales of the Juniors increased, sales of the big Packards fell away correspondingly. The Twelve was discontinued in 1939 and production of the Senior Eights effectively halved over the next couple of years.

In 1941, Howard "Dutch" Darrin produced a smart and forward-looking

design which was named the Clipper; it was hoped this might provide a much needed boost to sales as the entire line was beginning to look distinctly outdated. The Clipper was a resounding success and outsold all other models in the range. In 1941, Packard built more cars than Cadillac and during World War II they sold the machine tolls for the production of the old Junior and Senior

Above: The Essex made its debut in 1919, and in August 1920, set a new record carrying mail from San Francisco to New York in 4 days, 14 hours, and 43 minutes.

models to the U.S.S.R., to become the Z.I.S. After the war, the only model offered was the Clipper in various forms, and the company folded in1958.

1921

SPECIFICATIONS

OLDSMOBILE
MODEL 43-A

Engine:
Cast iron - 4 Cylinders
in line

Displacement:
224 cu. ins.

Bore and stroke:
3 11/16 x 5 1/4 ins.

Horsepower:
43

Body styles:
Roadster; Tourer;
Coupe

No. of seats:
2-5

Weight (lbs):
c. 2,800 lbs

Price:
$1,325 - $1,895

Produced:
13,876

Proof of the rapid development of the automobile's place at the very heart of the American way of life is shown from several incidents during this year. Warren G. Harding became the first US president to travel to his inauguration in a car – a Packard Twin Six, and, at the other end of the scale, was another first – the Pig Stand, a drive-in restaurant in Dallas, Texas, where barbecued pork sandwiches were served to people to eat in their cars. Meanwhile, in an effort to regulate the ever-increasing flow of cars on the streets, the Detroit police were experimenting with synchronized traffic lights, having introduced the three-colored light two years earlier.

But the economy was still depressed at the start of the year, with 5 million people unemployed. As Ford slashed the price of the Model T to stimulate demand, grabbing over 60% of the market, the need for cheaper cars was recognized by other manufacturers. Oldsmobile had established itself as a builder of medium-priced, good quality automobiles, but reacted to the down-turn in sales by bringing out a four cylinder car – the Model 43-A. Since 1916, Oldsmobiles had all been powered by either a six or eight cylinder engine and the four was a welcome addition.

At under $1400 in price, the 43-A was the cheapest Oldsmobile by a wide margin (their eight cylinder models cost nearly twice as much), yet they couldn't hope to approach the rock-bottom prices set by Ford. The cost of the Model T Runabout eventually sank to $325 in 1921, but a 2-door sedan was $760 – which was still half the price of the new Olds. The difference in price is reflected in the annual production. While Ford churned out nearly 1.3 million cars, Oldsmobile's output was a modest 19,157, of which 13,867 were the Model 43-A.

Despite the reduction in price compared to earlier models, the four cylinder Oldsmobile remained a quality automobile, far more sophisticated and better equipped than the Ford. While the cheaper open models were more popular, the Olds 4-door sedan looked more in keeping with the times, sporting the fashionable sloping windshield, but all featured smoother body work lines, especially where the hood joined the passenger compartment.

Mechanically too, the Oldsmobile was in a higher class, with its 224 cu.in. engine putting out 43 horsepower, over double that of the Ford four.

And, featuring a simple manual transmission with a single plate, dry disc clutch, torque tube drive and spiral bevel gear rear axle, the Olds was as conventional as could be. Dimensionally, the Oldsmobile was also unremarkable, sitting on a wheelbase of 115 inches with 32 x 4 tires on wooden spoke artillery wheels. It all added up to a straightforward package that appealed to those drivers who wanted a bit more from an automobile and were prepared to pay extra for it.

Oldsmobile might not have had the commanding presence in the market enjoyed by the overwhelming Ford juggernaut but, as a small part of the complex General Motors organisation put together by Billy Durant, it would survive and prosper. Pierre du Pont had taken over as president of GM, but it was Alfred P. Sloan who directed the essential rationalization programme needed to unravel the mess created by Durant. Part of the restructuring meant a clearer definition of the market levels in which each marque sold its products

and it was decided that Oldsmobile's future was to be with bigger and better automobiles. As a consequence, the four would be discarded after 1923 and, thereafter, the Olds would use only six and eight cylinder engines.

For 1927, just the six-cylinder engine was on offer. The major advance was the introduction of Oldsmobile's first four-wheel braking system. Prices were pegged and all models were offered in either "standard" or "deluxe" trim. The deluxe package offered front and rear bumpers, locking moto-meter and a choice of steel disc or wooden wheels. 1927 was the last year that the "30" model designation would be employed. Total sales for the year were 54,234, almost unchanged from the previous year.

Below: Although cheaper open cars were more popular, this Oldsmobile 4-door sedan exhibits several fashionable trends in early Twenties automobile design, including the sloping windshield, which was also used by other manufacturers.

SPECIFICATIONS

RAUCH & LANG

Engine:
Electric displacement

Power Source:
40 x 2 Volt wet cells

Range:
30 miles

Bore and stroke
-

Horsepower:
3

Body styles:
Taxicab

No. of seats:
2-6

Weight (lbs):
-

Price:
$3,500

Produced:
-

As we are currently progressing in the 21st century, it seems possible that the electric car will become a significant part of daily transport in the future, yet at one period it was the most favored method of automobile propulsion. The reasons for this were obvious – the electric car was clean, ran smoothly and quietly and didn't require either the vigorous hand cranking of the gasoline engine, or the laborious firing of a steam boiler to get it started up in the morning.

Electric power was also a familiar technology, with Thomas Edison having introduced electric lighting to New York in 1881, and most large cities had electric streetcars. The gasoline engine, on the other hand, was still in its infancy and suffered from plenty of teething troubles. The downside was that electric vehicles were expensive, heavy, and had a limited range before the batteries needed recharging.

For use in the city streets, however, the electric car was unsurpassed and so it became extremely popular with the wives of the wealthy, even indicating a certain social status and, at one time, there were many makes available to the discerning buyer. One of the more famous of these was Rauch & Lang. Formed as a carriage building company in Cleveland, Ohio, in 1884, Rauch & Lang entered the automobile business in 1903 by taking on an agency for the Buffalo Electric car. The first Rauch & Lang electric followed in 1905 and things progressed from there, the marque establishing itself as a supplier of quality automobiles. One of the largest electrics ever made was the 1912 Rauch & Lang six person town car, costing $3,800.

Sales of electric cars, or "juicers" as they were sometimes called, peaked in 1914 with 4,669 units. These were mostly elegant carriages, very tall, with large areas of glass and plush interiors. The major problem with the electric car was battery life and this is still true today. Although a range of between 30 and 75 miles was possible, depending on the speed driven, overnight recharging was necessary which meant plugging in to special equipment in the owner's garage. Another disadvantage was the sheer weight of the batteries, around 1,000 pounds on an average car, which slowed acceleration

somewhat. In addition, the batteries generally needed replacing after about three years and this also proved expensive.

All Rauch & Lang electric cars were similar in appearance. With no need for a radiator, they had a rounded-off nose and almost all had a very upright stance and a virtually flat roof with sharp corners. This design was common to almost all electric cars of this period. But travel horizons were expanding and, whereas a top speed of 20mph and a range of under fifty miles was fine for local journeys, long distance trips were another matter. Lengthy promotional journeys were mounted by electric car manufacturers to counteract these shortcomings, and a Detroit Electric even managed to exceed 200 miles between charges on one trip, but the need for more frequent recharging remained the norm.

By 1919, the market for electric cars was in decline, mainly due to improvements in the gasoline engine and the wider availability of the self-starter.

Above: Electric cars were much favored for city use because of their smooth running and silent operation. Rauch & Lang were one of the most successful builders of electrics, but turned to taxis as the market went into decline and the gasoline engine took over. The rounded nose and upright style were typical features of most electric cars of this period.

Even so, Rauch & Lang were still producing 700 cars a year. In 1920 the passenger car part of the business was sold to the Stevens-Duryea organization and moved to Chicopee Falls, Massachusetts.

In 1922, Rauch & Lang Inc. (as the new company was called) started producing electric powered taxi cabs, and this seems to have been the mainstay of their production for the few remaining years of the business, which closed in 1928. Towards the end they were building as many, if not more, gasoline powered taxis as they were electric cars.

SPECIFICATIONS

STANLEY STEAMER

Engine:
Pressurised steam
- 2 Cylinders in parallel

Displacement:
56.5 cu.ins

Bore and stroke:
3.0 x 4.0 ins.

Horsepower:
10 - 30 (depending on
steam pressure)

Body styles:
Tourer; Roadster;
Brougham; Sedan

No. of seats:
2-7

Weight (lbs):
1,400lbs (minimum dry)

Price:
-

Produced:
181

Whenever steam-powered cars are mentioned, the name Stanley springs to mind, so it is somewhat startling to note that during the early years of this century, there were over 100 successful companies building steam vehicles in the USA.

However, it is the Stanley Steamer that is remembered above all others. Stanley was one of the more popular makes, lasted longer in the business than its rivals, and is the only steam-powered machine to hold the World Land Speed Record (127.659mph over the flying mile at Daytona Beach in January 1906) – a remarkable feat.

Whilst operating a photographic equipment manufacturing company in Watertown, Massachusetts, identical twins Francis E. and Freeland O. Stanley produced a highly effective steam car in 1898. After a demonstration, where the Stanley out-performed all other entrants on a hill climb contest, the brothers received orders for 200 cars.

Early in 1899, the Stanley factory was visited by John Brisbane Walker, a publisher, who liked what he saw and offered to buy the company. Having just got things off the ground, the Stanleys were reluctant to sell and put a huge price on their operation hoping to put Walker off. He agreed to pay the $250,000 asked and, in partnership with Amzi Lorenzo Barber, established the Locomobile car company building steamers to the Stanley design. Walker and Barber soon disagreed and Walker left to set up his own steam car production

using the Mobile name. Walker's Mobile only lasted until 1903, and Locomobile switched exclusively to gasoline power the following year.

Meanwhile, having made a financial killing from their initial venture into auto building, the Stanley brothers had been busy developing an improved steam engine and formed the Stanley Motor Carriage Company in 1902. Litigation over patent infringements and breach of contract were overcome, and by 1912 over 5,000 Stanley steamers had been sold, the body design evolving into a rounded "coffin-nose" style concealing the front-mounted boiler, with the two cylinder engine driving directly on the rear axle.

Despite updates, such as condensers and flash boilers, the main drawback with steam power remained its slow warm-up time and, as gasoline engines improved, Stanley's sales declined. In 1917, the brothers retired from active involvement with the company. By 1920, Stanley cars had a flat radiator with a dummy filler cap and looked much like any other automobile, but this wasn't enough to overcome the basic problems associated with steam propulsion. When Stanley went into receivership in 1923, it was offering a range of six Series 740 models including tourers, sedans, a roadster and a brougham. Based on a 130 inch wheelbase chassis, all were powered by a 20 horsepower two cylinder engine.

The Steam Vehicle Corporation of America bought the factory and assets for $572,200 in 1924, continuing production at the Newton, Massachusetts, plant until 1927. Thereafter, the Stanley name and its steam-powered automobiles were consigned to history.

Although steam cars would survive into the Thirties, 1923 effectively marked the end of the golden age for this type of automobile. The year also saw the untimely death of president Warren Harding in San Francisco in August; vice president Calvin Coolidge took over in The White House.

Other Steam Cars included the Moore, which became the Westfield, and the Maryland, the story of whose rise and demise is worthy of note... The Maryland Automobile & Manufacturing company was founded in the spring of 1900, in Luke, Maryland. At the end of the year the factory was blown down by a tornado but it turned out that the owners were the only people in the county with insurance against such an eventuality. The factory was rebuilt and production resumed. Sadly, the same foresight was lacking with regard to the future of the steamer. Maryland lasted but a year.

Left: To all intents, the Stanley Series 740 Tourer looks like a conventional automobile. The dummy radiator grille and filler cap hide the boiler, while the two cylinder steam engine drives directly on the rear axle. Although good performers with smooth running characteristics, steam-powered cars lost out to gasoline because of the inconvenience of the slow warm-up from cold. In 1923, Stanley was in receivership and the company never really recovered, the last Stanley steamer being built in 1927.

SPECIFICATIONS

CHRYSLER

Engine:
Cast iron - 6 Cylinders
in line

Displacement:
201.5 cu. ins.

Bore and stroke:
3 x 4 3/4 ins.

Horsepower:
68

Body styles:
Roadster; Coupe;
Tourer; Phaeton; Sedan;
Brougham; Town Car

No. of seats:
2-7

Weight (lbs):
2,730 lbs - 3,225 lbs

Price:
$1,395 - $3,725

Produced:
76,500

Walter Percy Chrysler proved to be a man with an outstanding talent and flair for the business of manufacturing automobiles. Since his background was in engineering, in the railroad industry, his first connection with cars was as works manager for Buick in 1910. By 1919, the frustrations of working with the volatile Billy Durant proved too much and Chrysler abruptly left the Flint, Michigan, factory, settling on a $10 million pay-off for his stock. Chrysler's next task was to try to sort out the troubled Willys-Overland Company on behalf of the Chase National Bank, for an annual fee of one million dollars. During his two years with Willys, Chrysler became convinced that a six cylinder engine being developed at the Elizabeth, New Jersey, plant, by three engineers who had formerly been with Studebaker – Carl Breer, Owen Skelton and Fred Zeder – showed some definite promise.

1921 saw Chrysler at Maxwell, which had merged with Chalmers and was facing difficulties. After both the New Jersey Willys factory and the six cylinder prototype were bought by Durant, Chrysler took the opportunity to acquire the services of Zeder, Skelton and Breer and brought

Right: The styling of the first Chryslers was hardly inspired, but their performance made up for it. The 201.5 cu.in. six cylinder engine produced 68hp thanks to a higher 4.7:1 compression ratio, giving a 70mph top speed, unheard of in such a car.

them to Detroit in 1923 to produce an improved version of their engine.

The resulting power plant provided Walter P. Chrysler with the means to make an immediate success of a car bearing his name, which replaced the Maxwell. Displacing 201.5 cu.in. the L-head six produced 68bhp at 3200rpm thanks to a much higher than average compression ratio of 4.7:1 with a Ricardo-type cylinder head, giving the new Chrysler a very comfortable top

speed of 70mph. Performance of this caliber in a car costing only $1,395 was a major breakthrough, and the Chrysler got an enthusiastic reception with 32,000 cars sold in 1924 – a record for first year sales by a new nameplate.

Competition success followed the car's launch, with Ralph Da Palma winning the Mount Wilson hill climb and setting a record two minutes quicker than the previous best by a stock car. Later that year, the same car and driver would cover 1,000 miles on a board track in California, establishing even more performance records. Yet the Chrysler was not just about speed. It had hydraulic brakes on all four wheels, air cleaner, oil filter, a tubular front axle

and several other features not normally found on mass-produced, medium priced automobiles. If the engineering of the Chrysler was both excellent and innovative, the same cannot be said of the body styling, which was both conventional and entirely devoid of any imaginative flair. For years to come, the Chrysler's sound engineering practice

Below: The 1924, V-63 Series, with its refined, ninety degree V8, now producing over 80 horsepower, continued to set the standard in both styling and performance, even though Henry Leland had left the company after a dispute with William Durant in 1917, over the proposed production of Liberty aero engines.

would dominate the aesthetic design.

Outwardly, the only hint of speed on the '24 Chrysler was the winged radiator cap, but it was enough to mark the beginning of a major force in the auto industry for the rest of the century. Less of a long term force was Calvin Coolidge, who won the presidential election in 1924 using the slogan "Keep Cool With Coolidge" to emphasize his laid back attitude. Also keeping his cool was Clarence Birdseye who introduced frozen food to the world and thereby established another enduring household name.

Chrysler's reputation for dowdy

styling would, of course, be completely reversed and the corporation would go on to become a style leader in the post-war period. One of the most dramatic examples of revolutionary Chrysler design came in 1934 with the arrival of the Airflow, styled, with the aid of wind-tunnel testing, by Oliver Clark.

Below: Cadillac was bought by General Motors in 1909 for five and a half million dollars. During World War I, more than 2,000 V8's were sent overseas as staff cars. When Henry Leland and his son, Wilfrid, left Cadillac to found Lincoln, managership of the division passed, eventually, to Lawrence P. Fisher.

SPECIFICATIONS

FRANKLIN

Engine:
Cast iron - 6 Cylinders
in line (air-cooled)

Displacement:
274 cu. ins

Bore and stroke:
3 1/2 x 4 3/4 ins

Horsepower:
95

Body styles:
Sports; Sedan; Coupe;
Cabriolet; Tourer;
Limousine

No. of seats:
2-5

Weight (lbs):
3,750 lbs - 4,000 lbs

Price:
$2,500 - $3,000

Produced:
c. 5,500

*Right: The Franklin
Series 11 with a false
radiator was designed by
J. Frank de Causse at the
insistence of dealers
who wanted a
conventional-
looking car to
sell. As well as
unusual air-cooled
engines, Franklins also
used a wooden chassis
and full-elliptic
suspension.*

Herbert H. Franklin was a foundry operator in Syracuse, New York, when, in 1901, he was introduced to a young graduate engineer named John Wilkinson. Upset because he had not been paid for building two prototype air-cooled cars for the New York Automobile Company, Wilkinson took Franklin for a ride in one of them which convinced the foundry owner to enter the automobile industry.

The first of a dozen Franklin automobiles produced in the initial twelve months was delivered in July 1902 and, from then on, the company prospered and grew. Development and improvement of the air-cooled engines continued over the years, and subsequently many endurance tests were carried out to prove the superiority of the Franklin over a standard water-cooled car. One such arduous undertaking happened in August 1915 with an 860 mile drive in bottom gear between Walla Walla in Washington and San Francisco. High and second gears were removed from the transmission and the unit sealed before the start, and the engine was never stopped during the running time of 83 hours and 40 minutes – representing an average speed of over 10 miles per hour through some of the most testing terrain.

Up until 1923, the front of a Franklin was readily distinguishable from most other makes of automobile because it didn't have a radiator. Being air-cooled, it obviously didn't need one, and the engine cover was a single cowl, hinged at the front and easily removed for maintenance work. In some respects it bore a passing resemblance to the electric and steam-powered cars of the day. However, in the summer of 1923, a group of Franklin dealers visited the Syracuse factory and threatened to give up their franchises unless the company produced a more conventional-looking car with a dummy radiator grille.

Herbert Franklin was quickly convinced that the dealers were right, but John Wilkinson couldn't accept the idea of a false radiator and resigned in protest. After consultations with both the Walter M. Murphy company in California and J. Frank de Causse in New York, the task of creating a different body design was given to de Causse, and the new Series 11 cars were

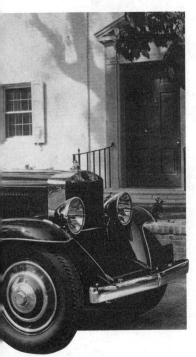

introduced in March, 1925. In addition to the sedan style that Franklin were already best known for, de Causse's new designs also included a boat tail speedster – a very stylish departure from any of their existing or previous models.

The construction of the Franklin engine bears some investigation. Without the shrouding to direct the air flow, the engine looks rather like a giant, old-fashioned motorcycle unit with six cylinders. Each cylinder is a separate item with the head and barrel cast as one and copper cooling fins attached to the outside. The cooling fan is driven directly off the front of the crankshaft and the air is fed directly to the top of the engine and forced down between the cylinders.

And if the Franklin engine sounds a bit oddball, the rest of the car has its share of quirks too. All Franklins used a wooden chassis exclusively up until 1927, long after other manufacturers had switched to steel frames. The suspension system was also rather special in that it retained the full elliptic leaf springs front and rear, but the cars were noted for an exceptionally comfortable ride. The restyled 1925 Franklins were a great success and the company continued producing air-cooled automobiles in quantities. It was only a disastrous attempt at an inappropriate V12 luxury car following on from the effects of the Wall Street Crash that caused Franklin to cease trading in 1934.

Quotable quotes of '25 include Calvin Coolidge saying: "The business of America is business," Henry Fords "Machinery is the modern Messiah," but probably the most telling was a judge who declared that the automobile was "a house of prostitution on wheels." John Wilkinson might well have agreed that the Franklin had prostituted its looks by adopting a false radiator, but even in his deepest disgust he would surely never have equated such a fine automobile to a whorehouse.

SPECIFICATIONS

FORD MODEL T

Engine:
Cast iron - 4 Cylinders in line

Displacement:
176.7 cu.ins.

Bore and stroke:
3 3/4 x 4 0 ins.

Horsepower:
20

Body styles:
Coupe; Roadster; Tourer; 2- and 4-door Sedan

No. of seats:
2-5

Weight (lbs):
1,655 - 1,972 lbs

Price:
$290 - 580

Produced:
1,431,795

In late 1925, the Model T received its first major makeover since 1917. The "Improved Ford" had new bodies, except for the Fordor, with reworked running boards and fenders. There were continual modifications to the chassis design. The length of the rear crossmember was increased, and the springs were modified to lower the car by one inch. In addition, US touring cars got a driver's side door for the first time.

The engine and running gear remained more or less unchanged—as ever—but this last revision provided 11-inch rear brake drums, operated by an "Emergency Brake Lever." The transmission brake was beefed up to provide more stopping power over a longer period, and the pedal increased in size to aid operation. The fuel tank was fitted beneath the cowl on all models except the Fordor,

Right: Production of the evergreen Model T finally would cease within a year, but engines would still be built, on a decreasing scale, right up to the beginning of World War II.

which continued to carry it under the driver's seat.

The Tudor and the coupe, originally only available in black, were now offered in Drake Green, while the Fordor was painted Royal Maroon. In mid-1926, the open cars received a coat of color paint too, with Gunmetal Blue and Phoenix Brown now available. Fawn Gray, Royal Maroon and Highland Green finishes were available on closed cars. By the beginning of 1927—the beginning of the end—any body could be ordered in any color. Commercial Green remained standard for the pickup, but Black was available on special order.

Wire wheels were offered as an option in 1926, becoming effectively standard equipment on closed cars for the final year of production. 21-inch balloon tires were now fitted as standard.

Model T production ended, officially, in May 1927, but engines were built, in diminishing numbers, until August, 1941. Between 1908 and 1927, over fifteen million Model Ts were produced. Henry Ford's "Tin Lizzie" is probably the most significant automobile ever produced. It had changed not only the face of the American landscape, but her labor and manufacturing policies, and thus the little car may truly be described as having altered the course of world history.

SPECIFICATIONS

LASALLE

Engine:
90 degree V8 - Cast iron with Alloy crankcase

Displacement:
303 cu. ins.

Bore and stroke:
3 1/8 x 4 15/16 ins

Horsepower:
75

Body styles:
Numerous, by Fisher and Fleetwood

No. of seats:
2-7

Weight (lbs):
3,755 lbs - 5,100 lbs

Price:
$2,495 - $4,700

Produced:
16,850

Another of Alfred P. Sloan's building blocks in his program to have General Motors offering a complete range of cars arrived in 1927. The LaSalle filled the gap between the top-priced Buick 6 and the cheapest Cadillac (a difference of $1700 existed between them). It was named after a French explorer who traveled the length of the Mississippi River in 1682. The LaSalle was also to be built as a junior to the Cadillac, another marque named after a French explorer who, in 1701, established a fort that became the city of Detroit.

But it is neither the French connection nor the fact that it was a failure that makes the car significant. What the LaSalle did was to bring stylist Harley Earl to Detroit and establish the practice of first designing a car to look good, then

Below: LaSalle Pace Car at the 1926 Indianapolis Speedway. Created to fill the gap in General Motors' range between the Buick and the Cadillac, the LaSalle was Harley Earl's brainchild and bore all the hallmarks of his unique talents. Launched at the Copley Plaza Hotel in Boston, in March 1927, the car was a sensation and 16,850 were built in the first year. Sadly, the LaSalle never really established itself as a separate marque but was regarded as a junior Cadillac.

making the engineering fit. Previously, the engineering had been dominant and the bodywork was definitely a secondary consideration, quite often produced by an outside supplier. Harley Earl and the LaSalle were to change that attitude forever.

Above: The Whippet was an aptly-named car produced by Willys-Overland. Small and quick, with either four or six cylinder engines, the Whippet was priced to take on anyone and 110,000 sold in 1927, helping Willys to third place in the sales charts.

Lawrence P. Fisher was general manager of Cadillac and had met Earl at a Cadillac dealership in Los Angeles where Earl was in charge of the custom body shop, producing special cars for celebrities. Fisher asked the young stylist to submit some design proposals for consideration. As a result, Earl came to Detroit early in 1926, as a consultant under a special contract.

Fisher outlined the project as being "that of designing a quality car of the same family as Cadillac but somewhat lower priced" - in other words, a production automobile that was as beautiful as the custom-bodied cars of the period.

Nowadays, it is hard to see how revolutionary the LaSalle was when it was launched, to great fanfare, in March 1927. Compared to other GM cars, the LaSalle was lower and longer, with deepdrawn Flying Wing fenders, better proportioned side windows and a new style of body moldings. It was a more integrated design, with few sharp corners and lines that flowed. The LaSalle was a huge sensation when it was exhibited for the very first time to the expectant, buying public at the Boston Automobile Show - as it proved impossible to get the car ready for New York, where it was planned to be unveiled.

Sloan was so impressed that he decided to employ Earl on the other GM

Below: Built in South Bend, Indiana, the Erskine was named after the founder of the Studebaker Corporation, Albert Erskine. Launched in Paris, it was subsequently shown in London and finally, with great fanfare, in New York. Europeans went for it but Americans didn't and the name was dropped in May 1930 after three years of production.

Above: The venerable Ford Model T came to the end of the road in May 1927 when the assembly lines were closed down after more than 15,000,000 Tin Lizzies had been produced. Buyers now wanted something more sophisticated than the old-fashioned (although slightly updated) Model T could offer – even at a bargain basement price.

models. In June, Earl headed a new department, called the Art and Color Section, to direct general body design and conduct research into special car designs. Fifty people made up the department at the start, ten of them designers, but it soon grew into a huge concern with hundreds of employees and it established styling as an essential part of the business.

Harley Earl had taken inspiration from the Hispano-Suiza, but the LaSalle was a car in its own right, even though it was promoted as a "Companion Car to Cadillac." It offered Cadillac qualities in a smaller package at a lower price and, with a splendid 303 cu.in. V8 engine, it could perform too. In a test at GM, a LaSalle roadster ran ten hours at an average 95.2mph - almost as fast as that year's Indy 500 winner!

The launch of the LaSalle, successful as it was, provided one sobering moment for the young Harley Earl. A photo shoot had been planned, outside the Copley Plaza Hotel. Earnie Seaholm, Cadillac's chief engineer, was to be seated behind the steering wheel, with the LaSalle factory manager, Bert Widman beside him. A platoon of General Motors dignitaries were ranged

on the sidewalk behind, including L. P. Fisher and Earl himself. A brace of Boston cops were on hand to hold back the expected crowds of excited onlookers, all anxious to get a look at the glamorous new automobile. Seaholm recalled that "Lo and behold - no one stopped to give it even a passing glance! Knowing Harley, I doubt if he ever went again to Boston!"

It was a year of sensational happenings – Lindbergh flew solo across the Atlantic, talking pictures arrived with Al Jolson in The Jazz Singer and Babe Ruth hit three home runs as the New York Yankees won the World Series. Against those events, the LaSalle must have seemed small potatoes, but it was the starting point of an amazing age in automotive history.

SPECIFICATIONS

FORD MODEL A

Engine:
Cast iron, 4 cylinders in line

Displacement:
200.5 cu. ins.

Bore & Stroke:
3.88 x 4.25 cu. ins.

Horsepower:
40 bhp

Body Styles:
Tudor (2 door) and Fordor (4 door) sedansRoadster, Cabriolet, Phaeton, Victoria, Wagon, Bus.

No. of seats:
2 - 5

Weight:
2,155 lbs - 2,525 lbs

Price:
$435 - $1,200

Produced:
1 million plus

Model T production ceased in the spring of 1927, after almost twenty years. Despite its longevity, reliability and undiminished popularity, Ford's beloved "Flivver" was being overtaken by its rivals. The model T's planetary gear set and two-wheel brakes were starting to look distinctly outdated, and so Ford, grudgingly, accepted the need for a new model and then threw into the project with gusto.

The model A, introduced in 1928, had—like the Model T—a four cylinder, side-valve engine. Displacing 200 cu.ins., the Model A's motor produced 40hp—double that of its predecessor. Top speed was a dizzying 65mph. The factory had been closed for six months prior to the car's eagerly-awaited debut, and so the workforce must have been as keen to get the production line moving again as the public evidently were to purchase the new car that came off it.

The Model A was far more "modern" in appearance than the model T. The car's styling was the work of Henry Ford's son, Edsel. Edsel Ford had been overseeing work at Lincoln, following Ford's takeover of the company in 1922 and Lincoln influence is clearly visible in the lines of the Model A. The wheelbase of the new car, however, was the same as that of the Model T—103.5 inches. Semi-elliptical, transverse springs were a carry-over from the Model T too.

The Model A had a high belt line and all body styles featured fully-crown fenders. Contrast color paint jobs, with coachlining were available and the radiator shell was reworked to make the new car instantly distinguishable from the Model T. Like the Tin Lizzie, however, the Model A offered extraordinary value for money, retailing from under $400 for the Phaeton and the Roadster. Chevrolet had managed to overtake Ford's sales during the factory closure prior to the model A's launch, but the new car proved as popular as its predecessor and Ford regained its crown in 1929 and 1930. Chevrolet went ahead again in 1931—before the Ford V8 arrived.

The Model T was a pretty hard act to follow, but the model A was universally regarded as a worthy successor.

Left: It is almost impossible to believe today but, in 1927, Ford closed its production lines for six months in order to introduce the Model A in early '28. What is equally unbelievable is that both dealers and customers were willing to wait for such a long time without defecting to other makes, such was the influence wielded by Henry Ford. Although a major advance on the ancient Tin Lizzie, the Model A was completely conventional, powered by a 200 cu.in. L-head four cylinder engine, and nearly five million would be built in four years.

SPECIFICATIONS

CORD L-29

Engine:
Cast iron - 8 Cylinders in line

Displacement:
298.6 cu. ins.

Bore and stroke:
-

Horsepower:
125

Body styles:
Sedan; Brougham; Convertible Coupe; Convertible; Sedan

No. of seats:
2 - 5

Weight (lbs):
-

Price:
$3,095 - $3,295

Produced:
1,819

It was the year of Chicago's St. Valentine's Day Massacre and the Wall Street Crash. But while rival gangs of hoodlums were bumping each other off in the Windy City, and ruined stockbrokers were hurling themselves to oblivion from the upper floors of New York's skyscrapers, in Indiana the Cord Corporation were putting the wraps on a new automobile with novel features and great styling that, in many eyes, would make it the most beautiful car of the period. That car was the Cord L-29.

Errett Lobban Cord was a colorful character, a wheeler dealer who, at the beginning of the Twenties, was a successful used-car salesman. By the middle of the decade, however, he had become president and major stockholder of Auburn. Shortly after, he acquired Duesenberg, and by the early Thirties he also had interests in the Lycoming engine plant, American Airlines, the airplane manufacturer Stinson, and various other businesses in the automotive industry. Cord was an empire

Right: *The L-29 was an impressive looking car from any angle, as this cabriolet shows. The final drive fits neatly beneath the Duesenberg-inspired grille and radiator surround.*

Right: The front-wheel-drive layout of the Cord L-29 was based on Harry Miller's 1927 Indy race car, with the final drive and transmission ahead of the engine. The latter was a Lycoming straight-eight similar to that used by Auburn.

builder, but the methods he used to gain controlling interests in companies were dubious.

By 1929, Cord perceived the need for a car that would fill the gap between the attractively-priced Auburn and the mighty Model J Duesenberg, which had recently been introduced by the Cord Corporation. The result was a car that bore his own name: the Cord L-29.

One of the most significant aspects of the L-29 was its front-wheel-drive layout, which had a dramatic effect on the overall styling of the car and made a major contribution to its rakish good looks. The L-29 was not the first American automobile to utilize front-wheel-drive, as for a short period prior to WW1, the Christie had been available with just such an arrangement.

Although that project did not succeed, by the late Twenties interest in front-wheel-drive had been revived again following the successful showing of several similarly-equipped race cars in the Indianapolis 500.

Cord employed race car builder Harry Miller and Detroit engineer Cornelius Van Ranst to design the front-wheel-drive set-up for the L-29. Miller's cars had already proved themselves on the track, while Van Ranst was also a keen exponent of the front-wheel-drive

Below: The long hood and flowing front fenders, coupled with the car's low overall height made even the sedan a stylish automobile. Sadly, the performance did not match the stunning good looks.

layout. Indianapolis race car driver Leon Duray would also act as an adviser on the project.

The team began with Auburn's 298.6 cu.in. flathead, in-line, eight cylinder engine, which produced 115 horsepower at 3300rpm, basing the driveline layout on Miller's 1927 Indy race car. This meant the final drive and transmission had to be ahead of the engine, which had to be turned around so that the flywheel, clutch and chain drive faced forward. The cylinder head was also modified to place the water outlet at the front. A three-speed, sliding-pinion transmission was fitted between the clutch and final drive, the latter having the drive shaft to each wheel equipped with Cardan constant-velocity joints to allow for suspension movement and steering. Miller also designed an

Above: The Cord's design was brilliant, its performance was shattering and its looks were stunning. Together with the Auburn it was one of the most desirable cars ever produced in America - or anywhere else. Tragically, the Wall Street crash effectively destroyed its market and production was halted on the last day of December, 1931. Four years later, however, the Cord would rise, like the fabulous Phoenix, from the ashes.

inboard braking system, using Lockheed hydraulic components. The front suspension comprised quarter-elliptic leaf springs and Houdaille-Hershey shock absorbers, which were also used at the rear with semi-elliptic leaf springs.

The car was based initially on a ladder frame, which was common practice at the time. However, when Cord himself drove the prototype over a patch of rough ground, the chassis flexed so much that it caused all the doors of the car to spring open. He immediately ordered Auburn's chief engineer, Herb Snow, to fix the problem, which he did by designing the industry's first X-frame chassis. This provided a much more rigid foundation for the car, and would be copied by other manufacturers as time went on.

Placing the transmission and final drive ahead of the long, straight-eight engine made for a long wheelbase, 137

Below: Built in Indianapolis, Indiana, the Duesenberg, in particular the Model J, was, and probably still is, the most desirable automobile ever made in the United States. Ab Jenkins drove a Duesenberg Special at over 150mph at Bonneville, Utah, and managed an average speed of 135.5mph for 24 hours. With over 300 horsepower coming from their twin over-head camshaft, 32 valve V8's, sometimes supercharged, and with custom bodies from the world's most exclusive coachbuilders, the Duesenberg was the ultimate status symbol.

Right: While the Whippet made a major contribution to Willys-Overland sales in 1929, it was another casualty of the Wall Street Crash and the Depression. Production ended in 1931.

inches in fact. This was much longer than any comparable automobile of the period, but it did have an advantage when it came to designing the bodywork. The Duesenberg-type grille, long sweeping hood and flowing fenders produced a rakish appearance, which was accentuated by the low overall height of the car. Because of the front-wheel-drive layout, no central transmission tunnel was needed in the floor which not only improved foot room for passengers, but also allowed the floor to be a low, step-down design. This ensured that the car retained good headroom for passengers inside while maintaining a relatively low overall height (61 inches for closed cars and 58 inches for open models – most other cars of the period were at least 70 inches high). At the same time, a generous ground clearance of 8 inches was also possible.

Not only was the Cord L-29 a good looking car, but it was also well appointed inside. The luxurious interiors of closed cars were trimmed in good-quality broadcloth, while open cars received leather upholstery. In both cases, this was set off by silver-plated interior fittings. In addition, the front seats and steering column were adjustable, while fingertip gear shifting was provided by a small lever on the dashboard.

Cabriolet, sedan, brougham and phaeton body styles were available, although many private coachbuilders, on both sides of the Atlantic, used the Cord as the basis for special bodywork. However, beautiful as the cars undoubtedly were, in performance terms they were somewhat sluggish. It took over 30 seconds for the L-29 to reach 60mph from a standing start, while top speed was not much more than 75mph. When compared to contemporary Cadillacs, Lincolns and Packards, the car was definitely a follower rather than a leader - but it did so in such great style.

Although, in theory, the front-wheel-drive layout should have ensured good traction on poor surfaces, in fact much of the weight of the L-29 was over the undriven rear wheels. As a result, the cars gained a poor reputation for dealing with loose surfaces. Furthermore, the constant-velocity joints were lacking in durability, and therefore rather frequent replacement was necessary.

Although many of the problems that beset the car could have been solved with a little more development work, Cord himself was impatient to put the L-29 into production and insisted that it be introduced before 1930.

Unfortunately, teething troubles were not the only problems that would affect the sales of the L-29. Two months after the car was introduced in 1929, the

stock market on Wall Street crashed, destroying the L-29's chances of becoming a commercial success. In an attempt to overcome the poor sales of 1929, the price was dropped by $800 for 1931, but this did not achieve the desired results. Production was halted at the end of the year, the last 157 cars being built as 1932 models. These had a more powerful 132 horsepower, 322 cu.in. straight-eight engine. This engine had originally been intended to power a new Cord, the L-30, but with the economic situation so poor, and so few L-29s having been built (around 5,000), it was never put into production. Indeed, there would not be another Cord for four years, and in the meantime E. L. Cord would concentrate on his other business interests. Even the new car would only last for two short years, after which Cord sold his empire for a reported $4,000,000, killing off Auburn and Duesenberg in the process.

Below: Chrysler produced three model ranges in the late 'twenties: the 65, the 75 and the Imperial. Two specially prepared 75 series roadsters ran at the Le Mans 24 hour race in 1928 and both completed the course, placing sixth and seventh in their class. All the cars had six cylinder engines in 1929, the four cylinder version being rebranded as the Plymouth. Custom bodies were available for these long, low, elegant automobiles, from Dietrich, Locke and, famously, LeBaron.

SPECIFICATIONS

CADILLAC SERIES 452 V16

Engine:
45 degree V16 - Nickel iron block on silicon/aluminum crankcase

Displacement:
452 cu. ins.

Bore and stroke:
3.0 x 4.0 ins.

Horsepower:
175 - 185

Body styles:
Numerous via Cadillac and Custom built

No. of seats:
2-7

Weight (lbs):
< c. 6,000 lbs

Price:
< c. $10,000

Produced:
3,251 in 1930 - 31

By just about any standards, the outlook in 1930 was bleak for the manufacturers of prestige automobiles. After the stock market collapse, demand for luxury cars had evaporated and many fine marques disappeared. Even though more people held on to their assets during the Depression than is usually suggested, it wouldn't have been acceptable to flaunt good fortune by driving around in a fancy car. So, of those that could actually afford to spend upwards of five thousand dollars on a car, few were willing to take the risk.

Into this atmosphere, came the most fabulous Cadillacs of all time – the Series 452 V16 range. It had a masterpiece of engineering, a 452 cu.in. sixteen cylinder overhead valve unit developing 165bhp and 320 foot pounds of torque. Arranged in a narrow Vee of 45°, with cast iron blocks attached to an aluminum alloy crankcase, the engine was the creation of Cadillac engineer Owen Nacker, and featured a completely unique system of hydraulically rotated eccentric bushings in the

Right: One of the V16 Cadillac models in 1930, the Fleetwood two-door convertible coupe had 19 inch wire wheels with specially balanced whitewall tires, dual sidemounts, twin spot lamps and a huge rear trunk.

rocker arms, to help silence the valve train mechanism.

No expense was spared to make it look impressive and the V16 engine bay was treated to extra plating and polishing. An uncluttered look was achieved by hiding the wiring and plumbing where possible. With smooth power rather than brute acceleration, Cadillac

Right: The badge bearing the coat of arms of Le Sieur Antoine de la Mothe Cadillac was registered as a trademark on August 7, 1906 and has been proudly borne on Cadillac automobiles to the present day. Hood ornaments, however, changed according to the fashions of the passing decades. The elegantly "art deco" Heron and Goddess mascots were available on both Cadillac and LaSalle models in 1930.

described the performance as "flexible and instantly responsive." Top speed was 90mph, and cruising at 70mph could be enjoyed at length, although a return of eight miles to the gallon may have been hard to tolerate in 1930 – even if gas was only 15 cents a gallon.

The car was built to majestic proportions, based on an enormous 148 inch wheelbase chassis (8 inches longer than the standard V8 models), and there were more than fifty body styles to chose from. Most of the V16 bodies were built to order by Fleetwood following the designs of Harley Earl, and advertised

by Cadillac as "Catalog Customs" but there were full custom models that came from the other famous coachbuilders of the day, and even a few bodies from GM's volume supplier Fisher. With such a plethora of styles and sources, it is no wonder that keeping track of all the variations that were constructed has proved to be a difficult task. One style name that frequently crops up in reference books is the "Madame X" – but opinions differ as to exactly what features this model had.

Even those buyers who ordered from the standard Fleetwood range could opt

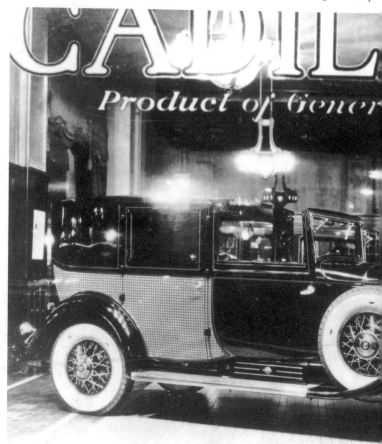

for their own modifications, and the degree of personalization probably means that every one of the three thousand or so V16 Cadillacs sold in 1930 was unique. One only has to look at the eight choices of windshield design that were available – flat vertical, sloping at five different angles, and the vertical Vee – with swing-out or crank-up options, to appreciate the selection facing the well-heeled buyer.

Had Cadillac been an independent company, and not insulated from the economy by General Motors, it is hard to believe it wouldn't have suffered the same fate as all the other manufacturers who were producing luxurious automobiles in small quantities. The V16 wouldn't survive very long, but it set a new standard of excellence that few would equal. That would matter little to the millions of unemployed who were hoping that president Herbert Hoover's measures of tariff controls and emergency job and relief programs would restore the situation, but things were destined to get worse before they got better.

Other manfuacturers, both at home and abroad, could only marvel at the jewel-like perfection of the V16. Cadillac's main domestic rivals: Packard, Pierce-Arrow and Lincoln, took a

Left: The Standard of the World and the envy of the world. Cadillac would survive when over 800 US banks collapsed, and go on to become the definitive symbol of success. The Cadillac V12 engine combined the reliability of the unimpeachable V8 with the performance of the slightly temperamental V16. Foreign competition in this configuration included such legendary names as Rolls-Royce, Mercedes, Maybach, Hispano-Suiza and Isotta-Fraschini. Beautiful and exclusive as these motors were, in engineering terms, they simply could not match the Cadillac's efficiency and finesse.

couple of years to rise to the challenge and then offered mere V12s. Marmon fielded a V16, which approached theCadillac's sophistication and matched its performance; the Duesenberg Model J was a performance contender as well. In Europe, neither Rolls-Royce nor Bentley could match the Cadillac. Rolls-Royce were forced to concede that their engine was no longer the quietest in the world and W.O.Bentley himself remarked that the word "automobile" was scarcely adequate to describe the Cadillac V16.

David Dunbar Buick had entered the automobile business in 1899, having famously developed a method of bonding porcelain to cast iron and thus giving the world the enamel bath tub. The company, based in Flint, Michigan, was the basis of the General Motors Corporation, founded by Billy Durant in 1908. Buick became the backbone of the GM corporate body and in the 'twenties it was one of America's most popular cars. In the 'thirties, however, Buick hit a bad patch, as did many other manufacturers.

1931

SPECIFICATIONS

MARMON SIXTEEN

Engine:
Cast iron - V16

Displacement:
490 cu. ins.

Bore and stroke:
3.13 x 4.0 ins

Horsepower:
200

Body styles:
Coupe; Sedan;
Convertible coupe;
Convertible sedan;
Close coupled sedan;
Limousine + Customs

No. of seats:
2-7

Weight (lbs):
c. 6,000 lbs

Price:
c. $5,000

Produced:
10,115 (all models)

Marmon not only suffered from being second to Cadillac when introducing a V16 engine, it also had to do without the protection of being part of General Motors. These disadvantages proved impossible to overcome and the Marmon Motor Car Company, of Indianapolis, Indiana, would go into receivership in May 1933, ending a history of building fine automobiles that went back to 1902.

The brainchild of Howard C. Marmon, a brilliant engineer, the Marmon Sixteen (it was never called a V16 by the Company) was destined to be the final chapter of a marque story that was nearly all about high performance automobiles. Indeed, what must rank as the most famous racing car of them all, the one that Ray Harroun drove to victory in the first Indy 500 in 1911, is the Marmon Wasp. Apart from being based in Indianapolis, Marmon's connection with the

Below: The magnificent Marmon Sixteen performed with an exhilaration that matched its looks, thanks to a 490 cu.in. V16 engine and a very lightweight construction. Sadly, it arrived at a time when the demand for luxury cars had evaporated, and the Marmon company would become extinct as a result.

speedway remained until the end: every Sixteen came with a guarantee that the car had completed two laps of the Indy track at over 100mph.

Above: By 1931, LaSalle was using the same 353 cu.in. V8 L-head engine as its Cadillac parent and was becoming more like Cadillac in other ways too – and suffering from the confusion of identity. A decline in yearly sales to 10,000 units didn't help future prospects much either.

Acceleration was brisk too, Marmon boasting that it would go from five to sixty miles an hour in 20 seconds, a feat few others could match. And, long before drag racing became a recognized sport, Marmon literature for the Sixteen proclaimed: "When the light turns green it leaves its neighbor far behind." The reasons for the superior performance came from extensive use of aluminum alloy in the 490 cu.in. 200 horsepower V16 engine which had a 6:1 compression ratio – the highest in the industry at the time. Although of a similar 45° narrow Vee configuration to the Cadillac motor, the Marmon unit weighed around 370 pounds less, giving a much better power to weight ratio. Lightweight construction was also a feature of the car as a whole, with hood and splash aprons, head light and tail lamp brackets, all made of aluminum.

Bodies were designed by Walter Dorwin Teague, built by LeBaron, and represented as big a departure from previous Marmons as did the V16 from the eight and six cylinder units seen in other company models. From the sloping V-shaped radiator grille to the low roof line, it represented a totally new concept for Marmon. But timing was its downfall. Not only did Marmon launch it at the beginning of the Depression, bad enough timing in itself, but following the display of the Sixteen at auto shows during the winter of

1930/31 it was April before the first car was delivered. The delay put Marmon even further behind Cadillac who were

Below: The Cadillac of 1931 was unmatched, except, perhaps, by the Duesenberg. Most Cadillac customers probably cared rather less about the remarkable performance that was available, than in the smoothness, silence and sophistication of the way they were conveyed.
Fuel consumption was obviously not a critical factor; a V16, cruising at a steady 60mph, would be giving the driver no more than 8 1/2mpg.

themselves struggling to sell their V16 in any significant numbers.

Pricing was another problem. While the Sixteen wasn't cheap, it undercut the

Above: A tiny proportion of Cadillac's V16 chassis were sold to independent coachbuilders, in the US and abroad. The vast majority of the "custom" body styles advertised, plus full customs, were produced "in house" by Fleetwood. Around 500 bodies a month were built, to a remarkably high standard.

Below: Cadillac's reputation for excellence was secure. Over the coming years, many of its competitors would gradually fade away, but Cadillac was to sail serenely on into the future, broadening its domestic market and creating new ones in some unexpected parts of the world.

Cadillac V16, and many believe that Marmon couldn't have made much profit on the cars they sold. Price cuts in succeeding years only served to make things worse. In the end, less than 400 Sixteens were produced in three years.

Marmon did produce other cars in 1931, and tried to move away from the limited production luxury market after George Williams took over as company president in 1924. The eight cylinder Little Marmon lasted one model year, 1927, and the Roosevelt (another eight cylinder car, this time priced at under $1,000) also failed to last after an initial demand saw production hit 22,300 units in 1929. Williams couldn't have forseen the economic catastrophe coming, and it hit the company hard. By '31, annual output was less than six thousand cars, and the Roosevelt had been dropped as a separate marque though the car itself remained in slightly revised form as the Marmon Model 70.

By 1933, the Sixteen was the only Marmon. Arriving in a year when over 800 banks failed, it's not surprising it was shortlived. It was also the year that Will Rogers said: "We are the first nation to go to the poorhouse in an automobile." The trouble was, no enough chose to go in a Marmon.

The Marmon V16 arrived about a year later than Cadillac's and is regarded by many as its equal or even its superior. The Marmon engine, however, lacked the silent, hydraulic valve system and the counter-balanced camshafts of the Cadillac and its all-aluminum construction was inherently more resonant - it lighter - than the Cadillac's cast iron block.

The Marmon is regarded as having had the edge in terms of acceleration and top speed over the Cadillac, but in the kind of cars that the vast majority of

Below: The influence of Harley Earl, who headed up General Motors' Art and Colour Section, opened in 1927, was already evident. New metal pressing techniques allowed Earl to develop flowing forms and to gradually dispense with the traditional strapped-on "trunk" by blending it into the bodywork, as seen in this splendid town car.

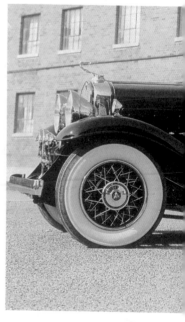

Below: The Roadster also came with a compartment for golf clubs as an option, accessed by a door set in the bodywork behind the driver. The luxury provided by Cadillac and the wealth of a small group of customers provided a demand for a traditional conveyance. Even in the depths of the Depression, there were still those who could afford not only to drive but to be driven and they liked to be driven in style.

buyers were ordering, these consider-ations were way down the list of prior-ities. The Cadillac's total silence and incredible flexibility - it would accele-rate smoothly from walking pace in top gear - were of far greater appeal. It is no doubt the case that, given time, Marm-on's engineers could have redefined their design even further and gone on to produce the definitive sixteen cylinder automobile. Sadly, time was not on Marmon's side and the commercial might of the General Motors Corpor-ation was on Cadillac's.

Above: As well as its two normal seats, the Cadillac Roadster came with a rumble seat as an option. Styling innovation had to be incremental rather than radical due to the innate conservatism of the customer, particularly at the upper end of the market. The "pregnant Buick" of 1929 was a hard lesson that taught Earl to be cautious. Over the coming years he revolutionized American auto design, surely, but slowly.

SPECIFICATIONS

FORD MODEL 18 V8

Engine:
90 degree V8 - cast iron block

Displacement:
221 cu. ins.

Bore and stroke:
3 1/16 x 3 3/4 ins.
Horsepower:
65

Body styles:
Coupe; Cabriolet; Roadster; Phaeton; Sedan; Victoria; Station wagon

No. of seats:
2-4

Weight (lbs):
2,422 lbs - 2,684 lbs

Price:
$475 - $640

Produced:
287,285

If we were to adapt a modern day saying to suit the circumstances of 1932, it might run something along the lines of: "When the going gets tough, Henry Ford gets things going." For, when it came time to making things happen or shaking up an established method of doing a certain task, nobody was as effective as the founder of the Ford Motor Company. It's true to say that he was also cantankerous, irascible, pig-headed, stubborn, and much worse besides on occasions.

It's also true that he had a vast army of men that he could command to do his bidding, and would often set them impossible targets to test out an idea

or prove a theory. Further more, history has a way of only telling us of the successes achieved by great men, and the mistakes they made along the way are often forgotten. There's no doubt Henry Ford made his fair share of errors while amassing a fortune from the Model T, but when old Henry got something right, it was usually a spectacular success.

Just such a brainwave was his decision to put a V8 engine in the 1932 models at the height of the Depression when thirteen million people were unemployed, the average wage had dropped by 60% since 1929 and even US President Herbert Hoover and baseball hero Babe Ruth had volunteered to take pay cuts. Henry's reasoning might not have been based on a very logical train of thought – the main purpose seems to have been to outdo his

Below: *Ford urged dealers to get customers to try out the V8, saying "Driving means buying."*

arch rivals at Chevrolet. "We're going from a four to an eight, because Chevrolet is going to a six," is what he is quoted as having said in 1929.

But although the idea came about from a fixation with competition, the execution of putting it into production was the stuff from which Ford legends were made. Early in 1932, when the foundry at the huge River Rouge plant was crying out for help to overcome the problems it had in casting the new V8 engine against incredibly short deadlines, it was suggested that extra draftsmen should be hired to get engineering drawings done. Ford's reply was: "Sorensen can make all you want just from a sketch on the back of an envelope," an attitude brought about by Henry's inability to understand proper drawings and his dislike of them being used. While "Cast Iron Charlie" Sorensen was undoubtedly a wizard when it came to solving the difficulties encountered with manufacturing large quantities of a complex new design, even he couldn't do it all from just a scribble on the back of an envelope. Nevertheless, Sorensen had to agree with his boss at the time, but the necessary blueprints were produced without Henry's knowledge.

Such subterfuge was often employed when Henry Ford was involved in making decisions about how something should be done, and as far as the mechanical side of the Model 18 was concerned, Henry was very much in control. An article published in the Detroit News in February 1932 carried this quote from Edsel Ford: "My father is never happier than when he is solving some big mechanical problem. When the Model A was brought out he left many things to others, but I have never seen him give such attention to detail as he is now. He works for hours at a time trying to eliminate a single part. He figures that the fewer the parts in a car, the less the risk of trouble."

But Henry's quest for fewer parts didn't stop him from holding on to old-fashioned ideas, long after they had been discarded by other manufacturers and often in complete contradiction to common sense. Hydraulic brakes were not acceptable, the mechanical rod system giving rise to the Ford slogan "safety of steel from toe to wheel," but hydraulic shock absorbers were deemed to be okay, despite being more expensive. Transverse leaf springs were another thing that Ford would insist upon in the car's suspension design for many years to come.

Fortunately, thanks to his preoccupation with the nuts and bolts of his cars, Henry left styling matters to his son Edsel, saying "He knows style – how a car should look." Edsel was assisted by Joe Galamb and Eugene T. "Bob" Gregorie, and although it has been suggested that LeBaron or body manufacturers Briggs also had a hand in the design, this seems unlikely apart from the usual small modifications that might be requested by any supplier to make a component easier to produce. When compared to its predecessor the Model A, the Model 18 (the Model B shared the identical bodyshell but used a four cylinder engine) featured a more rounded look, especially on the radiator grille, front fenders and roof leading edge – not streamlining but a definite move in that direction, away from the utilitarian school of thought.

After some of the most intensive development work ever seen in peacetime, the first of the new Ford V8 engines came off the line in March 1932 and was ceremonially stamped by Henry

Right: *In 1932, Cord fitted the Auburn with V12 Lycoming engine. At just over $1000, the Auburn Boat-tail Speedster Model 12-160 must be the cheapest twelve cylinder car ever produced - it was sold as a loss-leader for the eights and sixes lower down the range. Sadly, the Auburn went the way of the Cord and the Duesenberg in 1937.*

Ford with the numbers 18-1, representing the first eight cylinder and the first of its type. Displacing 221 cu.in. and rated at 65bhp, it was the first such engine in volume mass production. Despite predictions, initial V8 production was slow, with many rejects. Once the cars finally got into the hands of the eager customers (cars ordered at the launch in early April weren't delivered until August in most cases), it was found that the new engine suffered many shortcomings. Overheating, excessive oil consumption, bearings and pistons wearing out rapidly, blocks cracking, fuel pump problems and much else besides, brought in numerous complaints and the Ford Motor Company was forced to issue corrective remedies and free replacement parts which cost millions of dollars.

In an attempt to counter some of this negative feedback, Ford staged a test to demonstrate the durability and reliability of the V8. A car was driven night and day around a 32 mile course in the Mojave Desert, California, for 33 days. At the end of the test, the car had covered 33,301 miles – equivalent to going one and a third times around the world according to the Ford publicists – at an average speed of 41.8mph (including stops), achieved 19.64 miles per gallon, and used "only" 1.5 pints of oil for every thousand miles.

Whether this exercise had the required effect is difficult to judge, and in more recent times it is the recommendations that Ford received from notorious gangsters like John Dillinger and Clyde Barrow (of Bonnie and Clyde fame, who actually wrote Henry Ford a testimonial letter) for the V8's superior performance in getaways that have often been given greater prominence. That the Ford could provide previously unknown speed and acceleration in a low-priced car when its engine was running on song is undeniable, but the haste to produce it caused no end of problems – some of which took years to eradicate.

If engineering was causing Ford plenty of headaches, things were also far from tranquil on other fronts. Four demonstrators were killed during the Ford Hunger March to the Rouge plant on March 6, organized to protest at the lack of jobs – after being idle for months

Below: *Built by Hudson, the Terraplane Roadster was priced below both the Ford V8 and Chevrolet equivalents to attract buyers with reduced circumstances in the depths of the US economic depression.*

Above: *The 1932 Cords were in fact 1931s, as production had ceased on New Year's Eve. The price of the beautiful L-29 was cut to around $2,500 and the motors over-bored to give even greater power, but nothing, it seemed, could save the ailing company in an ailing market - at least not for the time being*

while the new car was being prepared, workers discovered that there were less than half the jobs on offer than before. And to cap it all, much to Henry's chagrin, Chevrolet still outsold Ford by a wide margin as the Dearborn company had its lowest calendar year production since 1914 and lost $75 million in the process. The V8 would go on to be a winner and the 1932 Ford would become an automotive icon, but few in those dark days could have guessed it.

The Model eighteen was a good-looking car, even if it suffered from teething troubles mechanically. The V8 logo, carried on the tie-bar between the headlights has become a design classic. To assist cooling, the number of louvers cut in the hood was increased from 20 to 25. Inside, the comprehensive instrumentation was mounted in an engine-turned oval-frame in the center of the wood-grained dash panel. The ignition key and ignition system incorporated an anti-theft device.

Henry Ford may have been a difficult man to get along with but his instincts, in the broadest sense, were infallible. He had, after all, put America on wheels with his immortal Model T. Had various

factors not conspired against him, it is probable that Ford would have moved directly from the T to the V8, having been experimenting with 8 cylinder engines since the mid-'twenties. With the advent of the Model 18, America would emerge from the Depression equipped to move on to an age of performance for all, able not merely to get around but to travel at speed and in comfort - at least where the roads (which in many rural areas were still in horse and buggy condition) and the local highway restrictions, permitted it.

The Ford V8s dominated stock car racing for years and were favored by the Automobile Racing Club of America. In 1935, Ford was rewarded for his efforts with the news that he most wanted to hear: he had outsold Chevrolet - at last.

SPECIFICATIONS

**PIERCE SILVER
ARROW**

Engine:
V12 - cast iron block

Displacement:
462 cu. ins.

Bore and stroke:
3.50 x 4.0 ins.

Horsepower:
175

Body styles:
Numerous: in-house

No. of seats:
5

Weight (lbs):
5,729 lbs

Price:
$10,000

Produced:
5 Silver Arrows
2,152 (all models)

*Above Right: The Pierce
Silver Arrow was
streamline styling at its
elegant best. Designed by
Philip Wright, the
curvaceous sedan was
capable of 120mph, but
at $10,000, it was one of
the most expensive on the
market.*

Most truly great automobiles have an exclusive styling feature that makes them instantly identifiable. For Pierce-Arrow, it was having the head lamps incorporated into the fenders. Designed at the Buffalo, New York, factory by Herbert Dawley and patented in 1913, ordinary head lights were an option until 1932, yet without head lamps on the fender, it just wasn't a Pierce-Arrow.

Famed for producing cars in the luxury car market, by 1915 Pierce-Arrow could count 12,000 automobiles that had found satisfied wealthy customers since the company's start in 1901. But, in the following years, things weren't to run nearly as smoothly as the silky six cylinder engines used in their cars. In fact, their insistence on staying with the six was the start of their problems, as most other prestige makers soon offered eights, or even twelves, and so Pierce-Arrow soon fell behind; it took until 1920 for Pierce-Arrow to shift the steering wheel from the right-hand side to the left to conform with the standard used by the rest of the industry for years.

In the early Twenties, a merry-go-round of management changes exacerbated the situation and, by 1926, Pierce-Arrow was in trouble. By

1928 company president, Myron Forbes, could see that Pierce-Arrow needed help and negotiated a merger with Studebaker. Things perked up considerably and in 1929 came a new eight cylinder engine. Sales doubled to 10,000 units that year, but this was not to last.

1933 proved to be the crunch year, although it might not have seemed so

Below: Oldsmobile called its 1933 models the "style leaders" and production more than doubled over the previous bad year. Six and eight cylinder models were offered, with shorter wheelbase sixes in the majority. "No-Draft Ventilation" with pivoting wind wings was developed by Fisher Body and featured on all GM models this year.

right at the outset. First there was the superb V12 engine. Designed by Karl Wise and introduced in '31, it was equal to any other twelve cylinder powerplant, with seven main bearings instead of four, as was used by Packard and Cadillac. Then there was the pioneering use of hydraulic tappets – another first for Pierce-Arrow, and ranking alongside its power braking system for technical

innovation. Sales increased in early '33, but a crippling strike by tool and die makers soon interrupted the recovery.

Studebaker protected Pierce from the worst effects of the Depression, but it had over-extended itself and went bankrupt in the spring of '33. Albert E. Erskine, president of Studebaker (and Pierce-Arrow too, following Forbes' resignation in '29) committed suicide in July and, in August, Pierce was sold off to a group of bankers and businessmen.

In the midst of all this upheaval, came Philip Wright's streamlined masterpiece – the Pierce Silver Arrow. Promising "in 1933 the car of 1940," this tapered-tail fastback 4-door sedan caused a sensation when it appeared at the New York Automobile Show. Said to be capable of 120mph, with a cruising speed of 80mph thanks to the 175bhp 462 cu.in. V12 engine, the wind-cheating shape foretold many future styling features. There were no running boards, the fenders were smoothly integrated into the body and every joint was precise.

Priced at $10,000, the Silver Arrow was the most expensive US car on the market, apart from Duesenberg, and only five were made. Some of its features were later incorporated in '34 models, but sales were in decline.

After Franklin D. Roosevelt was inaugurated as the 32nd President of the United States at the start of '33, he had set in motion his 100 Days program to boost the economy. Prohibition was abolished, but Pierce-Arrow had little to celebrate as, despite the first small signs of economic recovery, the days of such an expensive hand-made car were numbered. After several more attempts at reorganization, the company finally folded in 1938.

Left: Lincoln had by this time been absorbed into the Ford Motor Corporation and Edsel Ford, son of Henry was the company President. The improved V12 engine of 1933 featured light-weight aluminum pistons and a four-bearing crank. Custom bodies could be specified, from coachbuilders like LeBaron and Brunn.

SPECIFICATIONS

**CHRYSLER AIRFLOW
SERIES CU**

Engine:
Cast iron - 8 Cylinders
in line

Displacement:
299 cu. ins.

Bore and stroke:
3 1/4 x 4 1/2 ins.

Horsepower:
122

Body styles:
Coupe; Brougham;
Sedan; Town sedan

No. of seats:
5-6

Weight (lbs):
3,716 lbs - 3,760 lbs

Price:
$1,345

Produced:
8,389

For a company where engineering considerations were dominant, almost to the exclusion of styling innovations, the arrival of the Airflow from Chrysler in January '34 must have been a surprise to many people. But even more of a surprise, perhaps, is that the Airflow indeed came directly from a desire for better automotive engineering rather than a decision to create a design statement.

Unfortunately for Chrysler, the Airflow was proof that while good engineers can be relied on to crack difficult technical problems, even the best of them sometimes fail to appreciate that styling shouldn't be completely ruled by function. The engineer's view of what looks right is usually determined by what works best, not what appeals to the potential customer. Throughout modern history there have been numerous examples of ideas that were too far ahead of popular taste and had to be abandoned as a result – the Chrysler Airflow is just one such mistake.

Above: *The Chrysler Airflow Series CU 4-door Sedan came with an in-line eight cylinder L-head 299 cu.in. engine that developed 122bhp. Standard equipment included an automatic vacuum-operated clutch on a three-speed manual transmission. By far the best seller of the 1934 Airflow models, the CU Series was the cheapest range at $1,345, but only 7,226 of these 4-door sedans were ever built.*

Left: *Although featuring all the body trim of a 1934 example, the pointed grille of the car pictured is of the type introduced for the '35 model year by stylist Raymond Dietrich in an attempt to revitalize sales from the disastrous slump – it wasn't enough. There was also a range of limited production Chrysler Custom Imperial cars, which were the first to use a curved one-piece windshield in '34 and also had vacuum assisted brakes.*

Inspiration for the wind tunnel research that led to the creation of the Airflow is said to have come to Chrysler engineer Carl Breer back in 1927 when he saw a squadron of air craft flying in formation. It set in motion a train of thought about the lack of aerodynamics involved in the design of car bodies, so he had a small scale wind tunnel constructed where he carried out tests on wooden blocks. The next stage was to have a much larger wind tunnel built at the Chrysler Highland Park research center. One of the most interesting observations arising from the experiments was that most cars produced less wind resistance when placed backwards in the tunnel. In a later interview, Carl Breer said he remembered looking out of his office window at the parking lot and thinking: "Just imagine all those cars running in the wrong direction all this time."

One of the first elements he found to reduce wind resistance was a sloping back and this led to other fundamental design changes. In order to give sufficient headroom for rear seat passengers, they had to be moved forward, which in turn caused the front seat to shift and this had a knock-on effect of pushing the engine out over the

Below: Intended for export, the Chrysler Airflow six was, in fact, a DeSoto. The CU - eight cylinder - model incorporated the improved design with unitary body construction and there was an extended "Imperial" version as well. The curved, single-piece windshield, introduced in 1934, was an industry first.

front axle – a completely new idea. But important though streamlining had become, there were many other factors that the team of Breer, Owen Skelton, Fred Zeder and Oliver Clark were working on with the new car. Improved ride qualities through better weight distribution, more interior room and greater structural strength were also targets for the engineers.

With a conventional Thirties car, the majority of the weight was supported by the rear axle, typically in a ratio of 60:40%. By moving the engine forward, the Airflow had a much better front to rear balance, with 55% at the front and 45% at the rear. It wasn't simply a matter of moving the engine forward, however, it had to be tilted at an angle of 5° to keep the transmission tunnel profile down. This, in turn, required a special oil pan to cope with suspension movement as one third of the block was ahead of the front axle. Longer leaf springs were used to further enhance the ride characteristics and some reports concluded that the Airflow came close to fulfiling the "Floating Power" phrase in Chrysler advertising. Also, seat width was increased by a whopping ten inches, giving unrivaled room for six people to travel in comfort.

Structurally too, the Airflow differed considerably from the norm, using an all-steel cage fixed to the chassis rails, rather than the traditional method of wooden reinforcement members for the steel body panels favored by most other manufacturers. The lightweight cage, resembling a modern NASCAR racing stock car safety frame, closely followed the roof and body lines providing a rigid mounting for the panels and was a step along the road towards full unitary construction and the elimination of a separate body and chassis. One other feature of note was the first use of a one-piece curved windshield on the special

Custom Imperial limited production models.

But no matter what technical advancements were achieved with the Airflow, it was the body styling that would sell the car to the public. Today we can look at the "waterfall" grille and rounded front end and appreciate what they were doing, but back then it was seen as an ugly beast. That wasn't the case at the New York Automobile Show where the car made its debut, and enough of the more sophisticated metropolitan audience were sufficiently impressed to place orders which added up to several thousand in total. And several high-profile personalities in the fashion and design world expressed enthusiasm for the ultra-modern shape. It was a fairly promising start, but by no means all of the big city observers liked the design, and some warning signs might have been noticed.

The immediate problem faced by Chrysler was fulfiling these initial orders. Getting the radical design into production proved more difficult than had been envisaged and there was a three or four month delay (depending on the model) before deliveries began. This hold-up proved to be critical. In the interim, rival manufacturers were able to circulate negative rumors about the strange-looking Airflow and without any cars in use to counter this propaganda, Chrysler suffered from a loss of consumer confidence in the new automobile. It also has to be admitted

Below: 1934 Dodges came as Standard, Special or DeLuxe. The Ram hood ornament appeared for the first time, anticipating models far in the future. In the same year Dodge pioneered comparison road tests with the products of other manufacturers. The Dodge compared well with most, on price, performance, and styling.

that when the first cars were actually delivered there was some shortfall in the build quality, which didn't help at all.

It wasn't just Chrysler that was affected; DeSoto used the Airflow design exclusively for its '35 model range and sales tumbled as a result. The Chrysler marque fared slightly better because of the line of more conventional models with the Airstream name that were produced alongside the Airflow and so helped limit losses. In a year when auto industry sales rose by 40% the combined total for Chrysler and DeSoto dropped by almost 10% to about 50,000 units. Of those, only 15,000 were Airflow models – it was a dismal verdict on a technically superior vehicle.

Thankfully for the corporation as a whole, Plymouth and Dodge hadn't used the Airflow shape and their sales remained buoyant. The situation wasn't as disastrous as it might have been for Chrysler, partly due to sales of the standard Airstream models, but also to the fact that the Airflow had been designed to keep tooling and manufacturing costs down.

The Chrysler panic buttons were hit and stylist Raymond Dietrich was hired to rescue the situation. He introduced a grille with a peak to replace the original waterfall design for 35 but sales still declined. Chrysler kept faith with the Airflow until 1937, giving it annual facelifts to try and improve public acceptance but the resistance to the unusual shape just couldn't be overcome

and it was dropped.

Setbacks of a more permanent kind were suffered by the criminal fraternity during 1935 as bank robbers Bonnie Parker and Clyde Barrow were killed and became enshrined in folk lore. And Public Enemy Number One – John Dillinger – was killed by the FBI, as were hoodlums Pretty Boy Floyd and Baby Face Nelson. It proves that just like crime, it doesn't always pay to be first in the automotive field with a revolutionary idea, no matter how sound the engineering behind it!

Left & Below: The twelve cylinder Packards, originally designated "twin sixes" were beautifully built cars with excellent performance, if not quite in the league of the V12 Cadillacs. Custom coachwork was available from Dietrich and LeBaron and interior refinements included an optional radio. The engine was a monobloc design in cast iron, displacing 445 cu. ins. 160 Brake Horsepower was produced at 3200rpm. Most versions of the V12 weighed in excess of 5,000 pounds but could accelerate to 60mph in around 20 seconds.

SPECIFICATIONS

STOUT SCARAB

Engine:
Ford: 90 degree V8 -
cast iron

Displacement:
221 cu. ins.

Bore and stroke:
3 1/16 x 3 3/4 ins.

Horsepower:
85

Body styles:
Unique & Unitary

No. of seats:
4+ with adaptable lay
out

Weight (lbs):
-

Price:
-

Produced:
5

Sometimes the past can come back and hit you in the face, reminding you that it's all been done before. To use an automotive analogy, it's like looking in the rear view mirror and seeing that engraved message warning that "objects may be closer than they seem." Since Chrysler introduced the Plymouth Voyager and Dodge Caravan in 1984, minivans, MPVs or "people movers" have become some of the biggest selling models of the Nineties and nearly every manufacturer has an example. But look at the Stout Scarab of 1935,

read the specification and marvel at how farsighted was its creator William B. Stout.

While the Scarab was influenced by his pioneering work on all-metal aircraft, Stout's background also included automotive jobs. His first taste of car design was in 1913 when he was an editor on Motor Age, but his proposed cyclecar never made it into production due to lack of finance. Stout had better

Below: The minimum body overhang due to the wheels being positioned at the extremities and the aerodynamic shape were part of the futuristic Scarab's unique features, but poor rearward vision was a handicap. Stout Scarab advertising consisted of "A challenge and a prophecy..." but the prediction that the unusual car would be a major influence on automobile design was about half a century out.

luck with the Imp cyclecar when he was general sales manager for McIntyre, but that was a commercial failure and he moved to Scripps-Booth at the end of 1914 where he was chief engineer. That position was also brief, and in 1916 he joined the aircraft division of Packard.

All his life, Stout was a prolific inventor (he filed more patents than

Right: Ford's slogan for 1935 was "Greater Beauty, Greater Comfort, and Greater Safety," and the Deluxe Phaeton is a good example of the longer, wider and faster automobiles being produced by the company. The year's most popular Ford was the 2-door Tudor sedan which sold over 322,000; the more expensive Phaeton sold only 6,073, but the lack of roll-up windows probably didn't help. Note the front doors are now front hinged and this was the last year for outside horns and wire wheels.

Below: Oldsmobile 6 Station Wagon. The Olds' straight six had displaced 213 cu. ins, and developed 90 horsepower. 1935 was the first year of Olds' "Turret Top" body styles but traditional designs, such as this "Woody," were still available and still popular.

anyone else except Thomas Edison) and he introduced the internally-braced, cantilevered all-metal wing and corrugated aluminum outer skin to American aviation. Stout also had a gift for self-promotion, as shown by a letter he sent to Detroit industrialists, to raise money for a project, which said: "We want to build a metal plane. If you join us it will cost money. One thousand dollars. No more, no less. And for your thousand dollars you will get one definite promise. You will never get your money back."

But it was joining forces with Henry and Edsel Ford that really got things going. The Fords built Stout a new facility in Dearborn, Michigan, and the Stout Metal Airplane Co was established as a division of The Ford Motor Company. The result was the 2-AT, the first all-metal aircraft built in the USA, which had exceptional load carrying capabilities. In 1925, Henry Ford decided to buy out William Stout's share of the company, and Stout became the head of an independent airline while still developing aircraft. Stout Air Services operated Ford 4-AT Tri-Motor airliners, and was the first airline to offer in-flight meals (sandwiches and coffee) and employ uniformed Flight Escorts. Stout's aircrew also wore the company uniforms of blue trimmed with gold braid, a suggestion by Henry Ford that it would "lend dignity to their profession."

Stout sold his airline to the newly-formed United Airlines and turned his mind to other things. In 1932, he started Stout Engineering Laboratories in Detroit where he built the first Scarab prototype. It wasn't until 1935, however, that he deemed the Scarab was ready for production when he introduced a second, steel-bodied version (the original had a duraluminum alloy body). Everything about the Scarab was unusual – unit construction and streamlined in shape, it had a rear-mounted 85hp Ford V8 coupled to a transaxle/differential unit modified from a three-speed transmission, plus coil spring suspension all round.

The Scarab interior was equally unorthodox: in a huge 7ft 6ins by 5ft 7ins floor area, only the driver's seat was fixed, the others were loose to enable them to be moved to any position. A folding table was provided for eating or playing cards and there was a rear

davenport seat which converted into a full-length couch. One magazine described the Scarab's cabin thus: "The interior of the car is extremely comfortable and roomy, with a table and movable chairs. It gives passengers the feeling of traveling in a hotel room."

A very few cars were actually produced, and mainly offered "by invitation to a selected list." A couple probably ended up with movie stars but the main drawback of the car in terms of appealing to a mass market - or even to a specialist market - was that it was - let's face it - no oil-painting.

Below: Auburn's last, sleek and stylish, hurrah, shown here with auto designer Alexis de Sakhnoffsky, who designed the 1935 magazine ad campaign for the Auburn Automobile Company. Cord's attention was already elsewhere, having moved into Checker Cab. Despite a long list of speed records and amazing value for money, the Depression was biting and the writing was on the wall.

SPECIFICATIONS

LINCOLN ZEPHYR SERIES H

Engine:
75 degree V12 - cast iron block

Displacement:
267.3 cu. ins.

Bore and stroke:
2 3/4 x 3 3/4 ins.

Horsepower:
110

Body styles:
2 door sedan; 4 door sedan

No. of seats:
2-4

Weight (lbs):
3,289 lbs - 3,349 lbs

Price:
$1,275 - $1,320

Produced:
14,994

In October 1936, the first 300-mile international road race was held at New York's Roosevelt Raceway at Westbury on Long Island. The track had been built on the site of the airfield from which Charles Lindbergh had taken off on his daring solo transatlantic flight in 1927, and the racers were vying for the George Vanderbilt Cup. It was ultimately won by Italian Tazio Nuvolari in a Scuderia Ferrari Alfa Romeo. The highest-placed American finisher, however, was Mauri Rose, who took eighth place in an Offenhauser-powered Miller car.

Rose's placing was not much for American sports fans to cheer about but, earlier in the year, they had good reason to be happy. Black athlete, Jesse Owens, triumphed at the Olympic Games in Berlin, much to the chagrin of Adolf Hitler and his Nazi followers. Their racist doctrine could not contemplate the success of anyone other than a blonde, blue-eyed aryan and Hitler stormed out rather than present Owens with his gold medal.

Right: Lincoln offered two body styles for the Zephyr in 1936: a 2-door sedan and a 4-door sedan. The teardrop shape was in evidence throughout the car, including the rear lights and fenders.

It would not be long before the Nazi hordes would be storming through Europe, but such a prospect would be far from the minds of Americans that year. US car buyers, particularly in the luxury market, would be considering the new streamlined Lincoln Zephyr. This radical design employed a novel method of construction and was technically advanced in many ways.

The Zephyr began life outside the Ford Motor Co., being conceived by John Tjaarda, a stylist at Briggs Manufacturing Co. Briggs built bodies for Ford, and the new design was intended as a project to sell to Ford. An early prototype was constructed in 1934, but it was far too radical for production. Although it was powered by a Ford flathead V8, this was mounted in the rear with a swing-axle final drive sprung by a transverse leaf spring. The cost of making this set-up work, plus the likely buyer resistance to such an unusual arrangement, even if it were backed by the Ford name, made the idea a non-starter.

However, the overall streamlined shape of the car appealed to Edsel Ford, who felt that it had possibilities as a front-engined car. Edsel had been responsible for transforming the fortunes of Lincoln during the Twenties and early Thirties. When he took charge of the division in 1922, Lincoln had only recently been saved from receivership by his father, Henry Ford, and was building expensive, old-fashioned cars. Under Edsel, the company soon began producing some of the most beautiful automobiles ever created.

Henry Ford believed that a car should

Right Above: The new 267.3 cu.in. flathead V12 engine was similar in design to Ford's V8, but had its cylinders set at a narrower angle. Despite lubrication problems, it performed well giving the Zephyr a top speed of 90mph.

be engineered first, with the bodywork designed to suit. But Edsel had other ideas. He placed good styling first and foremost, so much so that he authorized the creation of Ford's first styling department under the direction of Eugene T. Gregory. The latter was now given the task of refining Tjaarda's design to allow for the installation of an engine and radiator at the front of the car.

In the original, rear-engined design, the nose of the car had been very narrow and pointed; Gregory managed to widen this sufficiently to accommodate the engine, radiator and radiator grille, while retaining the sense of a narrow, pointed nose. The result was a beautiful, streamlined body, based on a 122 inch wheelbase, that was quite unique for its day. Much use was made of the teardrop shape, not just in the overall style of the body, but also in individual features, such as tail lights, fender skirts and grille emblem.

The uniqueness of the car's styling was matched by its method of construction. Even in its rear-engined prototype guise at Briggs, the car had featured unibody construction, the body panels being welded together with various strengthening members to produce a strong structure that had no need of a separate chassis. The fabric roof insert, found on all other closed Ford cars at the time, was also disposed of and the Zephyr had a solid steel roof panel in its place.

The narrow tapering nose of the Zephyr needed a small, narrow engine.

At the time, all Lincolns were powered by V12 engines, and it was felt that the new car would have to be similarly equipped to be considered a Lincoln. However, the existing powerplant was too large for the sleek design, so Lincoln's chief engineer, Frank Johnson, designed a new engine to suit the car. While this was based on Ford's successful flathead V8, it naturally had four extra cylinders. To achieve the narrow profile, the cylinder banks were angled at 75° (they were set at 90° in the V8). The one-piece, cast-iron block was fitted with aluminum cylinder heads and alloy steel pistons. With a bore and stroke of 2 and 3 inches respectively, the new V12 displaced 267.3 cu.in. and produced 110 horsepower at 3900rpm.

Backing the engine was a three-speed manual transmission with floorshift. This was connected to a torque-tube drive, which was standard Ford practice.

While the engine and bodywork were completely new, some aspects of the car were definitely behind the times. Not only was the Zephyr equipped with mechanical brakes on all four wheels, but its suspension system was also outdated: transverse leaf springs were fitted at front and rear with solid axles. While the mechanical brakes would be replaced by Bendix hydraulic units in 1939, the transverse springs would soldier on for some time to come. Even the new engine received a lot of criticism, particularly concerning the lubrication system. To ensure that the engine ran reliably, owners were advised to change the oil every 1000 miles. Some engines never made it to the 30,000 mile mark before expiring.

Although sales were slow when the first Zephyrs appeared in November 1935, they soon picked up, and total production for the year came to 15,000 cars, a big improvement on Lincoln's performance for the previous year, which totaled 1,400 cars. No doubt, its revolutionary styling produced some initial resistance, but the Zephyr was well priced, at a fraction of the cost of earlier coach-built models offered by the company.

When the Zephyr went into production, Briggs built most of the car, while Lincoln carried out final assembly work, such as fitting the engine, transmission and suspension along with the hood and fenders, then painting and trimming the cars. However, this arrangement was terminated shortly after the car was introduced. When the Zephyr needed updating for 1937, this was handled by Ford's styling department, who made subtle changes to the design that not only significantly improved the car's appearance, but also kept costs to a minimum by utilizing most of the original tooling.

The Lincoln Zephyr would continue to be updated and restyled until 1949. Throughout, it remained a sleek, streamlined design in keeping with the original. In 1940 the gear shift moved to the now fashionable position on the steering column and various other improvements had been made.

Two years earlier, The old Lincoln K series was nearing the end of its life and Edsel Ford was enjoying a trip to Europe. On his return, he requested E. T. "Bob" Gregory to style a custom body for him that was to be "strictly continental." Gregory decided on the Lincoln as a basis for this car and produced a striking convertible.

The new car was shown to the public in October 1939 as the Lincoln Zephyr Continental Cabriolet and subsequently went into production. A coupe was added in 1940 and the name Zephyr was subsequently dropped from the model's designation.

Below: The performance of the Ford V8, with its domed, aluminum pistons and slick transmission system, was a lot more than adequate for the average driver. Ford won the 1936 Monte Carlo Rally and, closer to home, their engines were already attracting the attention of a young generation of Hot Rodders.

Above: *Franklin D. Roosevelt at the wheel of a 1936 Ford V8 Model 68 Phaeton. Ford were following the fashion by incorporating the separate trunk into the bodywork. The V8 range was subtly restyled for 1936, incremental improvement still being the Ford watchword. Looking at these surprisingly "modern" cars, with their V8 motors and refinements that included windshield wipers and radios, it is remarkable to think that it was a mere eight years previously that the Tin Lizzie had bowed out.*

Below: *Ransom Eli Olds left the company that he had founded and that bore his name, in 1904, having given America its first "volume production" automobile. The first REO was built in the same year. Olds' cars enjoyed considerable success, but by the beginning of World War I, the man himself was losing interest in the cut-and-thrust of the developing auto industry. Without his leadership, the company lost its way and the last cars were produced in 1936, when the company went over to building trucks.*

SPECIFICATIONS

LASALLE

Engine:
90 degree V8 - cast iron block

Displacement:
322 cu. ins.

Bore and stroke:
3 3/8 x 4 1/2 ins.

Horsepower:
125

Body styles:
Coupe; Sedan; Convertible sedan; 2 and 4 door touring sedans

No. of seats:
2-5

Weight (lbs):
3,735 lbs - 3,830 lbs

Price:
$995 - $1,485

Produced:
32,005

Disasters in the air were major news in 1937. After a successful transatlantic crossing, the massive German airship Hindenburg exploded while coming into land on May 6 with great loss of life. Out over the Pacific, pioneer aviatrix Amelia Earhart disappeared and no trace of her, her companion or her airplane was ever found. While ostensibly she was on a record-breaking flight, it was rumored that she was working for the government and spying on the Japanese, who shot her down. Whether or not this is true, no one will ever know, but it is far more likely that the weather, machine problems or simply fatigue caused her to crash and be swallowed up in the vastness of the ocean.

In the world of international auto racing, Americans faced a disappointing result in the

Vanderbilt Cup at Roosevelt Raceway. The first three machines across the finish line were all from Europe. In the lead was Bernd Rosemeyer, whose Auto Union averaged 82.5mph to win; in second and third places respectively were Dick Seaman (Mercedes) and the American, Rex Mays (Alfa Romeo).

In Detroit, the United Auto Workers union had settled a running dispute with GM. However, there were riots following labor disputes at Ford and US Steel.

But there were triumphs too in 1937, among them being the opening of the Golden Gate Bridge across San Francisco Bay. With its soaring towers, this stately suspension bridge was a master-piece of engineering that remains as impressive today as it was 60 years ago.

While many buyers of automobiles that year would have marveled at the Golden Gate Bridge, a significant number of them were also impressed by

Below: In 1934, the restyled LaSalle had been chosen as official pace car for the Indy 500 race. That honor was bestowed on the marque again for 1937, when a convertible coupe led the procession around the famous track. Although originally styled in 1934, and with only minor changes since, the LaSalle had a graceful, streamlined appearance that in no way looked dated.

the new LaSalle. With a longer wheelbase and a V8 engine, the car was snapped up and production rose to a record level. Total Cadillac production that year was 46,000 cars, and LaSalle accounted for 32,000 of them.

Interestingly, the styling of the '37 LaSalle could be traced back to 1934, when it had definitely been ahead of its time. The car received a completely new look in 1934, following a poor showing in the early part of the decade. While the car had originally been conceived to fill the gap between the bottom-of-the-range Cadillacs and the top-of-the-range Buicks, by the beginning of the Thirties, there was not much to choose between it and the less expensive Cadillacs. Altho-ugh the difference in price was about $500 (a substantial sum in those days), the Cadillacs actually seemed to provide better value for money, and their production outstripped LaSalle.

Rather than drop the LaSalle line altogether, GM executives decided to give it a more positive identity so that it was no longer perceived as simply a cheap Cadillac and, therefore, would appeal to a wider audience, other than the traditional buyers of luxury cars. LaSalle could trade on the prestige of being associated with Cadillac and the upmarket body builders Fleetwood, but there would be no doubt that it was not a Cadillac. Moreover, this was emphasized by the $1000 price differe-

nce between the LaSalle and the bottom-of-the-line Caddy.

The new streamlined body style had many features that would not be found on other automobiles until later in the decade. Among these were airfoil-shaped fenders that were full and low at the front, blending into the radiator shell and concealing the frame rails. The teardrop–shaped headlights were supported on the radiator shell and the grille was tall, narrow and oval. The hood sides featured a line of oval ports rather than the normal louvers. The windshield was raked to match the sloping grille and the doors were all of the suicide type, hinged at the rear.

Body styles comprised 4-door sedan, club sedan and convertible sedan, and 2-door coupe and convertible coupe. These were all mounted on a new

Below: *In 1936, Errett Lobban Cord had made a last attempt to move into the specialty market, with the 810. The new Cord had striking "coffin nose" styling by Gordon Buehrig and the range comprised two sedans, a phaeton and a convertible, all on a 125 inch wheelbase and powered by a 125 horsepower Lycoming V8. The car became the 812 in 1937, with an optional supercharger, but production was halted the following year, following Cord's departure from the auto industry.*

X-frame chassis with a wheelbase of 119 inches. GM's new "Knee-Action" coil-sprung independent front suspension was adopted, while semi-elliptic leaf springs supported the rear Hotchkiss drive, which replaced Cadillac's more traditional torque-tube arrangement. Double-action shock absorbers were fitted all round, while a rear stabilizer bar was also incorporated to improve ride and handling. Unlike Cadillacs that year, the LaSalles benefited from Bendix hydraulic brakes.

During the early Thirties, LaSalles had been given Cadillac's 353 cu.in. V8, but the new model had Oldsmobile's 240.3 cu.in. flathead straight-eight with aluminum pistons and five main bearings. It produced 95 horsepower (10 less than the V8) at 3700rpm and was backed by a three-speed manual transmission, also of Oldsmobile design. At the time, however, Cadillac were keen to conceal the source of the engine and other driveline parts, stating that they were built at the Cadillac factory, and they were prepared to allow potential customers to visit the factory to see for themselves. Of course, the individual parts may have actually been made by Oldsmobile and simply assembled by Cadillac.

The cars continued in this basic form for 1935 and 1936 with minor changes to styling and mechanical components. For example, the wheelbase was increased to 120 inches and all cars received a two-piece, V-shaped windshield. The engine was also bored out to give a capacity of 248 cu.in. and produce 105 horsepower at 3600rpm. The bodies were no longer built by Fleetwood, as production had been transferred to Fisher, who produced a new all-steel turret roof for closed cars.

Again, for 1937, styling changes were minimal, although the wheelbase had been stretched to 124 inches and the bodies were all-steel rather than of composite wood-and-steel construction. Changes included revisions to the front

fenders, lowering of the head lights, a new "egg-crate" grille and a windshield with a deeper V-shape. The hood side ports had also been dropped in favor of a line of deep rectangular louvers with horizontal moldings running through them.

A choice of five body styles was offered: 2- and 4-door sedans, a convertible sedan, a convertible coupe and a sport coupe.

The big news that year, however, was the return of a V8 engine. This 322 cu.in. flathead produced 125 horsepower at 3400rpm and had been used in the previous year's Cadillac Series 60. The three-speed manual transmission remained, but the Hotchkiss drive was replaced by a hypoid unit. A stabilizer was also added to the front suspension.

The improvements transformed the car, and sales took off. Sadly, a minor

recession in 1938 would cause them to fall again. Minor changes had been made to the cars for that year, including mounting the headlights on the tops of the fenders, but they were hung off the radiator shell again in 1939. LaSalles received several other changes that year, too, including increased glass area, a new narrower grille, and a steel sunroof, known as the "Sunshine Turret Top," for sedans. Running boards were optional. The wheelbase that year was back to 120 inches but, even so, sales remained uninspiring.

By 1940, the Buick range had expanded upward, catering for the market originally conceived for LaSalle. Despite new elegant body styling and a wider range of models than before, this competition, together with the fact that LaSalle was being pressed hard by Lincoln and lagging well behind Packard, meant that 1940 would be the last year for LaSalles. The name would appear again briefly in the mid-Fifties on a couple of GM concept cars but, other than that, it would be consigned to history. However, LaSalles would always be remembered as distinctive and refined automobiles.

Below: The New York Police Department employed DeSotos as squad cars in 1937, demonstrating the marque's reputation for ruggedness and reliability. A DeSoto acting as Official Car at the Indianapolis 500 underlined its performance. Styling was by former custom coachbuilder Raymond Dietrich and the '37 cars incorporated forward-thinking interior features including recessed switches and safety glass. All in all, at a base price of less than $800 for the S-3 six cylinder coupe, the DeSoto was an attractive proposition.

SPECIFICATIONS

DODGE

Engine:
Cast iron - 6 Cylinders in line

Displacement:
217.8 cu. ins.

Bore and stroke:
3 1/4 x 4 3/8 ins.

Horsepower:
87

Body styles:
Coupe; Rumble-seat coupe; Convertible coupe; Fastback sedan; Touring sedan; Limousine

No. of seats:
2 - 7

Weight (lbs):
2,875 lbs - 3,380 lbs

Price:
$808 - $1,275

Produced:
114,529

Unlike the previous year, 1938 proved a good one for aviation when millionaire Howard Hughes made history by flying his twin-engined Beech airplane around the world in a record time of 3 days, 19 hours and 17 minutes. He wasn't the only one remembered for achieving a remarkable feat that year. Orson Welles caused mass panic across the US, with his broadcast of The War of the Worlds radio play, and thousands of Americans truly believed that their country was under attack from alien spaceships. They need not have worried because, as anyone picking up an Action Comics' first edition would have found out, Superman also made his debut.

Among the technological developments that year was the invention of the Xerox photocopier

Below: The Dodge range was little changed since the major reworking of 1935 and was beginning to look just a little dowdy. Sales in recession-stricken '38 dipped severely, down from over a quarter million to just over a hundred thousand. A major overhaul of the company's image for its twenty-fifth anniversary in 1939, however, restored its fortunes, helped by sales to Canada and overseas markets.

by Chester Carlton, and the development of nylon products by Du Pont. Teflon and fiber glass also made their appearance.

The styling of the '38 Dodge was a mild reworking of the previous year's line. Dodge followed the Chrysler party line in overall look: the new, divided radiator grille incorporated narrower chrome strips, both vertical and horizontal, than that of the previous year. These echoed the slim, horizontal vent

Above: Better Looking, Better Built, Better Buy... Pontiac's advertising got straight to the point. Having been bred out of Oakland, Pontiac went on to outsell it and, in 1932, to outlast it. The company continued from strength to strength with sales peaking in 1937 at over a quarter of a million. In '38, however, with the recession really biting, they dipped, only to rise to new heights again, in '40 and '41, before the factory went over to war production.

trims on the sides of the hood. The headlamps were repositioned on top of the fenders, and 1938 was the last year that a Dodge Brothers badge was used on the radiator—the hood was embellished with a leaping ram ornament instead.

Ten body styles were available, ranging from the seven-seater sedan and the limousine (with divider), built on an extended wheelbase chassis, to the $800 business coupe. The all-steel, unitary bodies incorporated extensive sound insulation and were advertised as having "silent safety" construction. Autolite ignition was fitted as standard to the D8 Series, along with hydraulic brakes, a single windshield wiper and dual tail lights. Engine mountings were revised and a self-lubricating clutch was fitted, along with a sixteen-gallon fuel tank. Options included fender skirts and bumper guards, a clock and a cigar lighter, spotlights, whitewall tires and a radio..

The D9/D10 Dodges were based on the Plymouth P5/P6s, Dodge merely adding their own grille, badges and trim. These "conversions" were assembled in Windsor, Ontario and in the US Canadian production topped ten thousand, and more than half of the cars produced

in the US were right hand drive.

In the teeth of a vicious, economic recession, Dodge dropped from fourth to fifth place in the production league, having fallen to thirteenth a decade earlier, prior to the Chrysler takeover. The Dodge Brothers, John and Horace, had started out producing engines, axles and transmissions for Olds and Ford from the first years of the century. Their early cars, marketed from 1914, quickly gained a reputation for robustness and reliability, but both brothers died in the same year—1920. Their widows sold the company in 1921 for $146 million— the largest cash transaction to date in industrial finance—to New York bankers Dillon, Read & Co. Walter P. Chrysler bought it from them—via a stock transfer—for $170 million, in 1928.

Below: Ab Jenkins was back at the Bonneville Salt Flats with the massive Mormon Meteor II, seeking yet more endurance records. The venerable streamlined car was powered by an Allison V12 airplane engine, and had been used by Jenkins in a number of record attempts throughout the Thirties. During the course of 1938's 24-hour dash, he broke a total of 87 speed records.

SPECIFICATIONS

STUDEBAKER CHAMPION

Engine:
Cast iron block - 6
Cylinders in line

Displacement:
164.3 cu. ins.

Bore and stroke:
3 x 3 7/8 ins.

Horsepower:
78

Body styles:
3 & 5 seat coupes; custom cruising sedan; Deluxe versions of all styles

No. of seats:
3-5

Weight (lbs):
2,260 - 2,375

Price:
$660 - $800

Produced:
33,905

Right: The Mercury was to the Ford Motor Corporation what the LaSalle was to General Motors: it filled a gap in the range. In Ford's case the gap was between the V8s and the Lincoln. At its introduction in 1939, the Mercury had the Ford's flathead V8 and styling that echoed the Lincoln Zephyr.

As America celebrated the arrival of a new year on the eve of 1939, in Europe the ominous clouds of war were gathering. Later in the year, the storm would break: German Chancellor Adolf Hitler would send his troops into Czechoslovakia, then Poland, prompting Great Britain and France to declare war on Germany. This was the beginning of a terrible conflict that eventually would span

continents and last for six long years.

Although the United States took a neutral stance at this stage of the war and would not take a belligerent role until after the Japanese strike on Pearl Harbor in 1941, under President Roosevelt's guidance, she increasingly provided military aid of all kinds to the Allies, in particular the British. Without America's assistance in this way, the events of the early years of the war might have taken another direction altogether.

Helping to cement the special relationship between the US and Great Britain, King George VI and Queen Elizabeth toured the United States in 1939. Although they would cross the Atlantic

Above: Studebaker Commanders had replaced Studebaker Dictators to allay any suspicion of sympathy with a certain unsavory character in embattled Europe. They, like the Champion illustrated, were powered by a straight-six while the Presidents had a straight-eight. Despite a minor facelift, sales were low and the company was in trouble; total production of Presidents for 1938 was fewer than five and a half thousand cars. Better times would come, however.

by ship, other travelers could take advantage of a more rapid means of travel, for that year saw the inauguration of Pan American's regular transa-

Above: The Seventeenth Series Packards of 1939 were substantially unchanged from the previous model year, retaining their own dignified, if a little staid, style. Outside spare tires, though decorously covered, were still in evidence and a one-piece windshield was still to put in an appearance. The Six, with its new column shift, was the top seller, with over twenty-four thousand finding buyers, against seventeen and a half thousand Straight-Eights and a handful of Super-Eights.

tlantic air service, which made use of Boeing Clipper flying boats.

To escape the dreary news from Europe – and the stagnant economy at home – Americans could take in a movie; Clark Gable in Gone With The Wind, or Judy Garland in the Wizard of Oz. Or they could visit the World's Fair in New York.

"Economy" was a word that also played a major part in some of Ford's advertising that year, although in a different context. In an attempt to compete with the top-of-the-range Oldsmobiles and Dodges, and lower-range Buicks and Chryslers, Ford had launched a completely new model range

for 1939 under the Mercury name. The new cars – a convertible, a coupe, a 2-door sedan and a 4-door town sedan –

fitted neatly between the standard Ford offerings and the much more luxurious and larger Lincoln Zephyrs. Their overall styling was similar to both the Lincoln Zephyr and the de luxe Fords, but at 116 inches, the wheelbase was 9 inches shorter than the former and 4 inches longer than the latter. Apart from the slightly larger size, the immediate identifying feature between the Mercury and Ford was that the Mercury had horizontal grille bars, while the de luxe Fords had vertical bars. The Mercury coupe also had a distinctive roofline and side glass both of which were quite different from those of the Ford.

Mechanically, the Mercury was similar in construction to the Ford, but from the outset it was fitted with Lockheed hydraulic brakes, whereas

Below: The Series 61 replaced both the 60 and the 65 in 1939. Most Cadillacs were by now powered by ninety-degree, cast iron V8, bored to 346 cu.ins. The Sixty-Special, by Fleetwood, continued, as did the Series 75, riding a 141 ins. wheelbase. The Series 90 was also still in production, however, with a wide-angle (135 degree) sixteen cylinder engine displacing 431 cu. ins. Sadly, the mighty V16 would be dropped the following year.

both the Ford and Lincoln Zephyr had only switched to hydraulics that year. It was powered by a 95 horsepower version of Ford's famous flathead V8, and it soon gained a reputation as being hot performer for a big car. Despite this, Ford emphasized the fuel economy of the Mercury, which they claimed could be as much as 20 miles to the gallon and which few cars of any size could match at the time.

Like most of Ford's products, the Mercury sold very well from the outset, establishing the Mercury name, which would continue in the company's line-up from then on. A slight increase in the size of the wheelbase, to 118 inches, would follow in 1940 and the cars would continue to sell well until all civilian automobile production was stopped at the beginning of 1942 to devote capacity to the war effort. Up to

that time, the Mercury had always been regarded as an upmarket Ford. However, after the war was over, the parent company would form the Lincoln - Mercury division, and all future Mercurys would be offered as the less expensive versions of the company's luxury cars, rather than the more luxurious forms of their bread-and-butter automobile range. They were aimed squarely at middle-income, middle-aged, middle-of-the-road, Middle America.

Plymouth's tenth anniversary came around in 1938 and was celebrated, quietly, with a conservative styling overhaul. there were mechanical innovations, however: a high-compression head could be specified that increased the output from 82 to 86 horsepower. there was was also a "depression-sensitive" low-compression option that

delivered a measly 65 horsepower but gave considerably improved economy. The Business Line became the Roadking and Plymouth added their first in-house station wagon - the Suburban - to the line. Plymouth station wagons had previously been produced by US Body & Forge of Tell City, Indiana and sold as the Westchester Suburban. The 4-door body was largely constructed of wood.

1939 heralded a new look, courtesy of Raymond Deitrich, and headed by the distinctive, sharp-pointed front end treatment, reminiscent of the Lincoln Zephyr. The new, rectangular-shaped headlamps were faired into the fenders but the windshield reverted from a single pane to a "V" two-piece design. Convertibles had power-operated tops for the first time. Inside, the gear shift moved from the floor to the steering column, in line with current fashion.

Appearing in the range for the last time in '39 were a rumble-seat coupe and a four-door convertible. Plymouth sales had dropped off considerably in the recession, but bounced right back to above 400,000 for 1939.

Below: A 1939 Plymouth Prototype illustration, very similar to the later Series P8 Deluxe. Plymouth played the poor relation in the Chrysler Corporation in 1939. Whilst other divisions were rebodied, Plymouth had to get by with restyling. They managed to ring the changes with some neat details though, such as rectangular headlamps and the first power-operated convertible top on an American automobile. Prices were down and sales were up; Plymouth could look forward with confidence.

SPECIFICATIONS

BUICK SPECIAL SERIES 40

Engine:
Cast iron - 8 Cylinders in line

Displacement:
248 cu. ins.

Bore and stroke:
3 3/32 x 4 1/8 ins.

Horsepower:
107

Body styles:
Touring sedan; Phaeton; Business coupe; Convertible coupe; Sports coupe; Taxi

No. of seats:
2-5

Weight (lbs):
3,505 lbs - 3,755 lbs

Price:
$955 - $1,355

Produced:
100,000+

Right: Bottom of the Buick range were the Special Series 40 models. In addition to the 4-door sedan shown, the series included a 2-door sedan, a 4-door phaeton, a 2-door convertible, a business coupe, a sport coupe and a taxi. The parking lights above the head lights could be wired into the directional signal system.

As 1940 progressed, the news from Europe was increasingly gloomy; France and the Low Countries all fell to Germany. Meanwhile, the British had managed to evacuate most of their expeditionary force from Dunkirk. After a short lull, the German airforce began to attack targets in Britain in preparation for the expected invasion; the Battle of Britain had begun and would rage throughout the summer. Against all odds, the RAF inflicted substantial damage on the German airforce, such that they could not guarantee control of the air, which was essential for a successful seaborne invasion. Germany had experienced her first setback of the War.

Roosevelt, who would be elected as President for a third term, was in constant contact with Prime Minister Winston Churchill. At his urging, America moved from a policy of neutrality to one of non-belligerence, and much of industry,

Above: *A decade after the Dodge Brothers automobile had become simply the Dodge, and twenty years after both brothers had died, the company had recovered from its sad decline in the mid-'twenties to a position of strength and stability in the market place. Chrysler had bought the ailing company in 1928 and positioned it between the Chrysler and the Plymouth, roughly on a par with the doomed DeSoto. By 1940, production was up to 200,000 and the division's future was secure.*

particularly the auto industry, began to take on the production of armaments and other military equipment. Even so, substantial numbers of new automobiles were still produced. Buick broke their annual production record, exceeding 250,116 cars, and also built their 4,000,000th automobile.

Following the recession of 1938, Buick's President, Harlow Curtice, had ordered a 10% reduction in material and component costs across the board. When it came to the chassis of the small series cars, this was achieved by removing the portion that overhung the back axle. This rear section was considered unnecessary as Buick had switched from parallel leaf springs, which needed a mounting behind the axle, to coil springs that did not. Pre-production testing had shown no problems, but once the cars began to reach the public, collapsed trunk floors and distorted bodies caused by minor parking bumps were reported. The only solution was to restore the rear portion of the frame and rush out a reinforcing framework to be fitted to existing cars. This proved both costly and embarrassing.

As a result, Curtice eased financial restrictions on the 1940 models, which

Below: *The last of the V16s was produced in 1940. The engine was unchanged from '39 but the cars sported sealed beam headlights and direction indicators. Cadillac would not produce an engine in any configuration other than a V8 for the next 40 years.*

Above: Although the great majority of Cadillacs sold in 1940 came with standard "in house" body styles from Fleetwood, a number of custom coachbuilders were still supplying exotic one-of-a-kind care for those wealthy enough to be able to afford such indulgence. Among those few was William Knusden, president of Cadillac at the time, and his son, Bunkie, who was later to become General Manager at Pontiac and President of Ford. Their cars, a V16 and a V8 respectively, were individually styled at GM, but customers could choose from Vanden Plas, Bohman & Schwartz, Franay of Paris and Brunn of New York, who penned this elegant town car on the left.

received even more rigorous testing than normal, covering nearly 3,000,000 miles of cross-country driving. The resulting new cars were traditional with proven engineering.

The cars shared their general styling with the 1939 models, but received a face-lift that saw the head lights blended

Below: 1940 was the last year that the side-mounted spare remained an option. The coming of the war heralded the end of many formal body styles such as the "town car" with its open driver's "cockpit" and closed passenger compartment. Post-war models were aimed squarely at the owner-driver and coupe styling moved to the fore.

into the front fenders, and a wider grille with horizontal rather than vertical bars. In all, there were six series: Special Series 40, Super Series 50, Century Series 60, Roadmaster Series 70, Limited Series 80 and Limited Series 90. All shared the same front-end styling, but their wheelbase varied from 121 inches for the 40 and 50, through 126 inches for the 60 and 70, to 133 inches for the 80 and 140 inches for the 90. These sizes were common to the '39

models, but the Series 40 and 50 cars enjoyed a 1 inch increase to allow enough room for the front doors of cars, equipped with sidemount spares, to open fully! In addition, Series 50 and 70 cars were devoid of running boards.

Buick's range encompassed mid-priced bread-and-butter models and upmarket luxury cars that encroached upon the Cadillac market, which did not endear them to their fellow GM division. However, the top-of-the-range

cars gave kudos to the less-expensive models, the entire range having an air of quality. All the cars were powered by Buick's trusty ohv straight-eight engine, of either 248 or 320.2 cu.in., depending on the series. This was backed by a three-speed manual transmission with torque-tube drive to the rear axle. Oil filters were standard as were sealed-beam headlights, while a new option was Fore-N-Aft Flash-Way directional signals.

Above: The Lincoln Zephyr's V12 engine was bored out to 292 cu. ins. for 1940, raising its output to 120 horsepower. The body was restyled and, with the intervention of the war, would remain effectively unchanged for nearly a decade. The removal of the running boards gave the new car a strikingly modern look. The same year saw the introduction of what was to become another design classic, developed from the Zephyr, the Lincoln Continental.

SPECIFICATIONS

CHRYSLER SERIES 28

Engine:
Cast iron - 6 Cylinders
in line

Displacement:
241.5 cu. ins.

Bore and stroke:
3 3/8 x 4 1/2 ins.

Horsepower:
108 - 112

Body styles:
Coupe; Brougham;
Sedan; Convertible;
Limousine; Town &
Country station wagon

No. of seats:
2-8

Weight (lbs):
3,170 lbs - 3,740 lbs

Price:
$995 - $1,500

Produced:
136,701

By 1941, most of Europe was under the German jackboot; only Great Britain stood defiant, but bloodied, refusing to be subdued. Through the lend-lease scheme, America was providing military equipment and supplies to the embattled British, despite officially being non-belligerent. As an explanation, President Roosevelt argued that if there had been a fire in his neighbor's house he would have lent that neighbor a hose to put it out. In addition to actual equipment, the US also provided naval escorts for convoys carrying it across the Atlantic, helping to protect it from U-boat attack. Moreover, the US Navy and Coast Guard mounted their own anti-submarine patrols to protect Allied vessels when entering and leaving American ports.

Although Britain was holding out against German aggression, British Prime Minister, Winston Churchill, knew that there was no chance of turning the tide of the war against the German forces. He needed the USA to declare war on Germany, but America had not been attacked, nor were there any treaties that bound her to come to the aid of any victims of German aggression. That

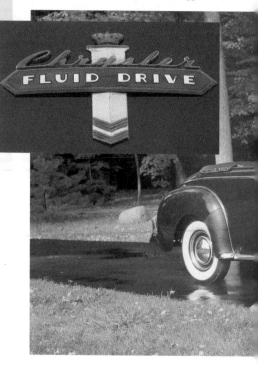

situation would change at the end of the year.

At the start of 1941, despite the ominous rumblings from across the Atlantic, it was business as usual for Detroit. At Chrysler, it was a face-lift year, the new models being similar in appearance to the 1940 offerings, although the bodies were wider and the cars had a lower stance. A six-bar grille replaced the previous year's nine-bar unit, and the cars could be ordered with or without running boards. Ever since the lack of success achieved by the radically-styled Airflow model which appeared in 1934, the overall styling of Chryslers had been conservative and, for 1941, the cars followed their rather staid image. However, in engineering terms, the company was always innovative.

The '41 models had a similar mechanical specification to their predecessors, the standard transmission being Chrysler's Fluid Drive, which had been in production for a couple of years. This was an unusual three-speed, semi-automatic transmission that incorporated a clutch mechanism. The clutch was used to select first gear, after which the pedal was released fully, then the accelerator depressed to move off, just like a normal automatic. Once on the move, the driver selected second gear by simply lifting his foot from the accelerator, yet when shifting into third, the clutch had to be used in the same way as with a manual transmission. Down-shifting was achieved in a similar manner.

Below: Although not spectacular, Chrysler's styling for 1941 projected the company's dependable image and steady progress through proven engineering. The standard transmission for all models was the Fluid Drive semi-automatic.

Above: The demise of LaSalle in 1940 heralded the reintroduction of the Cadillac Series 61. Similarly, the old Series 72 was replaced by the Series 67, riding a 139in. wheelbase. All Cadillacs now used the same V8 motor. The Series 62 line offered both a convertible coupe and a convertible sedan - the last one ever offered. In 1941, for the first time Cadillacs sported a styling feature which would become a post-war signature feature of the marque - the Dagmar. These bullet-shaped protrusions grew out of the front bumpers; at this stage they were mere buds, but by the mid 'fifties they would have developed to heroic proportions. The source of their inspiration can only be guessed at.

Although the technique sounds confusing, at the time Chrysler advertised Fluid Drive as being the transmission you could not make a mistake with. Obviously, plenty of people agreed, as the cars sold well.

Chryslers offered in 1941 were available in two basic series: 28 and 30. The former was powered by a new "Spitfire" sidevalve in-line six engine, which had a capacity of 241.5 cu.in. and came in low- and high-compression versions that produced 108 and 112 horsepower respectively, although the latter was increased to 115 horsepower later in the year. The 30 series models were equipped with a sidevalve in-line eight cylinder engine, which displaced 323.5 cu.in. and produced either 137 (low compression) or 140 horsepower (high compression) at 3400 rpm. The hood of these eight cylinder cars was slightly longer to accommodate the engine.

Within the two series was a wide range of styles, including coupes, convertibles, 2-door broughams, 4-door sedans, station wagons and long wheelbase limousines. These were sold as Royal, Windsor, Saratoga, New Yorker and Crown Imperial models.

Among the options available was a striking upholstery pattern, which cost an extra $20 and was similar to Black Watch tartan. This fancy stitchwork led to a completely separate series of Windsor and New Yorker models, known as Highlanders. To distinguish them they carried Highlander emblems on the dashboard and hood.

Despite Chrysler's less-than-flamboyant image, buyers in 1941 could

Above: Concealing the fuel filler beneath the tail-light was a neat piece of detailing that Cadillac continued to incorporate until the introduction of the shark fin in around '57.

choose from a list of 13 colors and 27 upholstery options. Also included in the list of options was a four-speed, semi-automatic transmission known as Vaca-matic, and power-operated windows, although the latter were only available on the top-of-the-line crown Imperial.

Compared to their poor performance during the recession of 1938, Chrysler were doing well in 1941, having more than tripled their sales. They were ranked eighth in the US auto industry that year, but still fell a long way behind Oldsmobile in sixth place, who had built their 2,000,000th automobile in 1941.

The Oldsmobile range of 1941 comprised three series – 60, 70 and 90 – as it had done in 1940 and, while they appeared similar in styling, they were all

Below: Whilst the stylists of other manufacturers struggled to find a defining 'forties look, Cadillac's, under Harley Earl's masterful direction and rigid discipline, produced designs that defined the period with confident elan.

based on longer wheelbase chassis. The bottom-of-the-range 60 series cars grew 3 inches to 119 inches, while the 70 and 90 series shared a 125 inch wheelbase, from 120 and 124 inches respectively.

All three series of cars could be specified with either a 238 cu.in. in-line flathead six or 257 cu.in. eight, being designated 66 or 68, 76 or 78, or 96 or 98 as appropriate. In fact, 1941 was the only year in which a top-of-the-line 90 series car could be ordered with a six, but few buyers took up the option and it was not offered again. What they did go for, however, was the Hydramatic automatic transmission.

The three series offered a range of body styles, including convertibles, business and club coupes, 2- and 4-door sedans and station wagons. An unusual offering was a 4-door phaeton, which had been introduced in 1940, but would be discontinued after 1941.

1941 was a good year for the auto makers and few realized what was in store for them. Indeed, few Americans had any inkling of what was to come until December 7, when the Japanese launched a devastating surprise attack on the Pacific Fleet, based at Pearl Harbor in the Hawaiian Islands. In a furious air assault, they virtually destroyed the Pacific Fleet, torpedoing five battleships and two cruisers within the first few minutes. Fortunately, two aircraft carriers were at sea when the attack took place and would prove to be a valuable nucleus around which a new fleet could be built. In the meantime, however, Japan would be almost unchallenged in her conquest of much of the Pacific.

America was now at war with Japan, and because the latter was part of a tripartite pact with Germany and Italy (the Axis powers), she was also at war with those countries too. The Japanese also struck at British-held Singapore,

while the Germans gave up trying to crack Great Britain and turned their attention east to the Soviet Union, ignoring the non-aggression pact they

Above: The 1941 Sixty-Special, styled by Bill Mitchell - under Harley Earl's tutelage - is regarded by many as the finest example of the model ever produced. The basic price was $2,195.00 and over four thousand of them would be sold in the model year.

had signed with that country. All the elements were in place for a world conflict, but both Germany and Japan had awakened sleeping giants which, ultimately, would cause their downfall.

Now all of American industry had to turn its attention to the war effort. Automobile production was cut by 20% as the factories began producing military equipment. Soon they would be making nothing else, as America concentrated her entire might on the common cause.

Left: Running boards had disappeared from the '41 Sixty-Special, but factory-fitted air-conditioning and Hydra-Matic transmission were offered as options. Although the basic specification of the 1941 Cadillacs would remain effectively unchanged until after the war, the Sixty-Special would have a final face-lift for '42.

SPECIFICATIONS

CHEVROLET FLEET-LINE AEROSEDAN

Engine:
Cast iron block - 6
Cylinders in line

Displacement:
216.5 cu. ins.

Bore and stroke:
3 1/2 x 3 3/4 ins.

Horsepower:
90

Body styles:
2 door Aerosedan; 4
door Sportmaster

No. of seats:
6

Weight (lbs):
3,105 lbs - 3,165 lbs

Price:
$880 - $920

Produced:
76,385

*Above right: Santa Claus
may well have been able
to prove his need for a
new 1942 model at the
end of 1941, but for
those Americans who
couldn't, owning a
Chevrolet Fleetline
Aerosedan such as this
was simply a dream.
Built before the
beginning of the model
year, this model has all
its brightwork intact.*

By the beginning of 1942, the Japanese were making steady progress in their conquest of the Pacific islands, while American industry was turning rapidly to war production. As a result, many raw materials were severely restricted for civilian use and some withdrawn completely. From January 1, the government had banned all brightwork on cars, with the exception of bumpers, bumper guards and windshield wipers. Such automobiles therefore had their trim painted a contrasting color instead, and were popularly known as "black-out specials." Then, from February 2, the production of civilian cars and trucks was banned completely – America was committed to total war.

With production curtailed so early in the year, few new models reached the civilian hands and potential buyers had to prove a specific need for a car. Most were impressed for military service,

including Chevrolet's face-lift model for 1942. Based on the previous year's design, using the same chassis, mechanical components and basic body shell, the updated Chevy appeared longer, wider and lower, yet the wheelbase remained the same at 116 inches. The new look was achieved by installing a more prominent radiator grille, by stretching the hood back to the leading edge of the doors, and by extending the front fenders well into the doors; the rear portion of the fender, known as a fender cap, opened with the door. From there back, the car was essentially the same as the 1941 model.

Chevrolet's two model lines – Special Deluxe and Master Deluxe – included sedans, coupes and cabriolets. The Special Deluxe versions had a few extra accessories to set them apart from the others. In 1941, a close-coupled 4-door sedan, the Fleetline, had been the top-of-the-range but, for 1942, it was upstaged by the sleeker, fastback Fleetline Aerosedan. This attractive 2-door body style had a low roofline that swept down in a continuous curve to the rear bumper. As a result, the windshield and side glass were shorter, and the seats were lower too. Both Fleetline models were distinguished by three stainless-steel moldings on each fender, but otherwise they were similarly equipped to the other Special Deluxe models.

Power for all '42 Chevies came from the trusty "stovebolt" in-line-six engine, the basic design of which had been in use since 1937. It displaced 216.5 cubic inches, had a 6.5:1 compression ratio and pumped out 90 horsepower. Chevrolet continued to use this same engine in their post-war models until 1953.

Despite the relatively short time that it was available, the Fleetline Aerosedan proved a winner, outselling all the other Chevrolet models. Nearly 62,000 were built before production was halted in February. For the rest of the year, Chevrolet concentrated on building military trucks. However, the fastback

Aerosedan styling would return after the war and continue in the Chevrolet line-up until 1952.

Although the lack of new cars and the advent of sugar and gasoline rationing made life less comfortable, not all the news of 1942 was bad. At the cinema, Humphrey Bogart was reminding Ingrid Bergman that they'd always have Paris and Dooley Wilson, who couldn't play the piano, was playing Sam and singing "As Time Goes By" in Michael Curtiz's Casablanca. On stage, a young skinny guy by the name of Frank Sinatra was

keeping the kids happy. On the war front, the Japanese navy had been severely mauled at the Battle of Midway in early June, losing several valuable aircraft carriers, General Dwight D. Eisenhower had been named commander of American forces in Europe, and those forces began to prove themselves when they invaded North Africa in November to harass German troops retreating from Britain's Eighth Army. This crucial amphibious assault was to be useful practice for the invasion of Europe, still two long years away.

Below: The '42 DeSoto's styling was very distinctive. The headlamps were concealed behind retractable covers and the car was given a heavy, chrome-laden, front-end treatment. The options list was extensive and included "Simplimatic" auto transmission, two-tone paint, custom colors and various trim variations, but the motor was still an in-line Six producing 115hp at 3,800 rpm. DeSoto slipped 10th to 14th place in the annual sales league before war intervened. Production was halted in February.

SPECIFICATIONS

**WILLYS-OVERLAND
MB JEEP**

Engine:
Cast iron - 4 Cylinders
in line

Displacement:
134.2 cu. ins.

Bore and stroke:
3.13 x 4.38

Horsepower:
60

Body styles:
Convertible

No. of seats:
4+

Weight (lbs):
"quarter ton"

Price:
Government Issue

Produced:
Willys: 358.489 by
1945
Ford: 277,896

After the dark days of 1942, 1943 was to see America and the other Allied nations pursuing the war against Germany and Japan with vigor. With the wealth of American manpower and industry behind it, the allied war effort was slowly making gains. In Europe, Allied troops invaded Italy as a prelude to the far more critical invasion of northern Europe – D Day – in 1944. In the Pacific, Japan's island conquests were wrested back one by one. Of course, there were setbacks, as the aggressors fought tooth and nail to retain the lands that they had seized. But progress on both fronts was inexorable. German forces would eventually be fought to a standstill by US, British and other Allied armies in the west and Soviet troops in the east, capitulating at the beginning of May 1945. Japan followed suit in August after Hiroshima and Nagasaki were devastated by atomic bombs.

Throughout this period, however, a "car" was still being built, although its purpose, not surprisingly, was purely military. In the army's parlance, it was known as a "1/4-ton, 4x4 truck," but it soon became affectionately, and officially, known as the Jeep. It was built by the hundreds of thousand and served in every theater of the war. The axis powers had nothing like it; nor indeed had there ever been anything like it. The Jeep was a light-weight, rugged, powerful, go-anywhere vehicle that served both on and off the battlefield. Without doubt, it was the most versatile vehicle of WW2. It could be used for reconnaissance missions, running supplies to front-line troops, evacuating wounded, towing artillery pieces, carrying radio equipment, transporting generals, and myriad other tasks. Equipped with machine guns, it was used for hit-and-run raids behind enemy lines; it was landed by glider with airborne forces. It could negotiate thick mud, climb steep inclines and ford deep water.

During the allied liberation of Europe in 1944, Jeeps were put ashore on the beaches of Normandy from landing craft and drove from there all the way to Berlin, becoming as indentifiable with the American GI as his Lucky Strikes and his Hershey Bars. A lot of European children probably had their first automobile ride in an American Jeep.

Designed by Willys-Overland to meet the requirements of the US Army for a lightweight scout car, the Jeep had a strong chassis and simple open bodywork with no doors and a fold-flat windshield. It could seat three, but in action it often carried many more. Its 134.2 cu.in. four cylinder engine developed 60 horsepower and was backed by a four-speed transmission with high and low ranges; two- or four-wheel-drive could be selected at will. The result was a vehicle with good highway speed (in excess of 60mph) and real stump-pulling power to deal with rough terrain.

To guard their source of supply during wartime, the military insisted that Jeeps be built by at least one other manufacturer, but that they be identical in every respect so that parts were interchangeable. The masters of mass-production, Ford, were given this role and built many thousands of the little vehicles.

The one controversial aspect of the Jeep is how it got its name. No one seems to know for sure. Some argue that it came about from its military designation, GP (General Purpose); others say that it was named after a character in the Popeye cartoon strip. Whatever the truth may be, the fact is that the Jeep not only helped win the war, but also was the forerunner of a whole line of four-wheel-drive vehicles (both military and

civilian) that has continued to this day.

It was common practice for soldiers to name their Jeeps, just as pilots named their planes. Soldiers being what they are, this often resulted in the amazing juxtaposition of a tough, ungainly, strictly functional piece of equipment, bristling with shovels and spares, bearing a title like Crystal Lady or Honey Child. Perhaps the ultimate accolade for this remarkable vehicle is that its name passed into the language to describe any rugged, utility, four-wheel drive vehicle. In the immediate post-war period, the British even referred to their Land-Rovers as Jeeps. Thus, along with the Stetson, the Tannoy and the Hoover, the name of an individual make could be applied to the breed in general and the meaning be universally understood....

Below: The Jeep was a no-frills, effective military vehicle; a purposeful design. It was used by all Allied forces and was looked upon with affection by the men who came to depend upon it. There is no doubt that it made a major contribution to victory on all fronts.

SPECIFICATIONS

CHRYSLER TOWN & COUNTRY

Engine:
Cast iron V8

Displacement:
323.5 cu. ins.

Bore and stroke:
3.25 x 4.88

Horsepower:
135

Body styles:
Sedan; Convertible coupe; Hardtop coupe

No. of seats:
5

Weight (lbs):
4,300 lbs.

Price:
$2,718 - $2,743

Produced:
2,042 in V8 form

As they emerged from the war, most manufacturers were only able to offer revamped 1942 models to the eagerly-awaiting public. It didn't matter. As long as it had four wheels and an engine, you could find a buyer willing to exchange their savings for it. This pent-up demand gave false hope to many entrepreneurs who attempted to enter what appeared to be an very lucrative business – most of these newcomers ended up losing their shirts.

But if the cars seemed familiar, much else had changed since Pearl Harbor. Global conflict led to huge advances in technology and America was propelled into the atomic era, with jets, rockets and computers. These space age influences would form themes in every automobile produced in the USA (and beyond) but, for now, a more conservative approach was necessary to get cars to

customers as quickly as possible.

There could be few more traditional people in the industry than Chrysler president K. T. Keller (the initials stood for Kaufman Thuma, but nobody ever dared use those names) who had taken over the reigns from Walter P. Chrysler in 1935. Keller's concept of car design was firmly rooted in the past, as can be judged by part of a talk he gave in 1947: "Automobiles are looked at and admired. The buyer is proud of his car's symphony of line; its coloring and trim express his taste; he welcomes the applause of his friends and neighbors. But he bought the car to ride in, and for his wife, and children, and friends to ride in... Though at times one might wonder, even headroom is important. Many of you Californians may have outgrown of the habit, but there are parts of the country, containing millions of people, where both the men and the ladies are in the habit of getting behind

Below: The convertible Town & Country provided some much needed glamor to boost an otherwise conservative selection of Chrysler post-war autos. The company was then dominated by the engineering aspect of a car's design and styling tended to be of secondary consideration. By far the most expensive Chrysler model for 1946, at nearly $3,000, only 1,935 ragtops were produced that year.

the wheel, or in the back seat, wearing hats."

Engineering took precedence over styling at Chrysler, and maintaining sufficient clearance for headgear obviously restricted the designer's options, resulting in a rather more upright look than most other cars. One commentator described the early 1940s Chrysler body thus: "It won't knock your socks off, but it won't knock your hat off, either."

And it is from this rather staid background that the magnificent Town & Country model was born. As the woodwork suggests, its origins lay with a station wagon, but not the usual rect-angular timber box built on the back of a sedan body. It was David A. Wallace, general manager at Chrysler, who decided to add a station wagon to the catalog – a model new to them. However, Wallace specified a wagon with the curved lines of a sedan and this somewhat perplexed the bodybuilders who normally manufactured the "woodies."

Faced with reluctance, Wallace decided to bring the project in house and gave the problem to his own team of engineers. The solution was arrived at after much hard work and, in 1941, the first Town & Country station wagons were produced at the Jefferson Avenue

plant in Detroit by a group of skilled workers who learned the techniques required for mating metal and wood in such close harmony. About 1,000 cars were made in the first year, followed by a similar number in 1942.

Chrysler's sales team concluded that it wasn't the practical aspect of the wagon that attracted customers, but its unique appearance and the elegant mix of steel, white ash and mahogany. Accordingly, it was decided to create a whole new luxurious selection of Town & County models utilizing the striking wood features. Although several prototypes were built of varying body styles, only two versions were to make it into production – a 4-door sedan and a 2-door convertible.

Mounted on a 127.5 inch wheelbase New Yorker chassis and powered by the 323 cu.in. L-head straight eight coupled to a Fluid-Drive transmission, the handsome Town & Country ragtop established a uniquely American model style. By far the most expensive Chrysler model for 1946, at nearly three thousand dollars, only 1,935 were produced that year.

Chrysler used such words as "thorough-bred" to describe the Town & Country in their advertisements; the car was shown in opulent surroundings as befitted such a model. At the sailing club, driving through big iron gates at the entrance to a colonnaded mansion or on the archery range – these were the settings chosen to add much-needed glamor to an otherwise fairly unremarkable range of cars.

The text accompanying the illustrations could be equally fulsome: "Chrysler's work or play convertible... magnificent in its utterly new styling..." ran an early advert, and later copy was even bolder: "...the industry's most dramatic, most exciting, most daring

Left: Although previously known for its passenger cars, following the resumption of civilian production after the war, Willys-Overland elected to build on the reputation gained by the Jeep. Several variants, in both two- and four-wheel-drive form, were offered – mostly for agricultural or commercial use – but in addition they introduced an all-steel station wagon which carried obvious styling cues from the famous war-time runabout. Using the 134 cu.in four cylinder L-head engine on a 104 inch wheelbase chassis, it was often regarded as more of a truck than a car. This was nevertheless the first true all-steel station wagon and 6,533 were produced in 1946, although over 71,000 Jeeps left the Toledo factory that year.

styling. A classic of the long, low, and lovely – with the most luxurious trim... With beauty that truly reflects the inspired and sound engineering and solid comfort inside."

Stylist Raymond Dietrich was warned about the emphasis placed on the engineering aspect of Chrysler products when he joined in 1932. Although he was to leave Chrysler in 1940, after yet another dispute with head of engineering, Fred Zeder, the foundation of the 1946 Town & Country design seems to have come from Dietrich with the contours of the 1941 models. Robert Cadwallader took over as head of design after Dietrich's departure, with Herb Weissinger and Arnott "Buzz" Grisinger playing major roles in styling.

Describing the situation following the end of the war, as manufacturers scrambled to resume production, Grisinger recalled in a later interview: "Postwar plans were pretty much a hurry-up thing. There weren't any clay models or production prototypes... We just designed a series of different styles and brushed on wood trim where we thought it looked best. Sales took it from there."

Aside from the "brushed on" wood trim, the most prominent feature of the '46 Chryslers was the "harmonica" grille and the unusual central overrider fitted to the front bumper. A less obvious innovation perhaps, although more significant in styling terms, is the manner in which the line of the front

enders was extended back into the doors, thereby achieving an altogether more updated look for an old body design. In this respect, at least, Chrysler were ahead of most of their rivals.

While the ash framework stayed throughout the Town & Country convertible's early life, the use of genuine mahogany for the insert panels was quickly dropped to save money. In 1947, Chrysler adopted Di-Noc decals but these were such good quality it was hard to distinguish them from the original wooden panels. The convertible Town & Country disappeared with the 1950 model, to be replaced by a hardtop coupe. From then on the name was applied to station wagons, until the idea of a wood-bodied ragtop was resurr-

ected with the 1984 LeBaron Town & Country.

The 1946 Chrysler Town & Country is a prime example of how a truly classic design can evolve, almost by accident. It started out as an idea for a practical wagon with style, and turned into a beautiful car (particularly in open-top form) that was unfortunately short-lived in its original form. Would it have happened that way without the interruption of the Second World War? We will never know.

Below: As was the norm, 1946 Oldsmobiles were updated prewar models. The 4-door sedan was the most popular of the Custom Cruiser 98 series, and Oldsmobile sold 11,031 of them.

SPECIFICATIONS

BUICK ROADMASTER

Engine:
Cast iron - 8 Cylinders in line

Displacement:
320.2 cu. ins.

Bore and stroke:
3.44 x 4.31

Horsepower:
144

Body styles:
4 Door Station Wagon

No. of seats:
6

Weight (lbs):
4,445 lbs.

Price:
$3,249

Produced:
300

The US auto industry lost two giants in 1947; William C. "Billy" Durant died on March 1 and Henry Ford on April 7. Both were founders of huge corporations, but only Ford and his family were to benefit. Durant wound up nearly broke and, in an attempt to spare the four million ex servicemen returning to civilian life the same fate, the GI Bill was introduced.

During the 1940s, Raymond Loewy Studios were consultants to several car manufacturers, including Studebaker, the British Rootes Group, and Austin. Loewy himself had been responsible for the sumptuous Derham-bodied '41 Lincoln Continental—with its gold-plated bumpers—and he later designed the stunning body of the Jaguar XK 140 sports car. One of his ex-designers, the talented Virgil Exner, was also a major influence on car design, having created the '47 Studebaker. He went on to start the Chrysler Advanced Styling Group in 1949, eventually becoming Vice President of styling at Chrysler.

David Dunbar Buick was a Scotsman with a flair

for innovation and a shrewd business sense. He made a fortune out of a patented process for binding porcelain to steel to produce the "enameled"

Above: Another model coming to the end of its life was the wooden-bodied station wagon. Buick was the last company to produce a true wooden wagon in '53, but this '47 shows how wood cladding had replaced a structural feature on the sides, although the rear door remained an all-timber construction.

bathtub, and plowed his profits into the infant automobile industry. In 1903 he produced a primitive, chain-drive buggy with a two-cylinder motor. The notable feature of his engine was its overhead valve design, which became a Buick hallmark. William Durant absorbed the burgeoning Buick motor Company into his own, embryonic General Motors Corporation in 1908.

The first Buick "Six" appeared in 1914 and the six-cylinder engine became a standard Buick feature from 1925 to 1930. The Straight-8 engine was introduced in 1931 and proved its worth by qualifying for the Indianapolis 500 at a speed of 105 mph. The engine remained a Buick mainstay for 22 years. Once referred to as "The Doctor's Car," Buicks were favored by the professional classes. This market was severely dented by the Great Depression but Buick's fortunes were restored and it placed fourth in the production league, behind the "Low-Price Three"—Ford, Chevrolet and Plymouth—through to the 1940s.

The end of the Second World War saw most American automobile manufacturers offering warmed-over, pre-war models. Buick, however, had been engaged on a totally new design in 1942, just before production was halted. This meant that their cars were, effectively, brand new for 1945 and the radical styling, inspired by Harley Earl's outrageous Y-Job, was still fresh. The distinctive "gun-sight" hood ornament rode on top of a range of Specials, Supers and Roadmasters that were genuinely exciting and innovative cars.

1948 saw the arrival of one of the great Buick innovations, Dynaflow transmission, a highly superior system for the time. A number of Harley Earl inspired styling features appeared exclusively on Buicks, notably the line of orifices in the fenders, known as "Venti Ports." On show cars, these housed lights that flashed in sequence with the spark plugs, but they have become a useful method of identification. Between 1949 and 1956, Supers and Specials had three VentiPorts, whereas the Roadmaster had four. These decorative lines of demarcation were blurred in '57 and disappeared altogether in '58, only to return in 1960.

Below: The Cadillac Series 62 convertible of 1947 illustrates perfectly the restraint of the division's immediate post-war designs. The rounded, voluptuous lines of these automobiles remind us of a more leisured age. The era of fins and chrome was just around the corner, however.

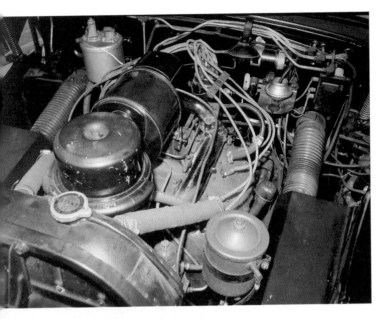

Above: With a vast amount of "war surplus" available at bargain basement prices, a lot of prospective Cadillac owners of limited means were tempted to re-adapt - often with disastrous consequences. Cadillac V8s, complete with their Hydra-Matic transmissions, intended for M24 tanks, for instance, had no reverse gear.

SPECIFICATIONS

HUDSON COMMODORE SIX

Engine:
Cast iron - 6 Cylinders in line

Displacement:
262 cu. ins.

Bore and stroke:
3.56 x 4.38

Horsepower:
121

Body styles:
Sedan; Club coupe; Convertible coupe

No. of seats:
5-6

Weight (lbs):
3,540 lbs - 3,780 lbs

Price:
$2,399 - $3,780

Produced:
27,159

Right: This 4-door sedan clearly illustrates the low roofline of the Step-down Hudson. Despite the shallow height of the side glass, a substantial windshield and back light were incorporated into the design, although they had to be laid down somewhat to fit. This is particularly obvious with the back light.

Americans had plenty to celebrate in 1948. The country was getting back on its feet after the war and life was returning to normal. To top it all US athletes picked up no less than 38 gold medals at the Olympics held in London, England. It was also election year and there was a new President in The White House – Harry S. Truman. Later in the year, Truman was to sign the Marshall Plan guaranteeing $6 billion for overseas aid. Some of that aid would be needed in Berlin, Germany, which was being blockaded by Soviet forces in one of the first moves of what would become the Cold War. Berlin was deep in the Soviet-occupied area of Germany, but the city itself had been split into zones administered by the Americans, British, French and Soviets. To keep their zones of the city alive, the Allies organized a massive, round-the-clock airlift, which kept the inhabitants supplied with all the essentials for daily life.

Back in the States, residents of San Bernadino, California, saw history in the making, as the first McDonald's hamburger stand opened. From this small beginning would grow first a nationwide chain of restaurants, then a world-wide chain that eventually would even penetrate the Soviet Union.

Fast food was not the only area of advance in 1948. The development of the transistor at the Bell Laboratories would soon lead to a burgeoning electronics industry, while the latest development in photography was the Polaroid camera.

In Detroit, the auto manufacturers were also making strides forward. In the years immediately after WW2, they had simply dusted off their pre-war designs,

made a few cosmetic changes, then built them as fast as they could to satisfy the demands of a car-hungry public. Buyers did not mind that the designs were four or more years old; after years of not being able to buy a new car, anything with wheels would do. Besides, they simply had no choice; it was the only way for companies to pick up the reins of business after years of wartime production.

By 1948, however, new models were beginning to appear, often resulting from development work carried out in secret during the war, and utilizing techniques of manufacture founded in the war work. Experience gained in the manufacture of non-automotive products, particularly aircraft and aircraft

components, opened the eyes of designers and engineers to new possibilities in automobile design and construction.

Hudson was one manufacturer that offered a new car for 1948 which was a real winner and, in some respects, unique compared to the rest of Detroit's offerings that year. It was known as the Step-down Hudson.

The new Hudson was based on a unibody design which, although not a new idea for an American car (Nash and Lincoln had already produced unibody designs), it was an innovative move at that time. As utilized in the Step-down design, the unibody arrangement gave greater passenger comfort and safety together with a sleek, attractive appearance. However, there were pros and cons to this construction. Without the heavy chassis, a much lighter structure could be built saving both materials and cost. On the negative side it was both difficult and expensive to make alterations to the design. This meant that the substantial changes in appearance, which had become an annual ritual in Detroit, were out of the question. This would prove to be a major problem with the Step-down Hudson but, in 1948, the rapturous reception afforded the car outweighed

Left & Above: The Tucker Torpedo was the brainchild of Preston Tucker, who had made a fortune during WW2 from the design of a gun turret mounting used in bomber aircraft. Fascinated by automobiles, after the war he set out to develop a car that would offer advanced engineering, styling, performance and levels of passenger safety. Powered by a 355 cu.in. rear-mounted, air-cooled, aluminum flat-six, the Torpedo could reach 60mph in 10 seconds and had a top speed of 120mph. For safety, its interior featured a padded dashboard and seatbelts, while a central third head light turned with the steering so that the driver could see around corners at night. Sadly, Tucker's enterprise failed with accusations of fraud and dirty tricks played by Detroit's "Big Three" automobile makers. Only 51 examples of the futuristic Torpedo were completed.

doubts about the future.

Based on a 124 inch wheelbase, the body was designed to incorporate box-section stiffeners, which effectively formed a strong cage around the passenger compartment and provided support for the engine, transmission and suspension. These formed perimeter rails that ran under the doors and outside the rear wheels keeping intrusion into the passe-

nger compartment to a minimum.

The "Step-down" name referred to the design of the passenger compartment itself. Aware that a low center of gravity would improve the car's handling and ride quality, Hudson designers arranged for the floor to be level with the bottom of the main perimeter rails, rather than sitting on top, which was normal practice with a separate chassis. To get into the car, it was necessary to step over the side rails and down onto the floor.

With a lower floor, it was possible to lower the position of the seats within the body and, consequently, the roofline while retaining good headroom inside. At 60 inches high, the new Hudson was four to six inches lower than most of its competitors, yet it provided as much, if not more, headroom. At the same time, ground clearance was not compromised. A two-piece driveshaft allowed the central floor hump to be quite low, improving comfort for passengers sitting

in the middle of the seats.

Hudson engineers also improved the ride for passengers by cradling them between the axles, rather than having them sit over the axle at the rear, so the rear seat was positioned ahead of the axle. This allowed for a wider seat without requiring a wider body. Further elbow room was provided by arranging for the side glass to drop down into the doors at an outward angle, which allowed recesses to be formed in the door trim panels.

Although the roofline was lowered, the beltline was of conventional height, making the side glass quite shallow in depth – the bottom edge of the glass was level with passengers' shoulders. However, the windshield and back light were comparable in area to taller cars, although these were canted somewhat.

Power for the Step-down Hudson came from a choice of six or eight cylinder in-line engines. The former was a new powerplant – the Super Six, which

Drive gave automatic operation of the clutch alone.

The suspension was conventional coilsprung independent at the front, with parallel leaf springs at the rear. However, a heavy front stabilizer bar and a rear panhard rod were both incorporated to assist handling and ride.

A very wide range of models was offered in the Super and Commodore series, which was comprised of 4-door sedans, 2-door broughams, club and standard coupes and convertible broughams.

Left: Chrysler's six cylinder Town & Country Sedan was deleted in mid 1948 but the straight-eight convertible continued in production, with the last few being numbered as '49s. Total production of this supremely elegant conveyance was in excess of 8,500.

Below: Having started out as a prototype station wagon in 1941, the Chrysler Town and Country series adapted the look of the "Woody" wagon to a luxury car and, in so doing, created a design classic. The T&C was surely the dream transport of anyone who had a country retreat for the weekends, instantly conjuring up images of foxhounds and polo ponies. A few hardtops were produced by grafting an elongated steel roof on to the convertible body.

had a capacity of 270 cu.in and developed 121 horsepower, while the latter was Hudson's tested Super Eight, a 254 cu.in. engine of 128 horsepower. Among the transmission options offered was overdrive, Drive-master and Vacumotive Drive, which had been available on previous models. Drivemaster was a form of automatic transmission, while the Vacumotive

149

When the Step-down was shown to Hudson dealers late in 1947, they could not believe their eyes. Worried about how long they could continue selling outdated pre-war designs in the face of steadily rising competition, they found the long, low and sleek automobile everything they could have wished for, and more. It was well received by road testers, too, who praised its styling, "roadability" and its comfort. For the next three years, the new Hudson would boost the small independent company's profits tremendously as the public stepped up to step down. The Berlin airlift came to an end and, still in the sky, James Gallagher made the first non-stop flight around the world in a Boeing B-50A Lucky Lady II, while another Boeing, the Stratocruiser, introduced new standards of airline passenger luxury. On the ground, more than 6 million cars poured out of factories and aviation influences abounded in the designs.

There was a momentous transformation in

Ford's fortunes as their output nearly tripled and they zoomed into the number one spot, overtaking arch rivals Chevrolet. On the face of it, this tremendous success can be attributed to the brand new automobiles they had to offer, but there's more to it than that.

For a start, the 1949 model year spanned almost eighteen months, as the restyled cars were launched in June 1948 and remained on sale right up until November 1949. This early announcement also shortened the '48 model year considerably and reduced sales of the pre-war designs on offer in that year, which were much the same as the '46 and '47 Fords.

Even taking all this into account, it has to be said that the '49 Ford was worthy of all the media attention and phenomenal sales that followed. The Ford is significant because it was the first low-price car with a slab-sided body devoid of any of the traditional fender lines. Other makes such as Hudson (another landmark in automobile styling), Nash and Kaiser-Frazer also produced similar concepts but they

Below: Despite a higher price tag, the 1949 Ford Custom Club Coupe proved itself to be a more popular choice than the standard version. Evidently most people weren't bothered about the possible saving of $96, and 150,254 Custom coupes were produced against only 4,170 of the cheaper ones. The extra money gave you such essentials as chrome window trims instead of rubber, a horn ring on the steering wheel, twin sun visors, dual arm rests and a chrome strip along the body sides.

were not as successful nor as cheap as the Ford. Chevrolet and Plymouth, meanwhile, still had pronounced rear fenders and an obvious dip between head lights and hood.

In fact, the slab-sided Fords were regarded as so flat that they soon earned the nickname "shoeboxes," though today it's hard to equate the curved lines with a shoebox. Engineering was revolutionary too (for a Ford!); this was the beginning of exciting times for the blue oval brigade. Following the death of founder Henry Ford in 1947, his grandson Henry Ford II introduced swinging changes and sought to rid the company of old-fashioned practices.

One of young Henry's most stalwart supporters was executive vice president Ernest Breech, and it is chiefly due to his efforts that the company won through. Breech also had a significant effect on the styling of the '49 Ford models, as we shall see later on. But the first things to disappear were the transverse leaf springs and beam axle suspension that old Henry insisted upon, to be replaced with coil spring independent front and longitudinal leaf rear suspension. Gone too, was the two-speed rear axle and in its place optional overdrive.

The engine was moved five inches

Below: Hail to the fin.... Probably Harley Earl's most celebrated styling innovation had arrived, quietly, the previous year, as an almost imperceptible bump at the trailing edge of the rear fender. Inspired by the twin tail booms of the Lockheed P38 lightning fighter aircraft, the incorporation of this detail may be credited to Frank Hershey who had designed the '48 model range. Earl ruled GM's Art & Colour studio with a rod of iron, however, and no innovation would have been permitted without his express approval. His love of all things aeronautical would manifest itself time and again in the coming years, but the "Cad Fin" was to become the defining style icon of the 'fifties.

forward to create a lower profile, yet provide greater internal space within a slightly shorter and narrower body. This

Above: *The long, low, purposeful styling of the late 40's Cadillacs had enormous influence, not only on American Automobile styling but across the world. The British Bentley, epitome of refinement and aristocratic breeding, was to follow Cadillac's lead with a series of custom bodies collectively known as the Flying Spurs.*

allowed more leg room for the people in the front seat, and with the rear seat now positioned ahead of the rear axle (instead of between the wheels), an extra six inches of width for the passengers in the back. Advertising emphasized this additional comfort by describing the seats as "Sofa-Wide" and promoting the "Mid Ship Ride" and HydraCoil front springs. The new Ford design also created 57% more trunk space, now denoted as a "Deep Deck Luggage Locker." And if that wasn't enough, then surely the Magic Air temperature control system, Magic Action brakes or Picture Window visibility would do the trick?

It's estimated that around 28 million

people visited the dealers' showrooms in the first three days after the new models were announced. What drew them were attractive cars that had progressed from initial design to production in just 19 months (in those days, average lead times were about three years). Haste wasn't without its problems, of course, and the build quality on the first '49s wasn't as good as it might have been. Body rattles plagued early vehicles and a number of alterations were made to alleviate problems. This situation persisted throughout the '49 model run and wasn't fully resolved until the 1950 models came along. But it didn't stop the '49 Ford becoming a huge hit and the company outsold Chevrolet by a large margin, with 1.1 million cars coming off the assembly lines.

Indeed, the success of the 1949 models is often credited for saving Ford from oblivion – it really was that desperate. Whether an organization of such magnitude would have disappeared completely is open to conjecture but this

automobile has warranted a special place in Ford's long and varied history.

The genesis of such a ground-breaking model was not without complications and there have been many claims as to how the design came about. The first stage in the saga began when Ford's head designer, Eugene T. "Bob" Gregorie showed his ideas to Ernest Breech in 1946. Breech liked the proposal, but felt it was too big to be marketed as a Ford, and in September '46 he pronounced that Gregorie's prototype would instead be used for the more upmarket Mercury range.

This naturally left a big hole in the planning process, and Gregorie immediately started work preparing an alternative design for the Ford. At the same time Breech contracted his friend George Walker (who operated a design consultancy that had done a lot of work for Nash) to come up with some ideas. On the staff were Elwood Engel, Joseph Oros, Richard Caleal, Holden Koto and Bob Bourke. When it came time to make

the presentation, Gregorie submitted one clay model and the Walker studio put up three for consideration.

Although there seems to have been very little to choose between them,

Below: One notable styling feature was that Indian head mascot on the front of the hood was illuminated at night.

Above: All that really changed on the Pontiac line to welcome the new decade was the addition of a mass of sparkling chromium trim. Even though all the innovation was entirely cosmetic, Pontiac's reputation for strength and reliability pushed sales in 1950 to record levels.

Breech picked one of Walker's designs. Gregorie left Ford a short time later although they remained on friendly terms. Walker's team proceeded to develop the design and developed the spinner in the center of the grille. Precisely who thought up this idea is debatable. Until recently it was accepted that the front end of the '49 Ford was the work of Caleal, Bourke and Koto – the latter two either working directly for Walker, or moonlighting from the Loewy studio (and the '50 Studebaker with its similar spinner was definitely a Bourke creation for Loewy). However, Oros had stated emphatically that the spinner was his creation.

Whatever the truth, it is apparent that there were many influences during what must have been a hectic period. George Walker took most of the credit at the time and used it to good effect to promote his agency, but it was Ernest Breech and Henry Ford II who had the final say on what went into production.

155

1950

SPECIFICATIONS

STUDEBAKER CHAMPION REGAL DELUXE

Engine:
Cast iron - 6 Cylinders in line

Displacement:
169.6 cu. ins.

Bore and stroke:
3 x 4

Horsepower:
85

Body styles:
Convertible coupe

No. of seats:
4-5

Weight (lbs):
2,900 lbs

Price:
$1,981

Produced:
270,604 (all models)

Above Right: 1950 was Studebaker's best ever year; they produced over 340,000 cars, of which 270,000 were Champions. The Champion styling was the product of a collaboration between Raymond Loewy and Virgil Exner. The joke was "Which way is it going?" but in fact it was way ahead of the field.

Henry and Clem Studebaker were building prairie schooners in South Ben, Indiana, way back in the eighteen-fifties. In 1902, with W. J. "Wheelbarrow Johnny" Studebaker at the helm, the company began building automobiles. The presidency of the company passed to Albert Russell Erskine in 1919. Erskine purchased Pierce-Arrow in 1928, just in time for the stock market crash, which decimate the market for luxury automobiles, and he had little more luck with the car named after himself. A bargain-basement model marketed as the Rockne fared no better.

Studebaker entered the 'thirties with a line headed by the Dictator, a name that would not survive the decade for obvious reasons. Sales ebbed away and the company went into receivership in 1933, after the collapse of a proposed merger with White. The unfortunate Erskine resigned and committed suicide soon after. Under the guidance of vice-president Harold S. Vance and head of sales Paul Hoffman, Studebaker managed to struggle back into the black in 1934. Pierce-Arrow was disposed of and production rose from a dismal 12,500 to a respectable 60,000. In 1938 Hoffman took on the inspired designer Raymond Loewy, who penned a radically revised Commander Six which had replaced the Dictator. There were also State Commanders and State Presidents. By the outbreak of World War Two, Studebaker production had reached over 85,000. During the war, Studebaker produced great numbers of aero

new line in 1946 while the bulk of the competition had only warmed-over '39 and '40 designs to offer.

In 1950, two years short of its centenary, Studebaker would record its highest ever output, with a production run of over 320,000 cars. The '47 model had been dramatically restyled and featured a distinctive, aircraft-inspired "bullet nose" that made the car an instant classic. Automatic transmission by Borg-Warner was offered for the first time. Both the Champion and the Commander were powered by L-head sixes, the former displacing 169.6 cu. ins and producing 85bhp, the latter bored and stroked to 245.6 cu. ins. and putting out 102bhp. A punchy, 232.6 cu. ins. V8 was to be offered the following year.

engines and personnel carriers while automobile styling was delegated to Loewy's studio. This resulted in the company being able to field a completely

Right & Below: The 1950 Mercury, with its curvaceous lines, was little changed from the face-lifted '49. However, the Mercury name was now proudly borne on a chrome strip on the hood, and sales were very buoyant.

SPECIFICATIONS

MERCURY ECONOMY/ CLUB COUPE

Engine:
V8 - Cast iron block

Displacement:
255.4 cu. ins

Bore and stroke:
3.19 x 4 ins.

Horsepower:
110

Body styles:
2 door coupe

No. of seats:
5

Weight (lbs):
3,345 lbs/3,430 lbs

Price:
$1,875 - $1,980

Produced:
151,000 (all models)

The war in Korea was dragging on, although the US Army was on the offensive and had recaptured Seoul, and it came as something of a shock when president Harry S. Truman sacked General Douglas MacArthur for defying the civil authority in April. Further shocks were felt when an atomic bomb was tested in Nevada, just 45 miles from Las Vegas, and the first hydrogen bomb was detonated on an atoll in the Marshall Islands in the Pacific Ocean. But probably the biggest explosion in America was the increasing television audience which had risen to 9% of all homes and continued to escalate at an ever faster rate.

Right: There were few major changes to the Mercury '51. The 4-door sedan was the top seller and one third of the buyers opted for Merc-O-Matic automatic transmission.

Truce finally came to Korea in November, and things became easier for some drivers who chose to buy a Chrysler with the auto industry's first viable power steering system, called "Hydraguide." At the lower end of the market, three-speed automatic transmissions could now be had on Ford and Mercury cars – the Ford-O-Matic and Merc-O-Matic units, built in conjunction with Warner Gear – but it was something of an exaggeration for Mercury to advertise its '51 models

using the slogan "Nothing like it on the road!"

The Mercury nameplate suffered from something of an identity crisis – it was usually looked upon as a fancy Ford rather than a junior Lincoln. The 1951 models (the last of a three year phase starting with the '49 designs) were more Lincoln in appearance, although beneath the bodywork there were mostly Ford mechanical parts.

In an attempt to give Mercury automobiles a more upmarket image,

the Lincoln-Mercury division was formed in October 1945. This also gave Lincoln an independent dealership network whereas its cars had previously been sold in selected Ford showrooms.

As we know from the story behind the creation of the 1949 Ford models, it was Ernest Breech who decided that Bob Gregorie's initial design should be used for the Mercury range. But the development of the shape that was to become inextricably linked with the Fifties wasn't quite as straight-forward as simply changing the name on the hood.

In fact, the evolution of the 1951 Mercury involved three generations of the mighty Ford dynasty and, in some ways, encapsulated the end of the old autocratic regime that had grown up under the ailing Henry Ford and the new beginnings heralded with the arrival of his grandson, Henry Ford II. Gregorie first started work on the design when Edsel Ford was in charge of styling and although the two shared many ideas.

Below: The Packard 250 convertible was a mid-year introduction, together with this companion 2-door hardtop coupe. It was based on the shorter wheelbase of the 200 series, but used the larger 327 cu.in. in-line eight cylinder L-head engine. Four dummy louvers on the rear fenders and fancy interiors featured in these models.

they were by no means in total agreement. Edsel Ford tended to favor a lighter touch, especially on details like bumpers and grille, whereas Gregorie was more inclined to use broader brush strokes.

The death of Edsel Ford on May 26 1943 was a turning point. Grief-stricken at the loss, Octogenarian Henry took even less interest in the cars bearing his name, and left important decisions to others – mainly Harry Bennett and Charlie Sorensen – as the battle waged

Above: Totally redesigned by John Reinhart, the 24th Series Packards for '51 were acclaimed as "the most beautiful car of the year" by the Society of Motion Picture Art Directors. The line up consisted of three main levels of models – the lower priced 200 (back) had a "toothless" grille with a 288 cu.in. engine and 122 inch wheelbase; the mid-range 300 (center) had a 5 inch longer wheelbase and bigger engine; the top of the line 400 Patrician (front) only came as a 4-door sedan.

for control of the Ford empire. Vice-president, "Cast Iron Charlie" Sorensen saw the Gregorie proposals and encouraged the stylist to make the cars even bigger and more rounded, equating size and luxury to the voluptuous curves of "those big Italian gals."

But Sorensen was part of the old guard and on his way out, eventually to be deposed early in 1944. However, the internal power struggle wouldn't be fully resolved until some time after Henry Ford II became company president in September 1945. Young Henry hired new management to replace Bennett and his cronies and, in one of his most crucial appointments, was to take on a group of ten young ex-USAAF officers headed by Charles "Tex" Thornton, who quickly became known as "The Whizz Kids" throughout Ford. Ernest Breech was then persuaded to join the company and things really started to happen.

One effect was a rationalization of the Ford, Mercury and Lincoln models. It was decided that Mercurys would now use a 118 inch wheelbase chassis (which was required for the larger body shell shared with Lincoln) of similar dimensions to pre-war designs although completely new in concept, while Fords would sit on a four inch shorter

platform. Meantime, Lincoln used tw slightly longer configurations – 121 an 125 inches – as befitted their status a the luxury marque.

Although Bob Gregorie had left For in 1946, his design for the 194 Mercury went into production with ver little modification. Subsequent face-lift in '50 and '51 improved the overa look, adding extended rear fenders an vertical tail lights. The bodywork ma have altered little, but a brand nev feature on the 1951 was of mor significance to the buyer – the Merc-O Matic automatic transmission.

Coupled to an outmoded Flathea V8, the automatic put the Mercury performance into the "leisurely" bracke

Below: Chryslers of the early 'fifties changed little in appearance. Chrome was gradually added and minor revisions made to radiator grilles and tail lights. The divided windshield eventually gave way to a single piece by '53, but the dazzling look that was to define the marque from the middle of the decade was still, literally, on the drawing board. Despite the arrival of the "hemi" V8, Sales were falling, probably due to the line's conservative styling. Virgil Exner, late of Studebaker, was about to change all that.

or, as Mechanix Illustrated tester Tom McCahill put it: "...the winged Mercury parked his track shoes outside the door and joined the ladies over a comforting pot of tea." Mercury adverts highlighted economy, promising to "Squeeze the last mile out of a gallon," and stressed that it wasn't expensive either, saying they gave customers "more car per dollar." The hot rodders' favorite had been turned into something different, something more comforting to Mr and Mrs Joe Average – for it was they who were buying new automobiles. The difference appealed and, with sales over 310,000, raised Mercury to number six in the charts.

But if the '51 Mercury was a success with the older generation when new, it would gain a far more long-lasting image as a Fifties icon from a most unlikely source – the death of a film star. Had he lived, it is impossible to predict what would have become of James Dean, but one thing is certain – he would never have driven a Mercury except in a movie. The fact that his second starring role in *A Rebel Without A Cause* (released in 1955 shortly after his fatal car crash) featured him as a

Above: Nash's six-cylinder, seven-main-bearing motor dated from 1928 and remained in production until 1956. A reputation for bullet-proof reliability, combined with its "compact" body, made the Nash, and its partner, the Rambler, to which the engine was also fitted, hugely successful despite its distinctly tin toy styling.

super cool teenager fighting the establishment and driving a mildly customized Mercury was to endow the car with a presence that endures today.

The association with James Dean fixed the "bathtub" Mercury as an automobile with attitude – performance didn't matter, it was all about looking cool as you cruised to the drive-in. Over the years, Hollywood has periodically reinforced this image, notably in the 1970s blockbuster movie American Graffiti in which the customized Mercury was used by a delinquent gang of youngsters.

From comfortable family transport for the suburban dweller to an everlasting symbol of teenage rebellion, surely no other car has made such a remarkable transition as the Mercury?

SPECIFICATIONS

KAISER "HENRY J"
CORSAIR DELUXE

Engine:
Cast iron - 6 Cylinders
in line

Displacement:
161 cu. ins.

Bore and stroke:
3.13 x 3.5

Horsepower:
80

Body styles:
2 door sedan

No. of seats:
4

Weight (lbs):
2,405 lbs

Price:
$1,664

Produced:
9,000

Many US industrialists profited hugely from government contracts during the Second World War, and one of the most famous was Henry John Kaiser who had interests in ship-building and construction. Like other tycoons who made vast fortunes over the years, Kaiser thought he could take on the established Detroit auto makers and beat them at their own game. And, just like all "outside" attempts to launch a new postwar car, Kaiser's venture ended in failure.

Henry Kaiser's dream was a small, cheap car that would provide basic transportation for everyone. In the early 1940s, he had predicted that he would produce a new car for $400 – a suggestion which proved to be totally unrealistic, yet one Kaiser often repeated in his quest for publicity. It was in an attempt to revive the flagging fortunes of his auto company, that he decided to launch the new small car in September 1950 and borrowed 44 million dollars to finance the tooling required.

Stylist Howard "Dutch" Darrin produced a prototype based on his 1951 full-size Kaiser design but, instead, Henry decided to go with another concept put together by American Metal Products of Detroit. Based on a 100 inch wheelbase chassis, the compact Henry J (as it came to be called) 2-door sedan was notable for its sloping fastback and small tail fins. The fins were part of Darrin's

However, that seems to have saturated the market, as sales more than halved in '52, despite a deal with Sears Roebuck to market the car using their Allstate brand name. The Allstate had a different grille and interior, but despite aggressive promotion, less than 1,600 were sold in 1952, and the scheme was dropped in '53 after fewer than 800 orders had been taken. In '53, sales of the Henry J halved again, and in 1954, the car's last year, only 1,123 in total were sold, and that proved to be the end.

Henry Kaiser's mistake was to believe that there was a huge market for a cheap car with no trimmings. He was quoted as saying, "We feel that we have accomplished our goal at a price which will be within the budgets of millions who have never been able to afford a new car." But Kaiser had failed to

attempt to improve the looks of the car, and he made several other changes, including his trademark feature – a slight dip in the bodywork just behind the door. Power for the Henry J came from either a 68hp flathead Willys 134 cu.in. four cylinder engine or a 161 cu.in. six that gave 80 horsepower.

Initially it seemed as though Kaiser had come up with a winner as almost 82,000 Henry Js were sold in 1951.

Left & Below: The small Henry J 2-door sedan was launched as an economy car that anyone could afford. Priced at $1664, the top of the line Corsair DeLuxe version came with glove box and opening trunk lid – items that came as standard on even the most basic cars. The 161 cu.in. six cylinder engine gave a 0-60mph time of 14 seconds. The central bar of the grille should be chrome, not painted.

understand that most Americans in the early Fifties preferred to own a car that looked glitzy and expensive, rather than one that classed itself as "a poor man's automobile."

While Kaiser's aim was to produce a cheap, no-frills automobile, that didn't prevent his advertising copywriters from filling the company sales literature with fulsome descriptions. Calling the mundane flathead engines "Supersonic" was pretty par for the period, but stating that the feeble four cylinder "Lunges like a lion (without the roar!)," was definitely over the top! Other animal connotations were used, such as "Tough as an Ox, nimble as a Kitten" but, in a misguided attempt to make the Henry J appeal to as wide an audience as possible, there were also statements like "You'll be the object of envy at the doors of the smartest shops."

As well as being a family car, the Henry J also saw some international competition use. Three cars were entered in the 1952 Monte Carlo Rally, and one actually finished in 20th place – an incredible achievement considering its lack of performance. But even had a Henry J won the event outright, it would not have been enough to stop Kaiser's dream becoming a nightmare.

Sales plummeted and debts mounted. Kaiser amalgamated with Willys-Overland in 1954, and the following year Kaiser-Willys ceased manufacture of passenger cars. Henry J. Kaiser's venture into the automobile world was estimated to have lost 100 million dollars in a decade.

Right: In an attempt to boost flagging sales in '52, Kaiser managed to persuade department store chain Sears Roebuck to market the car using their Allstate brand name. Little more than a Henry J with a different grille and interior, despite aggressive promotion, less than 1,600 Allstates were sold in 1952, and the scheme was dropped in '53 after fewer than 800 orders had been taken.

CHEVROLET CORVETTE

Engine:
Cast iron - 6 Cylinders in line

Displacement:
235.5 cu. ins.

Bore and stroke:
3.56 x 3.94

Horsepower:
150

Body styles:
Sports roadster

No. of seats:
2

Weight (lbs):
2,700 lbs

Price:
$3,513

Produced:
315

Ford and Buick shared 1953 as their Golden Anniversary Year and Charles E. Wilson, president of GM, made his famous (and often misquoted) statement: "...for many years I thought that what was good for our country was good for General Motors, and vice-versa." What eventually turned out good for Chevrolet was the arrival of a brand new sports car.

Whenever the reasons behind the birth of the

Below & Above: The Corvette grille with thirteen teeth was designed to carry the Chevrolet family identity, though standard Chevy's in '53 only had three! the lack of a full front bumper caused many to express concern over the lack of protection afforded the fiber glass bodywork, particularly when parking. The mesh stoneguards on the head lamps were deleted when it was discovered that they fell foul of local vehicle regulations in some states.

Corvette are chronicled, it is usually suggested that it was GIs returning from Europe with an enthusiasm for British or Italian sports cars that led to the creation of America's favorite two-seater. While not wishing to diminish this idea, it is worth pointing out that, in 1952, little more than 11,000 new sports cars were registered across the

entire USA – approximately 0.025% of the nation's new car market.

Given this perspective, it is easy to understand why the big Detroit automobile makers were not exactly fighting each other to enter such a small, specialized sector of the marketplace. That it should be Chevrolet – traditionally a purveyor of affordable, yet mundane, family sedans – to introduce such a bold departure from the norm, is almost entirely due to the efforts of two men – Harley Earl and Ed Cole.

As the stylist supremo at General Motors, Harley Earl used his considerable influence to mount almost a personal crusade to prove that his company could build a car as good as the Jaguars and Ferraris he so admired. Chief engineer Cole, on the other hand, saw a sports car would boost the Chevrolet name and give it a more youthful image. In addition to the two major players, the names of Robert McLean and Maurice Olley should be added. Newly arrived from Cal Tech, when laying out the chassis design, young McLean decided to reverse the

normal procedure and started at the back axle, then worked forward to obtain the 50:50 weight distribution specified. Most of the suspension and steering details came from Olley (an ex-Rolls Royce engineer) and their efforts helped give the Corvette its road-hugging profile, thanks to the lower slung engine and drivetrain.

Following the debut of the prototype EX-122 Corvette in the GM Motorama – a glamorous cavalcade of exotic cars that toured the USA throughout the Fifties – Chevrolet dealers found themselves inundated with enquiries about the sporty two-seater. It seemed Earl and Cole had produced a winning concept and the car was put into production without many alterations. This wasn't so easy. Using glass-fiber for a concept car was fine, but adapting the design and building techniques for the assembly line was another matter.

Compromises were inevitable; the Chevy engineers and designers were further hampered because they were forced, in the most part, to use existing mechanical components to save time

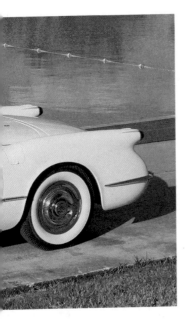

manager, described the new two-seater thus: "In the Corvette we have built a sports car in the American tradition. It is not a racing car in the accepted sense that a European sports car is a race car. It is intended rather to satisfy the American public's conception of beauty, comfort and convenience, plus performance."

On June 30 1953, the first ever Corvette (one of only 300 built in that year) was driven off the end of a short, six-car-length assembly line tucked away in a corner of the Chevrolet plant

The convertible top for the first (above left) Corvette was very much an afterthought and looked awkward and inelegant. It was also difficult to erect, with separate side windows that needed to be stored in the trunk when removed. With the hood up, the driver's all-round vision was severely impaired and the rakish, low-slung lines of the car were greatly compromised. A factory hardtop (above) looked like a great improvement! Earl's fascination with airplanes and rocketships may be seen in the treatment of the tail lights, but apart from this, the overall styling of the car is almost European in feel. Sadly, with its stove-bolt six motor and two-speed transmission, the first Corvette's performance was hardly in the Jaguar league.

and keep the cost of the project down to a minimum. This meant that the Corvette came with a six cylinder Stovebolt engine and a Powerglide two-speed automatic transmission. Of course, Cole's team tweaked the old Chevy six to produce 150 horsepower and push the speedo needle round to almost 110mph, but it just wasn't in the same league as Jaguar's twin overhead camshaft powerplant.

Thomas Keating, Chevrolet's general

in Flint, Michigan. Joining together the 46 separate glass-fiber panels that made up the body, getting them to cure and mounting it on the chassis was a labor-intensive task and, at times, the process was a slow and uncertain affair.

Because of the apparently huge demand and the shortage of cars, it was decided to allocate the available Corvettes to celebrities and prominent figures in the first instance. However, when the cars fell short of expectations, this method of selective distribution backfired and generated some rather unwelcome negative publicity. Only 183 Corvettes were sold in '53, and production had to be held in check the following year as manufacture was transferred to St. Louis. It didn't help that, priced at $3490, the Corvette was over a thousand dollars more than an MG and out of reach of the majority of young drivers it was supposedly aimed at.

Despite Thomas Keating's pronouncement, comparisons between European sport cars and the Corvette were inevitable. And, not unexpectedly, the Chevy two-seater didn't stand up well against such competitors. It wasn't just the less-than-exciting six cylinder engine, or Powerglide automatic, but also the dashboard and whitewall tires that didn't belong on a sports car. And even those people prepared to accept the lack of performance were far from satisfied with the level of standard equipment – no external door handles, clumsy clip-in side curtains instead of wind-up windows, a primitive convertible top that let in rain and dust – and distressing rattles from the glass-fiber bodywork.

Most other automobile manufacturers would have swiftly abandoned such a troublesome project as this. The fact that a huge company like Chevrolet kept the sports car alive and that the Corvette itself survives to the present day comes back, once again, to the influence wielded by Harley Earl and Ed Cole. Maybe some of it was simply a matter of pride and Earl protecting his reputation, unwilling to accept that his creation was, by most standards, a failure. Or perhaps Cole realized that when the new V8 engine arrived, Chevy would take on a whole new performance image – he certainly never lost his

enthusiasm for the car.

In many ways the 1953 Corvette is an anachronism. At the time it was a car that Chevrolet should never have made. A giant company busy churning out 1.3 million family cars a year had no logical reason to undertake the construction of a tiny quantity of hand-built vehicles, using a curious combination of special materials and stock components. But among many other facets of his character, Harley Earl was a dedicated car enthusiast and designing a sports car that would be internationally acclaimed obviously represented to him a challenge that he just couldn't resist.

His first attempt, while regarded as a Fifties classic today, fell woefully short of the type of car he wanted to emulate. But at least it was built and, in time, it would develop into a true sports car and one that Harley Earl, Ed Cole and all those Corvette designers and engineers that followed them could truly be proud of.

Left & Above: The 1953 Cadillac Eldorado could be distinguished from the standard series 62 by - among other details - a distinct dip at the beltline, a disappearing hood that was concealed, when lowered, by a hinged lid on the top of the rear deck, rather than being covered with a canvas cover as previously, and the world's first wrap-around windshield.

SPECIFICATIONS

NASH HEALEY

Engine:
Cast iron block - 6
Cylinders in line.

Displacement:
252.6 cu. ins.

Bore and stroke:
3.50 x 4.38

Horsepower:
135

Body styles:
Convertible roadster; Le
Mans coupe

No. of seats:
2

Weight (lbs):
2,750 lbs - 2,990 lbs

Price:
$5,688

Produced:
506 (total from '51 -
'55)

A ten year, $50 billion expansion program of the US highway system was announced by Vice President Richard Nixon, and General Motors produced its 50 millionth car (a Chevrolet) on November 23rd at Flint, Michigan, which was paraded through the city streets in front of huge crowds.

Not all production was on the grand scale, however. There were, in the 'fifties, as now, a number of brave souls who were willing to go it alone in pursuit of a dream, of perfection, or simply of fat profits. Some weird and wonderful cars were produced, among them the Gaylord, the Kaiser Darrin and the Nash-Healey. The last named was the product of a collaboration between George Mason and Donald Healey. Mason came from Kelvinator electrical appliances and arrived at Nash just before World War II and, in 1945, followed Charles W. Nash himself as president. Healey was an urbane Englishman, amateur engineer and racing driver who dreamed of producing his own sportscars. The two of them met on the liner Queen Elizabeth, bound for New York. They immediately hit it off and, by the time the ship had docked, had agreed to explore the possibility of building sportscar to Healey's

*Right: The Nash-Healey
was one of the first
Euro-American cross-
breeds, the product of a
chance meeting on a
luxury liner between
and American
industrialist and a
British gentleman
amateur. The result was
a classic sportscar.*

specifications, based on the engine of the Ambassador six. This was a robust, up-to-date, six-cylinder, overhead-valve unit that formed a good starting point for Healey's tuning genius. Reprofiled camshafts were fitted, along with British SU carburetors and a high-compression, aluminum cylinder head. The result was an output of 125 bhp @ 4,000 rpm. This engine was mated to a three-speed Nash manual transmission with Borg-Warner overdrive. Fitted with competition bodywork, the result was the first of many Euro-American hybrids that would, in time, include such legendary automobiles as the Jensen, the Bristol, the AC, the Gordon-Keeble, the De Tomaso and the Facel-Vega.

Healey ran the new car, effectively untested, in the gruelling Italian Mille-Miglia - a thousand miles of often dusty, public roads that were only closed on the day of the race. He finished and was placed ninth in class. Two cars were entered in the Le Mans 24 hour race and were creditably placed also. For the production car, a British company called Panelcraft built bodies in aluminum, based on Healey's own designs, and assembly was carried out by Healey's own company. The car was badged as a Nash but the styling was unmistakably English. it was exhibited at the annual motor Shows in London and Paris and production began in the middle of 1950. The cars were slow in coming - at the rate of about 10 a week - and expensive, at $4,063. They got Nash a lot of publicity but Mason wasn't happy with the styling. He engaged the Italian master coachbuilder Pinin Farina to submit a new design which incorporated a curved, one-piece windshield, inboard headlights and an altogether more curvaceous, typically Italian, line. The Italian-styled, 1952 model sold for $5,688 and production increased to 150 cars for the year.

Healey continued to expose the car to competition and it continued to perform successfully, despite his wrecking a coupe in the '52 Mille Miglia. The '52

Below & Above: The Kaiser Darrin of 1954 had been designed by Howard "Dutch" Darrin two years earlier. Based on the Henry J chassis, the fiberglass body was elegantly styled, though the small, protruding radiator opening may be a little too quirky for a lot of people's taste. The car featured sliding doors and a three-position "landau" hood. Darrin persuaded Henry Kaiser to market the car at $3,600 but only 435 were completed before Kaiser operations ground to a halt. Darrin bought out the last 100 and installed Cadillac V8s, giving the car a top speed approaching 140 mph, and sold them - for $4,350 each - through his own Los Angeles dealership.

Le Mans race was a real triumph, as cars entered by Jaguar and Aston Martin fell by the wayside, the Nash-Healey stormed on to finish third overall behind two works Mercedes Benzs, having averaged better than 90 mph. 163 cars were sold in 1953, including a longer-wheelbase coupe named the Le Mans in honor of their remarkable achievement.

In 1954 the roadster was dropped and the Le Mans coupe was restyled. Less than 100 were built before production was abandoned. Nash had been selling the cars for around half what it cost to produce them. Just over 500 examples of this labor-of-love were produced. The rugged and reliable Nash-Healey was a truly great sportscar by any standards.

Another great automobile that never made it into the big league was the Kaiser-Darrin. Like the Nash-Healey, it was the product of a collaboration between an auto manufacturer and a designer with a dream, but in this case the relationship was a lot more stormy.

Howard "Dutch" Darrin had resigned from Kaiser-Fraser, claiming that his original designs had been changed without reference to him. He returned, to design the '51 Kaiser, and then walked out again when an alternative design to his was selected for the Henry J. He retreated to his studio in California to work on a sportscar design based on the Henry J. chassis - without reference to Kaiser. This resulted,

Above: Starfire was the new name for the Oldsmobile 98 convertible in '54; it originally came from the Lockheed F-94 jet fighter, but was used on an Oldsmobile dream car displayed in '53. Apart from the obligatory annual body changes, the most noticeable styling feature is the Panoramic double curvature wrap-around windshield that appeared on all '54 Olds models. The Starfire engine was a 185 horsepower version of the 324 cu.in. Rocket V8, and 6,800 were sold, with a factory price of $3,248.

understandably, in a blazing row, when his plans were uncovered, but the beauty of the design won Kaiser over.

The car was a long, low two-seater, with a three-position convertible top and unique, sliding doors. The lines of the body were beautifully proportioned and the only possible question as to its beauty was in the very small, fan-shaped radiator grille set high in the center of the front panel. The body was to built in fiber-glass and be powered - or rather under-powered - by a 90hp version of the Willys six-cylinder engine. The interior fittings were of a high standard and the instrumentation was extremely comprehensive for the period. Although the hood was good, the sliding doors turned out to be a drag: it was impossible to stop them rattling and they didn't open very wide so getting in and out wasn't easy, particularly for anyone wearing a skirt. As cars like this were

supposed to appeal to skirt-wearers, this was a distinct drawback. The other great drawback was the performance of the Willys motor. Cars like this are meant to be swift but the Kaiser-Darrin was, frankly, pedestrian, compared to a Corvette, even with the stovebolt six. A supercharger was added to boost output to 125 hp but that motor still wasn't going to set the world on fire.

Kaiser-Willys had ceased production before 500 cars had been completed. Darrin bought out the last hundred or so bodies and fitted them with 300 hp Cadillac V8s, providing them - too late, alas - with the level of performance their elegant design had always promised but never delivered. He sold the cars, for $4,350 each, through his own Los Angeles dealership. A few of these last, Cadillac-powered cars were actually taken racing, with limited success, proving that had a credible power-plant been fitted in the first place, the car might have been a winner.

1954 was a year of unlikely couplings. Apart from the Nash-Healey and the Kaiser-Darrin, Marilyn Monroe married Joe DiMaggio and a jazz festival took place in Newport, Rhode Island, for the first time. Among other doomed designs that year were an atomic-powered locomotive, courtesy of the University of Utah. Dwight Eisenhower announced a plan to modernize the nation's highways with the costs being borne by both state and federal government. The New York

State Thruway was opened, running 559 miles from New York to Buffalo - and Mercedes Benz introduced the first car with fuel-injection - the 300SL. Within a couple of years, this innovation would be helping to boost the performance of American cars, being fitted as an option to the Corvette in '57. Otherwise, the main thrust of mainstream auto design in the United States was in the styling department. The '54 - '56 run of Cadillacs would be the last to bear the flowing coachwork that harked back to the 'forty-nines. The fin was itching to burst free of the fender line and the dagmars were already swelling ripely from the front bumper: the shape of things to come.

The 1954 Cadillac Eldorado was far closer to the Series 62 Convertible than the Grand Original of '53 and hence the price was a little less Olympian at $4,738. To compensate, Cadillac were able to produce, and sell, a lot more examples: 2,150 against 532. Power was up to 230 hp across the range but from the following year, along with the first "shark" fins, the Eldo would have more power than its stablemates.

1955

SPECIFICATIONS

CHRYSLER C-300

Engine:
V8 - cast iron block

Displacement:
331.1 cu. ins.

Bore and stroke:
3.81 x 3.63

Horsepower:
300

Body styles:
Hardtop coupe

No. of seats:
5

Weight (lbs):
4,000 lbs

Price:
$4,110

Produced:
1,725

Back in '55, cars were generally regarded as being for family use and categorized by body style – sedan, coupe, convertible or station wagon. If you wanted a sports car, you could look to Chevrolet's Corvette or to the Ford Thunderbird, or maybe even consider one of those itty-bitty European jobs. Combining the two as a sports-type passenger car wasn't really an option.

However, then came the Chrysler C-300. Styled by Virgil Exner, engineered by Robert M. Roger and powered by the legendary Chrysler FirePower Hemi V8, it was a revelation. Fast enough in standard form to set speed records over 127mph, and win NASCAR races when modified, the 2-door hardtop coupe could also seat six people in comfort. Part of the completely new-look Chrysler line in 1955, dubbed the "100 Million Dollar Look," it heralded a massive upturn in the marque's success as sales leapt an astounding 50% over the previous year.

At the very heart of the C-300 was the Hemi

Right: Styled by Virgil Exner, the Chrylser 300 of 1955, with its Imperial grille and "clip-on" fins was the first in a long and illustrious line of luxury muscle cars

engine – so called because of its hemispherically-shaped combustion chambers – a configuration long regarded by engine experts as being the most efficient for producing maximum power. The problem with this design was that the valves were canted over at an angle to fit in to the hemi chamber and it required two rocker shafts and a complex arrangement of pushrods and varying lengths of rocker arms to make it work. This increased the cost of manufacturing the cylinder heads and the Hemi was replaced in 1959 by a more conventional wedge-head design.

Introduced in 1951, the Hemi displaced 331 cu.in. and

pumped out an impressive 300 horsepower at 5,200rpm – providing the inspiration for the 300 Series name. As fitted to the '55 C-300, breathing through twin four-barrel carburetors with a full-race camshaft and an 8.5:1

Below: The 300 model name came from the 300 brake horsepower produced by the 331 cu.in. FirePower V8 Hemi engine – so-called because of its hemispherical combustion chambers.

Above: The Hot One! Such was Chevrolet's advertising copy line for 1955 and such were the cars that they produced. The Chevys of '55, '56 and '57 are now probably the most commonly restored cars in the world and looking at this 1955 Bel Air it isn't difficult to see why. Combining 'fifties flair with perfectly balanced styling, plus a superb, overhead valve V8 these cars are almost impossible to improve.

compression ratio, the Hemi quickly earned Chrysler the "US Speed Champ" title. Naturally, the cars were great for racing and Tim Flock qualified a Chrysler on the pole at Daytona in 1955 and went on to win the race. He repeated the feat a year later and there's no doubt that the 300 Series would have been a major force in motor racing for some years if the manufacturers hadn't withdrawn it from competition in 1957.

The body design of the 1955 Chryslers evolved from a long line of concept cars built by Ghia in Italy under instruction from famed stylist Virgil Exner. The result was a complete break from Chrysler's previous "engineering-led" policy pursued by company president K. T. Keller, who had by now retired. His successor, Lester L. "Tex" Colbert, got rid of the old six cylinder engines and gave the styling department a freedom that was to produce some of the most striking automobiles of the Fifties under the "Forward Look" banner.

The C-300 was produced to compete with the limited-production Chevrolet Corvette and the Ford Thunderbird sports cars; not so much for sales purposes, but more to improve Chrysler's performance image. Unable to create a special 2-seater model (although Ghia show cars of this configuration had been designed by Exner), Chrysler used what they had

garish two-tone paint jobs and an excess of chrome was deemed the way to go. It had very little ornamentation, not even outside mirrors, and was only available in three colors – red, white and black. Even without its outstanding performance, this elegance would have set the C-300 apart from the rest. In 1955, this model represented status, luxury and performance in an exclusive package that was priced beyond the reach of the general public.

Rather surprisingly for such an expensive automobile (it was just about double the price of a Chevrolet or Ford), the C-300 didn't have air conditioning – even as a factory option. Another omission from the performance point of view was that the disk brakes used on the Imperial weren't included in the specification, although the drums all round with power assistance were thought to be more than adequate. Uprated springs and heavy duty shock absorbers helped put the cornering capability in a superior class when compared to the Chrysler models, and a

got. The starting point was a New Yorker 2-door hardtop body, with rear quarters from the Windsor and the grille from the Imperial to add prestige, although the New Yorker front bumper was retained.

The C-300 was a complete contrast to most other offerings of the time, when

Below: The Chevrolet Biscayne concept car, shown in 1955, demonstrates how difficult it was, even for General Motors' finest, to better the Tri-Chevys. The Biscayne featured a pillarless line, with centre-opening doors and a "Stratospheric" windshield.

beefed-up PowerFlite automatic transmission with a higher stall speed torque converter produced rapid acceleration – 0-60mph in under 10 seconds.

Options such as power steering, power windows, radio, heater, tinted glass, and four-way power adjustable front bench seat could all be used to enhance the tan leather and vinyl trimmed interior. Regarded as highly desirable today, was the possibility of having Kelsey-Hayes wire wheels fitted at a whopping $600 a set.

It goes without saying that this exclusivity would result in very few C-300 models being produced, only 1,725 in fact, and it is estimated that there are approximately two hundred survivors. But the influence of the C-300 went far beyond mere sales figures. It was to be the founding member of a legendary automotive dynasty – the so-called Letter Series Chryslers. Following the favorable reactions from the media to the '55

offering, the following year a face-lifted 1956 version was designated the 300B. This became an annual feature of the Chrysler model line-up, with a change of suffix letter, until the final 300L in 1965 – although the 300 Series itself lasted as a distinct model group until 1971.

As was the trend, all American automobiles were getting longer, lower and wide and size was an important aspect of the C-300 (and all the other 1955 Chrysler models). However, the extra inches on length and width had

Below: The '55 Dodges had "Forward Look" styling and 270 cu. in. V8s to recommend them. Additionally, in a particularly forward-looking moment of inspiration, Dodge decided to produce a version of the Custom Royal Lancer hardtop specifically for the ladies. This was finished in pink and white and designated "La Femme." Equipment included a folding umbrella and fitted handbags.

some unforeseen side effects. While a three inch longer car might not make much difference parked on the driveway, nose-to-tail on the assembly line it soon added up and manufacturers found themselves having to extend their production lines by up to 30 feet to accommodate the new designs. Police and city officials also voiced doubts over how these bigger cars were going to fit into

Above: Series 62 Cadillacs stayed classic for '55, though the Eldorado had already sprouted pointed fins. Cadillacs represented the zenith of luxury motoring, combining engineering excellence with elegance of design and benefiting from the very latest developments on all fronts. From tubeless tires to air-conditioning, the Cadillac driver got it first, just as with the self-starter in 1912.

existing parking places.

In purely economic terms, 1955 was a boom year in the auto industry with nearly 8 million cars being churned out by Detroit. Disneyland opened in California, the rock 'n' roll era arrived with Bill Haley and his Comets topping the charts with "Rock Around The Clock" and the minimum wage was raised to $1 per hour. On the flip side, Martin Luther King was leading a bus boycott in Alabama protesting against segregation, and James Dean died in an auto accident.

There were many great cars made that year, but the merits of the Chrysler FirePower Hemi engine cannot be denied and, equally, it is impossible to ignore the sheer class of Virgil Exner's design. If ever there was a prize for the perfect combination of performance and appearance, then the '55 Chrysler C-300 must surely rank as one of the top contenders of all time.

SPECIFICATIONS

FORD THUNDERBIRD

Engine:
V8 - cast iron block

Displacement:
292 - 312 cu. ins.

Bore and stroke:
3.80 x 3.44

Horsepower:
202 - 225

Body styles:
Convertible roadster

No. of seats:
2

Weight (lbs):
3,038 lbs

Price:
$3,151

Produced:
15,631

We like Ike. That was the message resounding through the nation as Dwight Eisenhower was returned for a second term as President in a landslide victory over Adlai Stevenson. Yet to be crowned "The King," Elvis Presley was hitting the charts and grabbing headlines thanks to songs like "Heartbreak Hotel," "Don't Be Cruel" and "Blue Suede Shoes." Another title holder, world heavyweight boxing champion Rocky Marciano, announced his retirement from the ring.

The phrase "cause and effect" is something that comes to mind when looking at Ford's Thunderbird. That it was made in response to arch rival Chevrolet bringing out the Corvette isn't in doubt, but that it would also have the consequence of ensuring the survival of the GM model was certainly something that was far from Ford's intention. It is also ironic that, having rescued the Corvette from oblivion and provided evidence of a viable market for a US-built sports car, the Thunderbird would quickly be taken out of that sector and turned into a luxury four-seater.

The reason for the decision was numbers, and it

the European sports cars on display, Crusoe is supposed to have asked Walker why Ford didn't have anything similar, and the consultant (probably to keep his paymaster happy) replied that they were already working on just such a design. Immediately following this conversation, Walker was then said to have phoned his office back in the USA and told them to get something put together in time for his return.

It seems unlikely that these events ever actually happened. George Walker was a deft manipulator of the facts and often claimed credit for car design work that he personally was only involved with on an administration level. It has also to be remembered that there were an awful lot of young designers in the industry and their enthusiasm for the sports car would have generated many

Left & Below: Several changes were made to 1956 Thunderbirds following feedback from owners of '55 models. The externally-mounted spare wheel is the most obvious feature – intended to give more luggage space in the trunk – but weight distribution was affected. Other alterations to improve driver comfort included wind wings on the windshield to prevent buffeting when enjoying topless motoring, and vent doors in the front fenders to feed fresh air into the passenger compartment. The real bumper also had exhausts exiting through slots in the corners.

proved to be correct direction for the second generation Thunderbird to take in 1958, but that's taking us away from the original concept. There is a story that the idea for the T-Bird first came about following the visit by Ford general manager Lewis D. Crusoe and styling consultant George Walker to the 1951 Paris Auto Show in France. Seeing all

illustrations and drawings on the "what if we built one of those?" basis. Therefore, it can be assumed that Ford (in common with most other manufacturers) had, over the years, been carrying out various design studies on sports cars but not progressed them any further because of the perceived limited sales potential.

When Chevrolet brought out the Corvette in 1953, Ford had to respond quickly, and unveiled a full-size wood and clay mock-up of the Thunderbird at the Detroit Auto Show in February 1954. At a press conference held in the Ford Styling Rotunda at Dearborn, Ford's sales manager L. W. Smead announced: "The Thunderbird is a new kind of sports car. We are convinced it will set a new trend in the automobile industry. It provides all of the comforts, conveniences and all-weather protection available in any of today's modern automobiles. It represents a successful combination of graceful, low-silhouette styling, spirited performance and outstanding roadability with dependable all steel body construction."

The references to the Corvette's features are obvious enough. In addition, the T-Bird came with a V8 engine and the choice of manual or automatic transmission, an attractive glass fiber removable hardtop, wind-up windows (power optional) and, using standard Ford components, it could be serviced at a regular dealership.

Production of the Thunderbird wasn't due to begin until September 1954, by which time Ford was placing much more emphasis on the level of driver and passenger comfort than speed or handling when discussing the model, possibly giving a slight hint of where the

company thought its future might lay. W. R. Burnett, chief of passenger car engineering said: "Although the Thunderbird has the performance and attributes of most sports cars, management also felt that it should have a few more comforts to make it more appealing to a wider segment of the public." Burnett also used the term "personal car" to describe the T-Bird, this being the Ford's way of elevating it above the other run-of-the-mill sports cars.

Compared to the Corvette, Thunderbird sales were incredible – almost 16,000 a year in 1955 and '56, compared to a paltry 700 1955 Corvettes and only 3,400 of the revamped '56. It was clear that Ford had a better grasp of what the American buyer of the Fifties wanted from a sports car.

In this respect, a great deal of credit for the Thunderbird's acceptance must go to Ford's chief of styling Frank Q. Hershey and his design studio team, headed by Rhys Miller. Also involved in the creation of T-Bird were Damon Woods, David Ash and Bill Boyer. Between them, they produced a car that echoed the best features of European sports car design yet could be easily identified as American in origin with immediate connection to the rest of the Ford model line-up. Key elements were the proportions of a long hood and short

Below: The '56 Cadillac Sedan de Ville was the division's first four-door hardtop. This design, combining the line of a convertible with the comfort and convenience of a full-size sedan, is uniquely American and proved to be a massive success. the Sedan de Ville outsold all other '56 Cadillac models by a ratio of almost two to one.

rear deck, combined with the low profile found in all classic Fifties front-engined sports cars, plus embellishments that could only have come from Detroit.

But Hershey and his designers weren't infallible and for the '56 Thunderbird, there were a few minor alterations that had to be carried out for purely practical reasons. The most easily-spotted of the changes was the Continental Kit mounting on the spare wheel to make more trunk space available for luggage, but this wasn't universally approved of – some critics said it detracted from the car's appearance and added wind resistance. On the other hand, this set-up was also said to help give a better balanced weight distribution. Small vent door flaps were introduced behind the front wheel arches to feed the interior with cool air after complaints from over-heating drivers and passengers! In a similar vein, "wind wings" were added to the sides of the windshield to help reduce buffeting when the top was down.

If you chose to drive with the hardtop in position, in '56 this would more than likely come with the famous portholes on either side. These little round windows were apparently copied from car designs of 1930s, and some writers have said that Bill Boyer was the man behind this idea. Non-porthole hardtops were still available but the porthole version offered as a no cost option proved to be

far more popular and has become indelibly associated with the '56 T-Bird.

Long forgotten is the fact that Ford were also using safety as a selling point in those days. Okay, maybe a Life Guard package consisting of collapsible steering column and anti-burst door

Below: Even before the Sedan de ville was introduced, the Coupe de Ville had already succeeded in establishing its name as a by-word for classy personal transport.

locks isn't in the same league as dual air bags, but we are talking 1956 here! The offer of seat belts was another item that didn't prove too enticing to potential buyers, who were more likely to ask, "Why are you fitting seat belts – isn't the car safe?" How times have changed!

American Indian folklore was said to describe the Thunderbird as a good luck omen, being a mythical bird supposed to cause thunder, lightning and rain. A 1954 Ford press release went on to state that, among many

Above: The 1956 Plymouth Suburban Station Wagon was available in no less than four variants, including a sports version. Engines ranged from the standard straight six to a 200 hp V8, they combined high style with total practicality - and they sold like hot cakes.

things, the Thunderbird symbolized "power, swiftness and prosperity." If that is true, then Ford could hardly have picked a more appropriate name.

SPECIFICATIONS

CHEVROLET BEL AIR CONVERTIBLE

Engine:
V8 - cast iron block

Displacement:
283 cu. ins.

Bore and stroke:
3.88 x 3.0

Horsepower:
245 (250 with auto)

Body styles:
Convertible coupe

No. of seats:
5-6

Weight (lbs):
3,278 lbs

Price:
$2,229

Produced:
166,426

Headlines were dominated by racial integration conflicts, the radio was reverberating to the sound of rock 'n' roll and Russia launched Sputnik 1 to take a commanding lead in the space race. Hollywood mourned the deaths of silver screen idol Humphrey Bogart and comedian Oliver Hardy. But in the realm of automotive history, 1957 will forever be the year of the Chevrolet Bel Air.

Left & Above: *Among the most striking features on the 1957 Bel Air was the massive front bumper, which became an integral part of the body shape rather than an add-on. The convertible shows the low profile to great effect; the hood height was reduced by introducing fresh air vents above the headlights and eliminating the need for intake at the base of the windshield. In place of the traditional central hood emblem, twin spears also helped achieve*

In terms of styling, the 1957 Chevrolet is almost a unique example, for it has enjoyed undiminished affection since its introduction. It has been the subject of numerous songs, featured in films whenever a Fifties classic is required and was once dubbed "the most popular used car in history." Today, four decades on, there are enough suppliers of restoration and reproduction parts that it is practically possible to build a complete new car. Surely no other car from the 1950s can boast such an enthusiastic following.

A look at the outline specification doesn't explain the reasons behind this phenomenon – a face-lift of a three year old bodyshell and a smaller V8 engine

than both the Ford and Plymouth rivals – but that simplistic description doesn't do the '57 Chevy justice. It is, quite simply, a styling and performance classic. Not that this was apparent to the designers and engineers working on the car, far from it. In fact, studio head Clare MacKichan has been quoted as saying that there didn't seem to be much continuity of thought from one year to the next, and even some of the ideas that weren't used on the 1956 models somehow got resurrected and put on the '57.

The massive new front bumper had even earlier origins, with sketches dating back to 1949 and in 1953, designer Carl Renner produced an illustration that looked almost identical to the final '57 bumper. Apart from the bumper and front end, perhaps the most striking aspect of the 1957 Chevrolet is just how much longer and lower it seems in

Above: The Ford Ranchero offered sedan comfort and performance in a utility, pick-up package. Based on the Ranch Station Wagon, the Ranchero had the station wagon's rear section cut away and replaced with a flat cargo bed. This idea - basically a car crossed with a truck - was to set a trend that would continue to be followed by a dedicated band of American motorists for decades to come

comparison to the previous two years, despite sharing the same basic bodyshell. This was due to Earl's quest to reduce height and increase length in the belief that it produced a better looking automobile. To keep the cowl profile low, a revolutionary ventilation system was devised which drew fresh air from inlets in the front fenders above the headlights, rather than at the base of the windshield.

The hood had dual lance-shaped "wind-splitz" instead of the typical central jet aircraft-style ornament, used by other cars, for a low, smooth look. Elsewhere, the body revamp for '57 was so clever that, not only did it look different to the 1956 models, it was considered a great improvement. Undoubtedly one of the Fifties' most memorable and recognizable styling details is the ribbed aluminum panel used as part of the rear fender decorative trim on the Bel Air – it is an image, almost a trademark or a logo that couldn't be mistaken for anything else.

The other big news for the '57 Chevy was the engine and fuel injection. With a .125 inch diameter bigger bore, the small block V8 now displaced 283 cu.in.

and was becoming a high performance legend. In standard two-barrel carburetor form, the compact power-plant was rated at a healthy 185 horsepower and, when equipped with fuel injection, the Chevy could produce one horsepower per cubic inch – an accomplishment at the time, although Chrysler had done the same with the FirePower Hemi engine somewhat earlier. It meant a very rapid car in a straight line – even a base V8 model with a Powerglide two-speed automatic could top 100mph and accelerate to 60mph in 11 seconds.

Priced at over $500 (very expensive in '57 when a basic Chevrolet was little more than $2,000) the optional Ramjet mechanical fuel injection unit initially

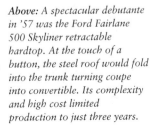

Above: A spectacular debutante in '57 was the Ford Fairlane 500 Skyliner retractable hardtop. At the touch of a button, the steel roof would fold into the trunk turning coupe into convertible. Its complexity and high cost limited production to just three years.

195

looked like a technical innovation – it claimed to improve fuel economy as well as horsepower. Designed by GM and made by Rochester Carburetor Inc, after they had tested and modified it, in everyday use the Ramjet started to show problems. In particular, the fuel nozzles would get clogged and heat absorption from the engine caused rough idling. So the fuel injection option was dropped from the Chevrolet family car catalog after 1958, although an improved version remained as a Corvette item until 1965.

Another unsuccessful Chevy development in '57 was the Turboglide automatic transmission. Modeled on the Buick Dynaflow, it was more expensive to make than the existing Powerglide unit and, while smoother-shifting when performing properly, it proved less reliable and hard to repair when faults occurred. The Turboglide lasted better than the Ramjet, surviving until the end of the

'61 model year, but both ventures were only relatively minor blemishes on the record of an automotive masterpiece.

It seems strange then to learn that, in 1957, Chevrolet failed to dominate the new car market in the same way as before. In fact, taking model year sales into account, Ford took first place. Competition was fiercer than ever and despite price reductions, '57 was not the great year the auto industry had anticipated. Indeed, come the fourth quarter of the year, the beginnings of the economic slump that was to devastate US car sales in 1958 started to have an effect and demand fell sharply.

Below: Similarities between the Oldsmobile Holiday sedan and the Chevy are obvious, but the Olds looks more refined. One curious feature is the three-piece backlight which seems in contrast to the huge double curvature windshield and hardtop style.

Another blow to Chevrolet came when the Automobile Manufacturers Association passed a resolution in June forbidding their members to participate in motor racing. However, while the men in the Chevy front office were following the AMA ruling and stating "they were no longer in racing," there was plenty of help out of the back door for those drivers who could put a Chevrolet into the winner's circle.

Using a racing driver to test a model was a device used by magazines in the Fifties, and *Speed Age* got stock car ace

Above: Plymouth's 1957 Fury is rightly regarded as a classic, and a true forerunner of the "muscle cars" of the '60s. The 290 hp, 318 cu. in. V8 came as standard and Chrysler's legendary torqueflite transmission was available. A stock Fury could hit 60 mph in 10 seconds and reach 110 mph; a modified example had managed 145 mph at Daytona beach the previous year. All this, combined with Virgil Exner's sensational styling, made the post '55 Plymouths almost unrecognizable compared to their predecessors.

Johnnie Tolan to test a '57 Bel Air 4-door sedan on the track and in the Los Angeles traffic. He reported: "I was really impressed with the new Chevy – liked its looks as well as its performance..."

Journalist Walt Woron writing for *Motor Trend* also liked the Chevy's performance, calling it "Appreciably faster on all counts" and, in a test carried out by the same magazine later in the year, the Chevy came out ahead of both Ford and Plymouth. Fast cars gave rise to doubts about people's ability to cope, however.

James Whipple of *Car Life* suggested that drivers would need "quicker

Above: *Though the styling clues range from the Corvette to the Facel Vega, the Gaylord was a highly original concept, laden with advanced technical features that were totally unique. Constructed around a "spaceframe" chassis, the car featured a tuned Cadillac V8 and performance-enhanced transmission.*

reactions and better judgement than ever before," but concluded: "Beneath the excitement created by the sensational (for light, low-priced cars) horsepower, the '57 Chevy is an excellent automobile with a tested, stable design and a very satisfactory level of quality and workmanship."

With all this talk of power, it is easy to forget that Chevrolet then offered three models – starting with the One-Fifty, Two-Ten, and top of the range Bel Air – and the cheaper models came with much less horsepower.

And while today's collector car money would go on the more expensive Bel Air coupes and convertibles, in 1957 it was the 4-door sedans that sold better than anything else.

Below: Jim and Ed Gaylord were very rich kids. They could have anything they wanted. They wanted the best sportscar in the world, then they wanted something better - so they built it themselves. Luxury features included a neat, disappearing steel roof and instrumentation of almost contemporary quality. Tragically, the brothers were let down by their manufacturing partners and what might have been one of the great cars of all time was stillborn.

1958

SPECIFICATIONS

FORD EDSEL PACER

Engine:
V8 - cast iron block

Displacement:
361 cu. ins.

Bore and stroke:
4.05 x 3.5

Horsepower:
303

Body styles:
Sedan; Hardtop coupe;
Hardtop sedan;
Convertible coupe; 6
seater station
wagon; 9 seater
station wagon

No. of seats:
5-9

Weight (lbs):
3,773 lbs - 3,919 lbs

Price:
$2,735 - $3,247

Produced:
21,292

The banner headline in the Detroit Free Press read "Reds claim their missile can reach the whole world" as America was smarting after the Sputniks demonstrated the Soviet lead in the space race, but the main picture on the newspaper's front page was of an Edsel. However, the economy was in recession and car sales in '58 dropped by about 20% compared with the three previous boom years.

In automotive terms, the Edsel name has become associated with spectacular failure – almost since it was launched in September 1957. Yet the surprise is, the Edsel disaster happened not by chance, but following years of solid market research and meticulous planning by the Ford Motor Company.

At the start of the 1950s, it seemed to Ford that it didn't offer enough models to cover the entire market and was losing out in certain sectors, particularly the middle price bracket. Back then, if

Left: Named for Henry Ford's beloved son - who was, in turn, the father of the man who took over the company's reins after his untimely death at the age of 49 - the Edsel turned out to be one of the great unloved cars of all time. It's not easy to know why but it probably had something to do with the strange styling of the radiator. "Like a Buick sucking on a lemon," was a common description. Four levels were offered, with the Citation at the top, grading down thru Corsair, Pacer and Ranger.

an owner was happy with a car they would buy a replacement from the same manufacturer. And if they had become more prosperous (or just wanted to give the neighbors the impression that they had – keeping up with the Joneses was quite an obsession that the dealers happily exploited), they traded up to a more expensive, and therefore more prestigious, make from the same corporation.

According to a company executive: "Ford was actually growing future prospects for the competition." In order to fill the hole, a Special Products Division was set up to develop a new mid-range to augment the offerings of Mercury. The code name given to this project was the "E-Car." This led to press speculation that the new car would be called the Edsel. Ford strenuously denied this, saying the E was for "Experimental" and not Edsel! But, no matter how large the company, making a 100% new car is unlikely to make economic sense so the E-Car was planned as a hybrid of existing Ford and Mercury major components with its own front and rear end sheet metal, its own engine, interior and dash panels.

The one thing the E-Car wouldn't share would be the Ford or Lincoln-Mercury dealerships, it would have its very own sales network. A vast recruiting campaign was organized and dealers were signed up from the competitors across the country.

The pressure was now on to give the car a name. Over six thousand suggestions were considered from all sorts of sources – including poet Marianne Moore who came up with humdingers like "Mongoose Civique" and "Utopian Turtletop!" Four names that got a more favorable reaction were: Ranger, Pacer, Corsair and Citation. Although these were eventually chosen as the model names, Ford chairman Ernest Breech didn't like them or any of the alternatives and, early in 1956, he made the decision to call the car the Edsel – named after Henry Ford's son who had died in 1942. Initially the Ford family were against the suggestion, but Breech managed to persuade them.

This choice of name was the first

mistake. Outside Detroit's inner circle, the word Edsel had no significance. While certainly no worse than Buick, that General Motors marque had, by then, been in existence for over fifty years and was well established in people's minds.

Then came the second mistake. The Edsel had probably the biggest new car build-up in history. The publicity was so widespread that the public were expecting a miracle machine to appear, not just yet another new car.

The third problem with the Edsel was timing, and this would prove to be crucial. The plan was to launch the 1958

Edsels in June 1957, thereby pre-empting the competition – traditionally cars were launched between September

Below: The 1958 Corvette incorporated twin headlamps that really didn't suit the clean lines of the '56 restyle. Much additional decoration had crept in to the front end treatment, and even in to the side coves. The basic purity of the overall design remained, just, though the car was now longer and wider - and heavier. Happily, power was up to 290 hp, courtesy of a fuel-injected, 283 cu. in. V8 that could propel the 'Vette to 60 mph in under seven seconds.

and November. But Edsel production didn't start until July and the launch was put back until September to ensure that dealers would have cars on display for the big day.

This three-month delay was a huge setback. After strong early 1957 model sales, the market suddenly slowed up in midsummer and dealers had to offer discounts to clear stocks and make way for the new '58 models. The US economy went into recession and the demand for middle- to upper-priced cars evaporated in favor of smaller, cheaper models. So, at the very time the Edsel burst on the scene, the market went into a severe decline. In other words, the goal

Above: The experimental XP - 700 Corvette of 1958 featured a transparent, bubble top with a blind system to cut glare, plus a periscope-style rear-view mirror that allowed a panoramic view behind. The oval grille at the front was on floating mounts to act as a low speed bumper, with air scoops below. Vents in the fenders assisted brake cooling.

Below: The '58 Chevrolet Bel Air series included a sub-division with a name that was destined for iconic status: the Impala. Available as a hardtop coupe or a convertible, with engine options that ran to a 300hp V8, the elegant Impala was an appealing package.

posts had been moved! Despite these three problems, the Edsel could still have succeeded. And Ford's need for the car was still valid. But the final blow was the controversial styling.

The most famous feature is the "horse collar" grille. Although many European marques had a vertical grille for many years – Jaguar, Alfa Romeo, Mercedes – somehow the Edsel didn't have the same effect.

When an automobile is successful, people clamor to associate themselves with it. In the case of the Edsel, practically everyone who worked at the Ford Design Center denies any involvement with it. The man responsible was Roy A. Brown, promoted to chief designer of the E-Car project following his successful work on the Lincoln Futura show car. He recruited Bob Jones, Dick Steiger and Bert Holmes as his assistants. The team decided to go away from the horizontal grille with a wide opening used by most of the other marques and opted for the vertical look.

Enthusiastic approval for the concept was given by a gathering of top Ford executives in August 1955 and, from then on, the die was cast. On launch day, it seemed the Edsel was a winner as 2.5 million people crowded to see the new car. After a few days, the first alarm bells rang – everybody came to look, but nobody was buying. After predictions of over a quarter of a million sales in the first year, only 63,110 were ever produced.

The Edsel was discontinued in November 1959, after two years, two months and fifteen days. It was estimated to have cost Ford over 350 million dollars. Henry Ford II typically took it on the chin and said afterwards: "Hell, we headed right into a recession, and everything went kaput... A lot of people didn't like the styling of the Edsel. We had a very weak dealer organization... we couldn't sell them, we were losing money, so we made a decision, 'Let's quit' which was the right decision, I'm sure. I'd rather admit the

Below: *Conceived as the DeSoto Division's answer to the Chrysler 300 Series - Plymouth had the Fury and Dodge the D-500 - the Adventurer was the brainchild of Virgil Exner. First announced in '56, it was a superbly styled road burner with great performance - and handling .*

Above: *Oldsmobile produced 3,799 Super 88 convertibles in '58. Its chrome-laded design was satirized by Ford's Alex Tremulis - on a photograph of the car he decorated the four lines of chrome on the rear fender with a clef and several notes of music!*

mistake, chop it off, and don't throw good money after bad."

Since the demise of the Edsel, people have suggested bizarre reasons for its failure. A few years ago, one psychologist even went so far as to claim that the real reason for the Edsel catastrophe was that the horse collar grille represented the female sex organ, while all the other automobiles were masculine!

The real reason for the failure of the Edsel is simple. The combination of recession, too much hype, a poor choice of name and peculiar styling proved insurmountable. However, had Ford seen it through those initial dark days and kept it going until the market swung back in favor of bigger, more expensive cars in the Sixties – who knows? We might still have been able to buy an Edsel today.

What was the Edsel really like as a car? In truth it was no better, no worse than its contemporaries. And that probably just about says it all.

SPECIFICATIONS

CADILLAC ELDORA-DO BIARRITZ

Engine:
V8 - cast iron block

Displacement:
390 cu. ins.

Bore and stroke:
4.0 x 3.88 ins.

Horsepower:
345

Body styles:
Convertible coupe

No. of seats:
5/6

Weight (lbs):
4,800 lbs

Price:
$7,401

Produced:
1,320

Above & Right: The Cadillac Eldorado Biarritz convertible featured a special rounded off rear deck and fender panels. Plenty of superfluous brightwork included dummy louvers in front of the rear wheels and a fake air intake on the front fender; quad head lights were standard on all '58s.

The history of the twentieth century is, more often than not, divided up into decades and each ten year period given its own separate identity. It is curious that this convenient method of grouping so often, and in so many ways, reflects the changes that take place in society. In purely automotive terms, nothing can surely equal the 1959 Cadillac tail fin as a symbol of the end of an era.

The Fifties was the age of the tail fin and, after having reached such heights, there was nowhere to go but down. 1959 was also the year that Harley Earl retired from his position as head of styling at General Motors and the towering Cadillac fins are looked upon as his final extravagance before bowing out. It has to be said that Earl would have found it hard to adapt to a changing environment of simplicity and economy rather than outrageous, ever bigger automobiles. It was a problem that other designers, working at rival auto makers, would also struggle to come to terms with.

At the time, there were few, if any, signs of misgivings. Designer Bill Mitchell (who took over from Earl) described the tail fins thus: "From a design standpoint the fins gave definition to the rear of the car for the first time. They made the back end as interesting as the front, and established a long-standing Cadillac styling hallmark."

Whether the addition of a rear "grille" which closely resembled that of the front was such a good idea is open to debate, but the feature didn't last very long.

Lower than ever before, though no longer or wider, the '59 Cadillac not only attracted comments about its styling it also drew some favorable reports about how it drove. Jim Whipple, writing in *Car Life*, said: "The car rode as level as any I've ever driven…" But it wasn't totally perfect, as shown by a report in *Motor Life* which stated: "Flaws are noted only at high speeds, when some swaying motion sets in, and in fast corners when the tires

protest loudly as the heavyweight goes through a bend." Of course, the Cadillac was built for luxury motoring and comfort, and not intended for slalom racing, so it can be safely assumed that few were ever pushed to the same limits by their owners.

Mind you, thanks to a new 325 horsepower (345hp in Eldorado models), 390 cu.in. V8 engine under that hood, the Cadillac was no slouch when it was time to get going, 0-60mph in under 11 seconds or thereabouts. And if you were in a real hurry, a top speed of close on 120mph was possible. Pretty impressive for a car weighing over 5,000 pounds and close to 19 feet in length. Sales moved ahead too, topping 142,000 and keeping Cadillac in the top ten (just) of US auto manufacturers.

The array of Cadillac models included convertibles, two-door hardtop coupes, and two different four-door hardtop sedans plus the Fleetwood limousines. Prices started at about $5,000 and went up to $7,400 for an Eldorado, with the Fleetwoods more than $9,500. But easily the most expensive was the Eldorado Brougham 4-door, the only Cadillac model of '59 that didn't have the huge tail fins and bullet-shaped lights, which was built by coach builders Pinin Farina in Italy, and cost a massive $13,000 – small wonder that only 99 made the transatlantic crossing this year. But underneath all the razzle-dazzle there were engineering improvements too, with better suspension, and revised power steering.

In May 1959, Motor Life compared the Cadillac to an Imperial and summed up with the following: "Cadillac's strongest claim to superiority is its unmatched feeling of luxury and quality. When riding in this car, the almost soundless operation coupled with rich materials and fine assembly produce the desired effect: you know that this is an expensive and luxurious automobile. One is never in doubt."

A smooth ride, luxury fitments, excellent performance and build quality – from almost any aspect, the 1959 Cadillac was a state-of-the-art prestige car of its day, but you cannot ignore the flamboyant body styling. Whatever your personal tastes, this is one car that it is impossible to be neutral about, you

Above: The array of Cadillac models included convertibles, two-door hardtop coupes, and two different four-door hardtop sedans plus the Fleetwood limousines. Prices started at about $5000 and went up to $7400 for an Eldorado.

either love it or loathe it.

To its detractors, the '59 Caddy has all the glamor of a Las Vegas hooker, while others regard it as the ultimate expression of Fifties space age design. Its styling is unique and the obvious associations with rockets, missiles and aircraft are clearly visible – from the dual jet intake shapes of the parking lights in the massive front bumper to the bullet-like tail lights (said to represent

exhaust flames) set in those soaring fins. It is a triumph of design over function. Nobody needed fins that tall, nor the lavish application of chrome, nor most of the other styling excesses included under Harley Earl's direction.

However, need and want are two entirely different emotions and Earl was a master at producing automobiles that were wanted in the highly prosperous USA of the Fifties. True, his obsessive pursuit of getting a car as low as possible had created designs that were at, or very near, the minimum height possible – given the agility of the average human being and ease of entry and exit required. And who knows how many knees were bruised in consequence, particularly negotiating a way around the bottom corner of the wrap-around windshields (another Harley Earl innovation) that protruded into the access opening. Ergonomics came second to styling, and product liability litigation was nothing like the rapacious

Below: Whatever your personal tastes, the flamboyant body styling means this is one car that it is impossible to be neutral about - you either love it or you loathe it.

industry of the Nineties, so such small inconveniences as these would be tolerated for the sake of owning the newest shape of automobile.

The annual model change that ultimately spawned the '59 Cadillac was regarded as part of the process that would provide what the Detroit public relations machine called "better transportation tomorrows." A false promise if ever there was one because, as every

Above: *The styling of the '59 Ford Thunderbird changed from the successful '58 only in details. These included a horizontal bar instead of a honeycomb pattern for the grille, a non-functional hood air scoop, taillight appliques, "bullet" moldings for the lower body "bombs."*

Left & Right: *Bill Mitchell was itching to restyle the Corvette by '59, but budgetary constraints meant that he'd have to wait a bit longer. Meanwhile, the 'Vette continued to gain chrome and cubes.*

child knows, tomorrow never arrives. We can look at these things with the condescension of hindsight, but caught up in the euphoria of the age it was hard to be completely objective. Without doubt, *Car Life*'s Jim Whipple echoed popular opinion when he enthusia-

stically described the '59 Cadillac as "...one of the sleekest jobs that ever came down the pike."

But to many fans, 1959 marked the beginning of the end of rock 'n' roll, and the most significant event of the year happened on February 3 when a Beechcraft Bonanza light aeroplane crashed near Mason City, Iowa killing Buddy Holly, Ritchie Valens and J. P. "The Big Bopper" Richardson. However, if three stars had been extinguished from the pop music firmament, at least there were two new stars on Old Glory as Alaska and Hawaii became the 49th and 50th States. And NASA was also aiming toward the stars – besides launching satellites and two monkeys into orbit, it also named the seven astronauts who would take part in the space race.

Automobiles might be about to get their wings clipped and the raw energy of Fifties rock 'n' rollers seemed to be giving way to slushy music exploited by large record companies in pursuit of a quick buck, but there was still plenty to look forward to!

SPECIFICATIONS

FORD FALCON

Engine:
Cast iron - 6 cylinders in line

Displacement:
144.3 cu. ins.

Bore & Stroke:
3.50 ins. x 2.50 ins.

Horsepower:
90 bhp

Body Styles:
2 and 4 door sedans; 2 and 4 door station wagons.

No. of seats:
5

Weight:
2,288 lbs - 2,575 lbs.

Price:
$1,912 - $2,287

Produced:
435,676

The Fifties had been a great time for the American auto industry – a period of design excess, during which automobiles grew ever larger fins and literally dripped with chrome. But as the new decade of the Sixties dawned, things were changing, the emphasis would switch from overstated looks to more efficient performance whether it be from smaller cars or bigger engines.

Changes in the auto industry were not the only news for 1960. In July, John F. Kennedy received the Democratic nomination for the Presidency, running against Republican Richard Nixon. Kennedy made it to The White House after a close race, but was tragically not to serve his full term. Meanwhile, relations with the Soviet Union received a major setback when a U2 spy plane was shot down over Soviet territory and its pilot, Gary Powers, captured. On a lighter note, Elvis Presley was discharged from his much-publicized spell in the US Army, while a young boxer by the name of Cassius Clay won a gold medal in the Rome Olympics. He would become one of the most famous boxers of all time, who would ultimately be known to millions around the world as Muhammad Ali.

Lovers of speed had plenty to talk about, too. At the Daytona 500, Fireball Roberts, driving a '60

Right: Ford's European experience of building small cars led to the Falcon compact, with its unibody construction. Later sporty versions provided the basis for the Mustang.

ontiac, had set the pace during qualifying at 151.556mph, while the ace proper was won by Junior Johnson n a 1959 Chevy. Pontiac products also eatured prominently at the Bonneville alt Flats in September, when hot rodder Mickey Thompson drove his Challenger treamliner to a speed of 406.60mph. The sleek projectile was powered by no ess than four Pontiac V8s, but a broken driveshaft prevented him from making a eturn run that would have put him in he record books.

Back in Detroit, however, high-performance automobiles were not the atest innovation from the major manufacturers – they would come later n the decade. For 1960, the auto ndustry was looking in a completely different direction. Since the 1930s, American automobiles had grown steadily larger, particularly in the post-war years. But during that time, small mported cars had begun to make nroads on the market, particularly sporty models. They were fun to drive and cheap to run. Concerned by the

impact these foreign cars were making, the major auto makers began to take a serious look at building more compact cars themselves. By the late Fifties, two smaller manufacturers were already in this sector of the market – Studebaker with the Lark, and Rambler with the American. In 1960, they would be joined by compacts from the big three – Ford, GM and Chrysler – who launched the Falcon, the Chevrolet Corvair and the Valiant respectively.

Of the three, the Falcon and the Corvair were the main contenders and were pitted against each other from the outset. They were two very different cars, the Ford simply being a scaled-down conventional car, while the Chevy was very definitely a radical departure in terms of both design and powerplant. Both had their beginnings in the mid Fifties and, more by accident than design, they both arrived on the market at the same time.

One aspect that was common to the Falcon and Corvair was unibody construction, a relatively uncommon

arrangement for American automobiles at the time which, in the main, relied on a separate chassis to support the various mechanical components and body panels. In a unibody design, the bodyshell itself is strengthened to accept the loads of the engine and suspension, making for a lighter structure overall. However, that is where the similarities ended.

As mentioned, the Falcon was of a conventional design. It was powered by a liquid-cooled, straight-six ohv engine, with a cast iron block and head, that displaced 144.3 cu.in. and developed 90 horsepower at 4200rpm. This drove through either a three-speed manual transmission or two-speed automatic to a live rear axle suspended on leaf springs. The Corvair was also powered by a six-cylinder engine, but it was a horizontally-opposed, aluminum, air-cooled unit mounted at the rear of the car and driving the rear wheels through a three-speed manual, or two-speed automatic, transaxle with coil-sprung, swing-axle suspension. The engine produced 80 horsepower at 4400rpm. Both cars had similar front suspension

arrangements, making use of unequal length wishbones and coil springing.

The cars were of similar sizes although the Falcon was slightly larger and taller, and both were intended as full six-seaters, being equipped with bench seats front and rear. However, the Falcon's transmission tunnel made it uncomfortable for anyone riding in the middle of the front seat, while the Corvair, with its virtually flat floorpan, was more comfortable, even though the manual transmission models had a floor-mounted shifter. This was curved to allow the center passenger leg room. Shifting was not a problem in the Falcon, since both manual and automatic transmissions had column shifters.

When first launched, the Corvair was offered in a 4-door body style only, while the Falcon came in a choice of 2- or 4-door models. The latter was conventional in appearance, while the Corvair, with its lack of radiator grille and somewhat tub-like styling, was less so. Both lacked the fins and chrome that had characterized cars of the Fifties. They were intended as economy cars

nd they looked the part.

In terms of performance, the makers quoted very similar top speeds – 87mph or the Falcon; 88mph for the Corvair. But the Falcon could out-accelerate the Corvair; *Road & Track* magazine found hat the former could reach 60mph in 17.7 seconds, while the Corvair was early a full two seconds behind at 19.5 seconds.

When the Corvair was launched, it was slow to gain acceptance; the unconventional rear-engine layout may have been okay in a foreign car, but it was downright unAmerican; the Falcon was a much more familiar concept, and it showed in the sales figures. Corvair sales were not helped by rumors that it tended to throw fan belts and that its handling was quirky. Indeed, if the tire pressures were not kept exactly as specified by the manufacturer and the car was pushed hard through a corner, it could switch from slight understeer to strong oversteer, kicking the rear end out with potentially disastrous consequences. Later in its life, a number of law suits were brought against GM for just this reason, although eventually the car was exonerated and would carry on in production until the end of the decade.

Later in 1960, in an attempt to boost flagging sales, Chevrolet introduced a 2-door variant, the Monza. This was a much sportier-looking car, a look that was enhanced by fitting front bucket seats, full carpeting and better trim. Where the Corvair had failed as an economy car, it succeeded as a sporty model and sales took off at last. Eventually, it was to receive ever more powerful engines and became an excellent all-round performer. Not to be outdone, Ford uprated later models of the Falcon too, eventually fitting a new 260 cu.in. small-block V8 that was to have a significant effect on the company's efforts in the sporty compact field.

Below: Fins and chrome still featured on another Chrysler product, the Plymouth Fury. Although incorporating the modern unibody construction, the old "jukebox on wheels" style led to poor sales of their 1960 models.

SPECIFICATIONS

AMC RAMBLER AMERICAN CUSTOM CONVERTIBLE

Engine:
Cast iron - 6 Cylinders in line

Displacement:
195.6 cu. ins

Bore and stroke:
3.13 x 4.25

Horsepower:
125

Body styles:
Convertible coupe

No. of seats:
4

Weight (lbs):
2,712 lbs

Price:
$2,369

Produced:
-

Above Right: Restyled and modern-looking, the Rambler American for '61 was smaller than the '60 models, but kept its spacious interior. The 2-door sedan was the most popular model.

Recycling is a familiar theme of the 1990s, and many of today's manufacturers emphasize how much material in their cars can be re-used. However, nobody can approach the audacity of George Romney, the head of American Motors Corporation, who, when facing the economic recession of 1958, decided to recycle an entire automobile!

The plan was simple: dust off the tooling of the 1955 Nash Rambler 2-door sedan, slightly modify it to open up the rear wheel arches and simplify the hood design, add a mesh grille and a little chrome – and launch it as the new 1958 Rambler American. The experts said it wouldn't work - after all the Nash design actually dated back to 1950 - but Romney had spotted a niche in the market for a US-built small car with a thrifty six cylinder engine at a rock-bottom price.

The Rambler American sold well, helping to put AMC in profit at a time when the competition was suffering losses. And, as frugal as the owners of the little car he was so enthusiastic about, Romney wasn't about to spend more money on building the American than he had to. It continued almost unchanged until 1960, with increasing sales, establishing itself as the leader in the compact car sector.

Although he was careful to control spending, Romney appreciated that this virtual monopoly couldn't last forever. The popular Volkswagen Beetle continued to dominate the import market, and the Studebaker Lark was the first American-made competition to arrive in '59.

When GM, Ford and Chrysler entered the fray in 1960, George Romney knew it was time to act in order to protect AMC's hard-won customer base. Even then, chief stylist Edmund Anderson was only allowed to re-skin the ancient bodyshell.

Given these constraints, Anderson's achievement is remarkable. While the inner panels remained untouched and so the interior dimensions of the American were exactly as before, the overall length was reduced by 5.2 inches and the width by over 3 inches giving a far neater package. Measurements aside, the squarer body now had a much more modern Sixties shape, and could therefore stand alongside the compe-

tition without looking old fashioned.

The distinctive trapezium-shaped grille, sharp leading edge "brow" that flowed into a gradually flaring side indent and simple round tail lights weren't to everyone's taste. Critics have called Anderson's design "boxy and truncated" while supporters claim the car is "a little jewel." One a feature that Anderson couldn't alter was the high beltline level, but this wasn't significantly detrimental. George Romney described the car as having "modern, enduring style."

Most customers were happy with the new look and, once again, AMC defied the detractors and sold 136,000 Ameri-

cans in 1961, and a total of 370,600 cars, lifting the Rambler to an unprecedented third place in the charts behind Chevrolet and Ford (albeit a long way behind, by something like a million units!). Styling was no doubt important, but the American was more about economy than prestige and AMC used the slogan "the top resale value among the low-priced cars year after year" to reinstate that Rambler buyers could expect a better price than other owners when trading in their car for a new model.

By 1961, there was more choice for the Rambler American driver too. From the one model "plain Jane" 2-door

Above: The Doge Dart Phoenix was restyled for '61 with curious rear tapering tail fins whereas the rest of the industry was getting rid of fins. It was completely revamped for '62.

sedan of '58, the range now featured three levels of trim – DeLuxe, Super and Custom – with a variety of bodystyles, including a new 4-door station wagon and a convertible. The top of the line Customs were also equipped with a modern overhead valve in-line six cylinder engine that produced 125bhp. This powerplant was available as a $59.50 optional extra on the lower specification models, otherwise you got the 90 horsepower antique flathead six. Both engines displaced 195 cu.in.

Not only was there a wider choice of models, Rambler American owners could now also specify extra creature comforts from an options list. You could jazz up the exterior with two-tone paint for $15.95, add front and rear DeLuxe foam rubber seat cushions at $19.90, or the ultimate has to be the Airliner Recliner Seats that folded down into Twin Travel Beds. If it was ease of driving you were after, there was always the lever control Flash-O-Matic automatic transmission ($165), power steering ($72) and power brakes ($38). The most expensive add-on was undoubtedly air

conditioning, which came with a heavy-duty cooling system and a hefty price tag of $359 – almost 20% of the cost of the cheapest American model.

The best seller was the DeLuxe 2-door sedan at $1,845, which compared favorably against $2,230 for a basic Chevrolet, and 28,555 were produced. But if the Rambler buyer got carried away and opted for too many extras, the "cheap little compact" soon became as expensive as a full-size automobile. Mind you, the Chevy salesman wasn't going to let a customer out of the showroom without ordering a few extras either, so the price differential was pretty much maintained at the end of the day.

Away from the motor industry, President Kennedy was promising to put a man on the moon before the end of the decade and Alan Shepard became the first American in space on July 21. Less memorable was the failure of the CIA-orchestrated Bay of Pigs invasion of Cuba in April, and the decision to send

Above: Cadillac style had anticipated the shift from the rounded curves of the 'fifties to the shaper lines of the 'sixties. Decoration was being deleted and the fins were slowly but surely folding themselves back into the bodywork. The V8 engine was still developing from the '49 and would last until '63, remaining a leader in the field for smooth and silent power delivery throughout its production run.

400 Green Berets to Vietnam. Also on the downside was an attack on the Freedom Riders in Alabama during a protest over segregation on buses, and a spate of airliner hijackings.

But there were plenty of winners to celebrate in 1961 too. Phil Hill became the first American to win the Formula One World Championship driving a Ferrari, A. J. Foyt took the checkered flag at the Indianapolis 500 (the first of four victories at The Brickyard) and Marvin Panch won the NASCAR Daytona 500 in a Pontiac. To compare the

success of a cheap, compact, family car from an independent manufacturer based in Kenosha, Wisconsin with some of the great names in motor racing might seem a bit presumptuous. However, finishing third for Rambler was an amazing achievement given their limited resources. By beating the might of Detroit, AMC, George Romney, Ed Anderson and the Rambler American deserve to be included in the list of winners in '61.

Below: Elwood Engel's 1961 four-door convertible version of Lincoln Continental is widely regarded as a design classic. He and his team were honored with an award from the Industrial Design institute.

1962

SPECIFICATIONS

**STUDEBAKER
GRAND
TURISMO HAWK**

Engine:
V8 - cast iron block

Displacement:
289 cu. ins.

Bore and stroke:
3.56 x 3.63

Horsepower:
210

Body styles:
Hardtop coupe

No. of seats:
4

Weight (lbs):
3,230 lbs

Price:
$3,095

Produced:
8,388

By 1962, the Studebaker-Packard Corporation was in serious trouble and the end of the road was in sight for the once-proud names of two long-established marques who had merged in 1954. In fact, the last cars bearing the Packard badge were actually produced in 1958 and Packard was dropped from the company name in '62, marking the final sad ending of a history of building fine automobiles that stretched back to 1899.

But Studebaker still struggled on, and even in their death throes, they managed to produce several rather remarkable automobiles. Probably the most notable of these was the Grand Turismo Hawk which was a face-lift of a design dating back to 1956 (the '56 was actually a revamp of the body shell first introduced in '53!). The updated design was produced at record speed and with very little expenditure. The car enjoyed a favorable reception and its success can be gauged by the comments in *Motor Trend* who called it: "A bold new approach to luxury and power – a man's car all the way." Technical Editor Jim Wright described the response

Right: Studebaker's Grand Turismo Hawk is the result of designer Brooks Stevens amalgamating several familiar styling themes taken from rival prestige cars and turning them into a highly effective design.

from other drivers by saying: "If the amount of interest generated in and around the Los Angeles area is any indication of what Studebaker-Packard can expect throughout the rest of the country, then we'd say their new Grand Turismo Hawk is definitely 'in'."

Other motoring magazines were equally supportive. *Car Life* stated: "In some ways, it was the most appealing car we've driven this year... It's very much the kind of car we'd be happy to own." *Wheels* magazine described it as "quick and handsome," while the reporter for *Modern Motor* magazine said about it: "...it's all motor-car, in the best sense of the term. The most advanced by far that I've driven." Judging from these reviews it would seem that Studebaker had created a triumph in spite of the prevailing doom, much in the same way as a conjuror

pulls a rabbit from a hat. Unfortunately, Studebaker needed some magic of a more powerful kind to survive, and even the most skilled illusionist couldn't hide the enormity of the task facing the company which eventually folded in 1966 – after closing the South Bend, Indiana factory and moving its operations to Canada toward the end of 1963.

The foundations of the GT Hawk were laid by the studio of extrovert stylist Raymond Loewy (whose long association with Studebaker resulted in some wonderful automobiles) with the new 1953 models which included the graceful Starliner hardtop and Starlight coupe – the work of designer Bob Bourke, assisted by Holden Koto. The Loewy studio also carried out the update for the '56 Hawk range, but this was to be a final collaboration and

thereafter the relationship ended. The main reason for the split was one of cost. Strapped for cash, Studebaker couldn't justify the expense of the high-profile Loewy organization and started to seek out cheaper freelance designers.

The task of rejuvenating the Hawk was given to Brooks Stevens who has, over the years, accumulated many great designs in his portfolio, but who is probably remembered most often as the man behind the Excalibur automobile.

At a time when the development of a new model (or even a relatively straightforward face-lift) was usually measured in years rather than months, Stevens worked something of a miracle in just a few weeks. The first hand-built example was put together at his Milwaukee workshop in June '61 and finished versions were in front of Studebaker dealers by September! It was a truly remarkable turn round.

What Stevens did in essence was to take a good, if out-dated, design, refine it and add a quality of style and

Above: Described as the "projectile look" by designer William Boyer, the third generation Thunderbird had a pointed nose, razor-sharp lines, round tail lights with vanes in the trim and abbreviated fins. This was a land-locked missile, thanks to a 300 horsepower 390 cu.in. V8 under the hood.

distinction that befitted a classic grand tourer. The rakish Fifties tail fins were quickly consigned to the rubbish bin to be replaced with far neater items, and the external re-skinning presented a flatter, more elegant body. Efforts were then concentrated on the roof section creating a squared-off, formal appearance which many people said was a direct copy of a Thunderbird, although Studebaker claimed it had been derived from the Packard Predictor concept car which had been built six years earlier.

Other styling elements that Stevens used to good advantage were altering the grille which gave it a slight

resemblance to the Mercedes (Studebaker was then the distributor for Mercedes-Benz cars) and adding a chrome strip along the belt line on top of the fenders, which ran the whole length of the car in much the same manner as the Lincoln Continental.

This device of using styling features to bring an association with recognized upmarket automobiles could have been a disaster, but Brooks Stevens managed to bring all the elements together and made it work beautifully. The only item that looks out of place is the false, stick-on trunk lid "grille" which was used to disguise a virtually unchanged compon-

ent. This was deleted for the '64 GT Hawks (the final in the series) and there's no doubt the smooth uncluttered panel works far better. The trunk lid apart, the decoration on the car is minimal and chrome trim is used in a restrained manner.

To back up the looks, a true GT

Below: Anticipating that people would demand smaller cars, Plymouth's design chief, Virgil Exner, reduced the wheelbase by eight inches and applied Valiant-like styling, as seen on this Belvedere. It was a disastrous mistake and sales plummeted.

needed some respectable performance, and here the Studebaker was able to take care of itself pretty well. The 289 cu.in. V8 engine might have been a touch on the heavy side for its capacity, but it was durable and, in standard form, it put out 210 horsepower which was sufficient to give a top speed over 100mph. For those who wanted to do some really "grand" touring, there was also a 225bhp option which included a four barrel carburetor and dual exhausts and, together with the four-speed manual transmission (three-speed was standard and automatic was also an option), this provided sufficient performance for one magazine to label the Hawk "an enthusiast's car." In subsequent years there were even more powerful choices available, including a supercharged Avanti engine, but these are rare finds today.

Another highlight for Studebaker in 1962 was having the Lark Daytona

Below: Chevrolet's dream offering for '62 was the prototype Monza Super Spyder. Based on the Corvair Monza, it was to have been fitted with a turbocharged 6 cylinder engine, have fully independent suspension and four-speed manual transmission.

chosen as the pace car for the Indiana-polis 500. However, while Raymond Loewy's radical new Avanti would also provide the company with plenty of publicity, it couldn't halt Studebaker's slide into obscurity.

Studebaker's own woes paled into insignificance compared to those facing the nation. The Cuban missile crisis saw JFK and Russian premier Kruschev bring the world almost to the brink of another war in October. Thankfully, everybody was able to breath a sigh of relief when the Soviet government finally backed down from the confron-tation. A tragedy that was mourned by red-blooded men around the globe was the death of Marilyn Monroe on August 5 – an event that is still shrouded in

Above: The 1962 Dodge Dart shared the unhappy and ungainly Exner styling of the Lancer and the Plymouth Fury and Valiant ranges. With the D-500 engine option, the Dart could top 100mph but even that didn't make up for the looks and sales fell by a quarter.

intrigue and mystery today.

There was no such mystery over the demise of Studebaker. A mixture of very poor management decisions following World War Two, inadequate investment for the future, and difficulties with controlling their work force had all contributed to their downfall. Even so, the company had built some excellent automobiles and the Grand Turismo Hawk still rates as one of the best.

227

SPECIFICATIONS

CHEVROLET CORVETTE STING RAY

Engine:
V8 - cast iron block

Displacement:
327 cu. ins.

Bore and stroke:
4.00 x 3.25

Horsepower:
250 - 360

Body styles:
Coupe; Convertible coupe

No. of seats:
2

Weight (lbs):
2,859 lbs - 2,881 lbs

Price:
$4,037 - $4,252

Produced:
21,500

During the life of the Corvette there have been some highs and lows along the way, but ten years after the model's first introduction came one of the truly great ones – the 1963 Sting Ray.

What makes an automobile great? In this instance it is a perfect combination of styling and performance. And the plaudits for achieving such an outstanding example of the automotive art must go to two men – Bill Mitchell and Zora Arkus-Duntov. Mitchell, as vice president in charge of design for General Motors, regarded the Corvette (and especially the Sting Ray) as very much his own baby, even to the extent of warning off other in-house designers from attempting to come up with new ideas for styling the car. Engineer extraordinaire and successful racing driver, Arkus-Duntov was responsible for transforming the Corvette's handling and giving it the horsepower needed to perform.

Above: *A split rear window was only used on '63 Corvettes, and has become an identifying feature of the model. The "boattail" fastback coupe was much more than a styling exercise, giving superb performance. However, the duck-tail rear was a carryover from the preceding model years to give continuity.*

Below: *Hidden head lights were a rare concept on US-built cars in the 'sixties, this Chevy sports car being the first since the 1942 DeSoto to use the idea. The razor-edge styling of the new Corvette Sting Ray was a sensation at the time, and is as striking today as it was in '63.*

Motor racing played a key role in the evolution of the '63 Sting Ray. To begin with, Bill Mitchell acquired the test vehicle from the abandoned Super Sport project (a factory-backed program developing a Corvette for endurance racing) and had Larry Shinoda design an open-top body for it. Shinoda took a lot of his inspiration from the Q-Corvette, an experimental rear-engined sports car that was the creation of Bob McLean – the designer who had laid out the very first Corvette. Mitchell christened his racer the Stingray Special and got Dr

Left: The tail of the Corvette may have been carried over from the previous line to provide continuity, but it blended perfectly into the new design which was - and is - an object lesson in fearful symmetry.

Below: The split rear window design of the original '63 Corvette gave the car a strong "spine" that ran from the top edge of the windshield to the tail. A controversial detail on its unveiling, it is now regarded as a masterstroke. The problem for owners was that there was no access to the stowage area in the tail from outside of the car...

Dick Thompson to drive it in the SCCA C-Modified class where it quickly proved to be a winner, taking the championship. At the end of the 1960 season, Mitchell decided he couldn't afford to keep funding the race car and so sold it back to GM, where it was rebuilt as a show vehicle.

By that time, progress was well in hand for what would become the sensational 1963 Corvette. Mitchell made no secret of his love for knife-edged styling and used it to great effect on the final production design which also incorporated the "triple hump" feature seen on the fenders and hood of the Stingray racer and Mako Shark concept car. But while the '63 Sting Ray was just about all new from the ground up (apart from engines and transmissions) Mitchell was careful to ensure some continuity of styling from the preceding years, and to this end had

Above: After the disasters of '62, Plymouth models like this Sport Fury Hardtop had a hasty redesign but, although sales improved, the Chrysler division was still well behind Chevrolet and Ford in the race for customers. Top of the range Sport Fury models came with bucket seats, central console, de luxe steering wheel and interior trim, and special wheel covers.

introduced the "duck-tail" rear on the '61 Corvette to give everyone the chance to get used to the theme.

At the Sting Ray's leading edge, the aggressive appearance was emphasized by the use of hidden headlights – the first time this device had been seen on a Chevrolet, and not used on any other US car since the 1942 DeSoto – but it was the rear window in the fastback "boattail" coupe model that would prove to be the most contentious feature

of all. Bill Mitchell was adamant that the split rear window should stay and he argued long and hard to get his way saying "...if you take that off, you might as well forget the whole thing." Mitchell won the day, but criticisms in the press about restricted rear visibility and further pressure from people like Zora Arkus-Duntov saw the central spine removed for the '64 models, giving the 1963 Sting Ray a unique identifying feature and instantly turning it into a highly collectible item.

It has to be said, however, that some '63 models subsequently had their split rear windows replaced with a one-piece window and, after the 1964 model

Below: Chevrolet's Impala for '63 was clean, uncluttered and elegant in its design treatment. The Impala range was establishing a strong individual identity and proved immensely popular. Chevrolet managed to stay ahead of Ford throughout the decade, topping their sales in every model year apart from '61 and '66

became available, Chevy dealers even offered a factory conversion – which immediately destroyed the car's value and it's certain that many Corvette owners today regret their actions.

As well as the split windows, Bill Mitchell also included several other non-functional styling ideas that met with disapproval and were dropped in '64. Dummy metal inserts in the hood copied lift-reducing vents used on Mitchell's Stingray race car and were deleted, and fake ventilation outlets behind the coupe door pillars were replaced with functional grilles. Another feature removed after the first year was the stainless steel trim on the windshield pillar.

But apart from stunning looks, a sports car is all about performance and the Sting Ray had that too, thanks to Zora Arkus-Duntov who stated: "For the first time I now have a Corvette I can be proud to drive in Europe." His starting point was a simple, but highly effective, steel ladder chassis that proved so good it remained in Corvette production for 20 years with only minor alterations. Coupled to the channel section frame was an all-round independent suspension system which endowed the Sting Ray with a cornering capability equal to the best of the competition. The most ingenious part of the suspension was the rear set-up which used a single transverse leaf spring and rugged, almost crude, construction to provide the equivalent of more sophisticated designs at a fraction of the cost.

Getting around corners efficiently is all very well, but the speed on the straights linking those bends is mighty important to the sports car enthusiast too. Once again, Arkus-Duntov had worked his magic and the Sting Ray could be had with horsepower aplenty. Standard was the 250bhp 327 cu.in. V8, but you could also order the optional 300bhp L75 version, 340bhp L76 or the fuel injected, 11.25:1 compression,

Duntov-cammed L84 specification which produced 360bhp at 6000 rpm. Car Life tested a 300bhp version with automatic transmission and recorded a 0-60mph time of 7.2 seconds which they reckoned compared favorably to the 5.9 secs achieved by Road & Track driving a 360bhp/4-speed manual car. Top speed was put at 130mph – fast enough for most, but there was potential for more if needed.

From the start of the Sixties, Corvette sales had begun to climb from an average of around ten thousand a year but so well was the '63 Sting Ray received that a second shift was taken on at the St. Louis assembly plant to fulfil the growing demand. Even so, there was a two-month waiting list, and buyers could expect to pay the full sticker price

as dealers weren't interested in offering any discounts. At the end of the model year, the Corvette Sting Ray had sold more than 21,500 units, split almost equally between the coupe and roadster, and virtually double the 1961 sales.

However, one event overshadowed 1963 and anyone who was alive back then can remember exactly where they were and what they were doing on November 22 when they heard the news that President John F. Kennedy had been assassinated in Dallas, Texas. Measured against such a tragedy, all other events pale into insignificance. It is impossible to say how differently things might have turned out had Kennedy not been shot, but the dynamic spirit of America survived and, in some small way, the Chevrolet Corvette can be viewed as a symbol of US determination to overcome all obstacles and produce something that is as good as anything manufactured elsewhere in the world – but at a price affordable by the majority. All Corvettes are great, but some are better than others and the '63 Sting Ray is undoubtedly one of the greatest.

Below: Bill Mitchell's classic 1963 Buick Riviera was originally designed as a LaSalle, in an endeavor to revive the famous name that had been in abeyance since 1940 - a previous attempt to do this had been made, in 1955. Various designs were tried but the hardtop coupe was the one selected. It was perfectly balanced and instantly recognizable and first-year production was 40,000.

SPECIFICATIONS

FORD MUSTANG (PRE SEPT '64)

Engine:
Cast iron - 6 Cylinders in line

Displacement:
170 cu. ins.

Bore and stroke:
3.5 x 2.94

Horsepower:
101

Body styles:
Hardtop coupe;
Fastback coupe;
Convertible coupe

No. of seats:
4

Weight (lbs):
2,583 lbs - 2,789 lbs

Price:
$2,372 - $2,614

Produced:
121,500

Right: The Ford Mustang established a new class of automobile called the "pony car" and set sales records that are unlikely to be bettered. The early ragtop had a 260 cu.in. V8 which gave lively performance in a smart, reasonably-priced package.

The first Ford Mustang is an automotive phenomenon that it would seem impossible ever to repeat. Just imagine suggesting that a new, but completely conventionally-engineered automobile based on an existing compact, economy model would sell nearly half a million in the first year and go on to set a trend affecting manufacturers for the next thirty years or more. Yet that's exactly what happened in 1964.

Ford certainly pressed all the right buttons with the Mustang, but had the good fortune to get some unintentional help from rivals Chevrolet and Plymouth. The Ford Falcon – introduced as a 1960 model following the success of the Rambler American and the demand for a cheap compact car – proved an immediate winner, taking up most of the spare production facilities left over from the Edsel debacle. The Chevy Corvair and Plymouth Valiant also entered this market sector, but a combination of radical rear-engined configuration (Corvair) and quirky styling (Valiant) gave the Falcon a distinct advantage. Ford were also able to utilize the compact's underpinnings in a way that was impossible for Chevrolet to do with the Corvair, and although Plymouth had a similar idea with the Valiant-based Barracuda their offering lacked the Mustang's glamor.

As the US economy started to improve in the early Sixties, customers began to ask for better performance from the smaller models and the auto makers were happy to oblige – after all, luxury and extra horsepower options meant more dollars! But though the uprated Falcon Futura Sprint and Corvair Monza models were acceptable, they didn't really satisfy the younger generation of affluent car buyers' demands for a true sporty compact that was just that little bit different from the usual run-of-the-mill Detroit products.

Whenever the history of how the Mustang came into being is discussed, one name always gets top billing – Lee Iacocca. Described as "The Father of the Mustang," Iacocca had the energy and foresight to get the project underway and the determination to see it through, even when Ford's top management kept refusing to approve the construction of such a car. Several Ford concept cars came under consideration for inspiration when the design parameters were

Above: The original Mustang would diversify and divide into endless variants, both factory Special Editions, performance options and Customs. These mid-engined concept cars were an exploration of a very different way in which things might have gone, with 2.0 liter, German-built Ford V4s developing 90hp, mounted in a glass-fiber bodyshell.

being set, but the most logical choice seemed to be for a snappy little four-seater based on the Falcon platform.

Before this, Ford stylists John Najjar and Jim Sipple came up with a sleek two-seater roadster body that was dubbed Mustang I and, powered by mid-mounted V4 engine, was demonstrated by Dan Gurney at the 1962 US Grand Prix. Although an interesting vehicle which contained several styling cues that would find their way onto the production version, Mustang I didn't really fulfil the requirement that Iacocca and his committee had laid down.

Above: The original Pony Car. The Ford Mustang was a uniquely American concept that proved a hit from its first introduction.

Further design development work was needed and this culminated in an internal competition between the Ford Studio, Corporate Advance studio and Lincoln-Mercury. The proposal presented by the Ford Studio team, headed by Joe Oros, Gail Halderman and David Ash, was unanimously chosen as the winning design, and this was eventually turned into a running prototype in 1963 called Mustang II, which is generally

Below: The first Mustangs were powered by a 170 cu. in. straight-six that produced 101 bhp. Top option was a 289 cu. in. V8 that could put out up to 271 bhp.

acknowledged as being the forerunner of the production Mustang.

Iacocca set the launch date for the Mustang as April 17 1964 at the New York World's Fair but, just over a month before that, the Motor City press were allowed an "accidental" sneak preview when Walter Ford (Henry Ford II's nephew) drove a pre-production Mustang convertible to a lunchtime meeting in downtown Detroit. The photos were quickly circulated to other magazines and newspapers and the corporate publicity machine swung into action to keep interest at a fever pitch until the official debut.

Pandemonium broke out wherever the Mustang went on sale and there are many stories of the chaos caused by Ford's new car – some of which had little foundation in fact, but it all added to the hype. Not that the Mustang needed much hyping – dealers couldn't write up the orders quick enough and it took only four months to reach 100,000 sales – a total which had been earlier forecast for the first twelve months! Demand was at such a pitch that the Ford assembly

Above: Elwood Engel had replaced Exner as head of styling at Chrysler and one of his first designs was the '64 Imperial Crown which carried several styling cues from the Lincoln: similar slab sides, sharp-edged fender lines and the hint of a spare wheel hump in the trunk.

plants at Dearborn, Michigan and San Jose, California were working flat out to keep pace. Early in the summer, a third plant at Metuchen, New Jersey was brought on-stream and ran around the clock pumping out Mustangs.

While it was clear that the Ford designers had created a car totally in tune with the times, a major contribution to the Mustang's popularity was the extraordinarily low base price of $2,368 f.o.b. Detroit for the coupe model. This was the price that Ford pushed in its advertisements, but it only bought the standard straight six engine with three-speed manual transmission – the big news was the lightweight V8 available at extra cost.

And it was the extensive options list

was aimed at younger drivers, owner-ship was opened up to anyone – there was no such thing as a typical Mustang buyer. They ranged from eighteen to eighty, and the car was equally welcome at the country club, fashionable restaurant and church, as at the local

Below & Above: Studebaker had retreated across the border into Canada by the end of 1963. The Avanti, designed by a team under the guidance of Raymond Loewy, was a fabulous performer, loved by enthusiasts, but unable to make an impression on the broader market. Eventually the name, rights and machine tools were bought by Leo Newman and Nathan Altman, the owners of a South Bend Studebaker dealership, who subsequently produced the custom-built Avanti II.

hat provided the opportunity for each wner to transform a docile, if stylish, tandard specification automobile into nything from a grand tourer in the lassic mold to a tire-shredding hot rod. his incredible variety of choice was ven more surprising when you remem-er that, underneath the bodywork, ost of the mechanical components ame directly from the old Falcon. It lso meant that although the Mustang

drive-in or drag strip. That remains true today.

What achieved such a broad spectrum of appeal? There's no doubt that the classic sports car "long-hood, short-deck" proportions set the right image, and the Mustang name evoked connotations of everything positive about the American way of life – but most of all it was about timing. The Mustang was simply the right car at the right time. Arriving at the precise moment when speed and performance were becoming major selling points as the "muscle car" era took off, even parked by the side of the road, a Mustang had the look of motion that Lee Iacocca had appreciated when he first saw the clay mock-up presented by Joe Oros.

The term "pony car" came to represent a new class of automobile, which Ford called "the family man sports car" in its adverts, and one that remains in use even today. And although the Mustang is still in production, the "Mustang generation" (a description first used by a California real estate

Below: The Chevrolet Corvair, introduced in 1960, was conceived in 1956 by Edward Cole, who was made divisional manager in July of that year. the car's layout and construction were unique on a US automobile: a horizontally-opposed, six-cylinder engine, mounted in the rear. To reduce costs, anti-roll bars were omitted and the tail-heavy, swing-axle design proved woefully inadequate , particularly when the car was driven with the kind of enthusiasm - that should have been foreseen - by its youthful, target buyers

Right: Along with designer Bill Mitchell, Zora Arkus-Duntov, a gifted engineer and experienced competition driver, was responsible for transforming the performance and handling of the Corvette. Sadly, his expertise was not brought to bear on the Corvair. The result was Ralph Nader's infamous and damning report Unsafe at Any Speed.

eveloper in a sales brochure promoting partments for young singles) belongs to the Sixties.

The Beatles brought pandemonium to the streets of New York when they rrived in February, and Lyndon Johnon's landslide victory to retain the residency over Barry Goldwater in November was seen as a vote to unify the nation but, in 1964, the one thing that all generations of Americans were united about was their love of the Mustang. And the streets and highways were filled with them.

SPECIFICATIONS

PLYMOUTH BELVEDERE SATELLITE

Engine:
V8 - cast iron block

Displacement:
318 cu. ins.

Bore and stroke:
3.91 x 3.31

Horsepower:
230

Body styles:
Hardtop coupe;
Convertible coupe

No. of seats:
5

Weight (lbs):
3,220 lbs

Price:
$2,649 - $2,869

Produced:
25,000

Speed was on people's minds in 1965, particularly towards the end of the year. On November 12, Bob Summers pushed the world land speed record for wheel-driven vehicles to 409.277mph at Bonneville, making his Goldenrod car the fastest on earth. Later, on the 15th, Craig Breedlove and his jet-powered "Spirit of America" took the world record for non-wheel-driven cars to 600.601mph, an absolutely phenomenal achievement.

Meanwhile, safety campaigner Ralph Nader was also looking at speed, when he published his book *Unsafe at any Speed*, which condemned, among others, Chevrolet's Corvair. But following in the hoofbeats of Ford's new Mustang, many manufacturers were scrambling to produce sporty models of their own to cash-in on the market for speed among car buyers of all ages. Since few were able to introduce completely new sporty cars like the Mustang, most updated more mundane looking intermediates from their existing ranges.

At Plymouth, 1965 saw the demise of the Sport Fury as the company's leading sporty model. The car had grown in size and had more luxurious appointments than before, something that did not really fit into the sporty image. To replace it, the company introduced the Belvedere Satellite, which came with a V8 engine as standard, albeit a small one, and had lots of performance options depending on how much muscle the buyer wanted

o flex – and, of course, on his pocketbook.

Before 1965, the Belvedere name was used on Plymouth's middle-priced, full-size cars, and it was more an indication of the level of trim and equipment than a model in its own right. In '65, however, the Belvedere series comprised a trio of intermediate-size automobiles, based on a 116 inch wheelbase. The three cars varied in their standard level of equipment and trim, being known as Belvedere I, Belvedere II and Belvedere Satellite, the last being the top of the range aimed at buyers who wanted a bit more performance than the norm.

Below & Above: The Satellite was the sporty version of Plymouth's Belvedere intermediate, and it came with enough engine and performance equipment options to turn it into a real tire-burner. In standard form, it came in hardtop and convertible models equipped with a 273 cu.in. V8 and three-speed. However, the buyer could choose between five optional engines, ranging from a 318 to the mighty 426 Hemi, backed by four-speed sports transmission.

Belvedere I and II models could be supplied with 225 cu.in. ohv, six cylinder engines or 273 cu.in. 180

245

Above: The Rambler Marlin was AMC's attempt at producing a pony car to match Ford's Mustang. It had sleek fastback styling that was decidedly stylish, but its standard 232 cu.in. six cylinder engine let it down.

horsepower V8s as standard, backed by a three-speed manual transmission with the option of a Torqueflite automatic. Body styles available comprised 2- and 4- door sedans, 4-door station wagons, a 2-door hardtop coupe and a 2-door convertible.

The Belvedere Satellite, however, only came with the V8 as standard, and in hardtop and convertible form. From the outset, it was given a sporty image, with front bucket seats, a center console and full wheel covers that incorporated center spinners. The hardtop also received all-vinyl trim. Emphasizing the performance look of the car, the rear fenders featured a row of louvers, while bright rocker panel moldings were also fitted.

The big news for the Satellite however, was the range of engine options listed. These began with the 230 horsepower Commando 318 cu.in. V8 equipped with a two-barrel carburetor followed by a similarly-equipped 361 cu.in. Commando engine that developed 265 horsepower, and a 383 with a four barrel carburetor that was good for 330 horsepower. If that wasn't enough, the buyer could specify the 426-S wedge-head V8, which displaced 426 cu.in. and had a four-barrel, and developed 365 horsepower. The amount these engines added to the cost of the car ranged from $31 to $545, depending on the engine.

price of either $1,150 or $1,800. This included the cost of a four-speed manual transmission. There were two prices because the engines were retrofitted at the factory, and the higher figure applied to cars that had originally been equipped with automatic transmission. The same arrangement applied to the wedge-head engines, with two prices being quoted. Given that the base price of a Satellite 2-door hardtop was $2,612, the Hemi represented a substantial investment and, in truth, these engines were really intended for competition use.

Although the four-speed came as standard with the 426 engines, it could also be specified with the 361 and 383 engines, while a positive-traction rear axle was also available for an extra $39. Other performance options included a choice of rear axle ratios (3.23 or 2.93:1) and a tachometer.

Not many Satellites had the monster

For those with deep pockets and an urge to burn rubber, however, there was the 425 horsepower, 426 cu.in. Hemi engine with dual four-barrel carburetors, and a

Below: The top of the Oldsmobile F-85 line was the 4-4-2, standing for four speeds, a four-barrel carburetor and two exhausts. Better handing than many of its "muscle-car" rivals, the 4-4-2 was introduced in 1964 as an option package on the Cutlass coupe but soon established itself as a force to be reckoned with in its own right.

426 wedge-head or Hemi engines. Most buyers opted for the more tractable 383 V8, which had power and torque aplenty and was much more user-friendly on the street. But the big engines, particularly the Hemis, were in keeping with Chrysler's interest in NASCAR and drag racing. In the former, the Hemi would be fitted to full-sized Dodges and Plymouths run on tracks of over a mile in length, while on shorter tracks, Dodge Coronets and Plymouth Belvederes would use it. In drag racing, too, the Hemi-engined Belvedere was legendary, being campaigned by the likes of Ronnie Sox and Buddy Martin and the "Drag-On-Lady" Shirley Shahan, who used it to set a National S/SA record of 127.30mph with an elapsed time of 11.21 seconds. Such was the company's interest, that they produced an altered-wheelbase drag package for Dodge and Plymouth automobiles so that they could compete

in the NHRA Factory Experimental class.

The actual body styling of the Belvedere models had been carried over from the previous year, when it had been common to all intermediate Plymouths. For 1965, it was changed by replacing the previous dual head lights with single lights, while the grille was given a cruciform trim with mesh background.

The sporting image of the Satellite that resulted from the company's NASCAR and drag racing activities, plus the undoubted performance of the car, helped boost sales and just over 25,000 of the 1965 models were built, most of them hardtops (only 1,860 convertibles left the factory). The car continued with this image for some time, and in 1966 was restyled with a swoopier roofline and more slab-sided contours. The big news for that year, however, would be a more refined 426 Hemi engine that was intended for street

Above: Top engine option thru' '66 was the 289 V8, but a 390 was added to the list in '67, producing 320 bhp.

Above: It is said that a lot of traffic accidents were caused by drivers turning their heads to look at the new Mustang, when it first began to appear in dealers' showrooms. The looks were certainly distinctive and, in the beginning, clean and well-defined. In the early years, the classic, hard-top coupe was the top seller by a massive margin.

Above top: The stylish Fastback Coupe accounted for a mere hundred thousand out of a total run of almost half a million Mustangs in 1964/65.

use. The Street Hemi had cast-iron cylinder heads rather than aluminum (although these were available as an option), while the inlet manifold was aluminum rather than magnesium. A wilder cam was available, and although compression was down to 10.25:1 from 12.5:1, output was still 425 horsepower. With this came a Sure-Grip axle, whether a four-speed or Torqueflite automatic was fitted.

The Street Hemi turned out to be a real winner, offering tractability as well as high performance. Car and Driver

said that the car offered the "best combination of brute performance and tractable street manners" that they had ever come across. In their test of the car, they recorded a 0-60mph time of 5.3 seconds, with a 13.8 second quarter mile time and terminal speed of 104mph. Stopping such a projectile needed substantial brakes, of course, and while front discs were not an option, 11 inch police-specification drums were.

Although it never looked particularly like a muscle car, Plymouth's Belvedere Satellite was definitely a force to be reckoned with. It would go on in this vein, eventually spawning the famed GTX and Road Runner.

SPECIFICATIONS

DODGE CHARGER

Engine:
V8 - cast iron block
silicon/aluminum
crankcase

Displacement:
318 cu. ins.

Bore and stroke:
3.91 x 3.31

Horsepower:
230

Body styles:
Hardtop coupe

No. of seats:
4-5

Weight (lbs):
3,500 lbs

Price:
$3,122

Produced:
37,344

Above Right: Hidden head lights and a full-width grille give the Dodge Charger an aggressive look, matched by ground-shaking acceleration thanks to the brutal horsepower of a 426 cu.in. Hemi engine. This was the car described as "...the hot new leader of the Dodge Rebellion."

If you're involved with the decision-making process at the upper end of management for a division of a large auto corporation, it is accepted that there will be a great deal of give and take. In all probability, you do not wield enough influence to insist on your division being able to produce a brand new model from the ground up – you have to share the basic corporate platforms with the other divisions and make as many alterations as is allowed within the constraints of the budget available. In this respect, Chrysler in the Sixties was no different from the many other large companies leading the automobile industry.

However, just once in a while, restrictions such as these engender creativity which produces something very special and the 1966 Dodge Charger is an outstanding example of what the art of compromise can achieve.

Around the mid-1960s, the fastback body style enjoyed a period of popularity as the result of the rest of the auto industry rushing to come up with their own versions of the ultra-successful Ford Mustang. Dodge were offered the opportunity to share the Plymouth Barracuda platform with this in mind but, instead, they decided to go their own route and use the larger Coronet model as a basis

for an entry into the burgeoning muscle car market.

The leading lights at Dodge behind this policy were product planner Burt Bouwkamp and stylist William Brownlie – both newcomers to the division and both self-confessed performance car buffs who simply loved the work they were doing.

Below: The Pontiac GTO started out as a variation on the Tempest. it is rightly regarded as the original, and definitive, "Muscle Car." Some people objected to the hi-jacking of Ferrari's revered initials, but the Pontiac was as fast, if not faster - in a straight line at least - and a cool $16,000 cheaper, even with all the add-ons.

Above: The handsome Oldsmobile Toronado was the division's most innovative car for a generation. It would set the trend for front-wheel drive that, by 1908, would be universally employed throughout the General Motors Corporation.

Even so, the merits of the Sixties fastback are hard to define from a practical point of view. Rear seat passengers had restricted headroom and minimal leg space, the large area of glass created a greenhouse effect causing the interior to heat up rapidly in the sunshine and, to cap it all, luggage space was abysmal. On the plus side of course, the fastback Charger does look great. Even when it is standing still, it seems ready to spring into tire-blistering action – and, when talking about muscle cars, that counts for a whole lot more than how much shopping can be accommodated in the trunk or the niceties of passenger comfort.

The starting point for the Charger actually came about almost by chance rather than being attributed to part of some grand corporate marketing strategy. Facing the lack of an attention-grabbing exhibit for an auto show in the summer of '65, Bouwkamp asked Brownlie to come up with an idea for a show car that could not only be built quickly, but at minimal cost. It was a tall order, but the designer rose to the challenge and suggested putting a fastback roof on the popular Dodge Coronet model. Following Brownlie's specifications, a 2-door hardtop was speedily modified and readied for the show.

Dubbed "Charger II" (Dodge had used the Charger name before on another show car a year or two previously), this car was not, as is often supposed, intended as an official prototype for a proposed new model but was simply created as a last minute showpiece. However, public reaction to the fastback was so enthusiastic that plans were immediately rushed through to put the Charger into production.

Brownlie's show car had, naturally enough for something designed to attract attention, several rather exaggerated styling features and it was deemed necessary to trim these excesses back for the version intended for sale to the public. Nevertheless, the production Charger retained all the good points of the original concept. The sloping fastback roof remained unaltered, and the

the four round head lights rotated into view but there was an override switch allowing the lights to be left exposed without being on. This feature was a clever Dodge engineer's solution to the problem of head light mechanisms being frozen shut in harsh winter conditions, which had blighted this feature on other makes.

The interior of the Charger, especially the dashboard and instrument layout, was taken almost directly from the show car and used unaltered, providing one of the most comprehensive packages on offer at that time. Elsewhere, it was luxury all the way with deep plush carpets and foam-padded bucket seats, plus a fake wood rimmed steering wheel as the final touch. In addition, the rear seats folded flat to give increased carrying capacity but, without a full hatchback, it didn't really help much on a practical level.

Because of the low budget allocated, the Charger II show car had a meek 318 cu.in. V8 under the hood, but the majority of '66 Chargers were ordered

full-width tail lights were incorporated in a flat rear panel with the slab-sided fenders neatly squared off at the back and a razor-sharp top edge picked out with a bright metal strip.

But it was the front end that provided the most radical departure from the show car's original appearance. In place of the simple grille with five thin horizontal bars and single rectangular head lights, the Charger presented a blank face made up of fine vertical lines interrupted only by the round medallion in the center. Hidden head lights, another Sixties styling fad, were in vogue and the use of them on the Dodge represented the first time that they had been seen on a Chrysler Corporation car since the 1942 DeSoto. When turned on,

Below: The Toronado's "split-transmission" system was elegant in its simplicity. A torque-converter mounted behind the engine was connected to a Turbo Hydra-Matic gearbox, mounted under the left-hand cylinder bank, via chains and sprockets. The system saved weight, reduced costs and was extremely robust. It also took up very little space, allowing more room for the driver and passengers.

Above: The arrival of the Ford Bronco Sports Utility pickup showed a new market was opening up for a 4x4 leisure vehicle that could "go nearly anywhere and do nearly anything." "Neither a car nor a truck, but a vehicle which combines the best in both worlds," the Bronco closely resembled the International Scout which had debuted in '61.

with the 325 horsepower 383 cu.in. engine. Thus equipped, the hefty fastback could reach 60mph in eight seconds, cover the quarter mile in sixteen at over 90mph and run on up to reach a 120mph top speed.

But for the serious performance devotee, there was only one powerplant – the mighty 426 Hemi. Fed by dual Carter AFB four barrels and rated by the factory at a very conservative 425bhp, this engine gave the Charger a 0-60mph time of six seconds, and quarter miles in the 13 second bracket. As befits a road-going race car, underneath everything about the Hemi Charger was heavy duty, from the vented four-pot front disc brakes, massive torsion bars and anti-roll bar to extra rear springs and Dana 60 axle.

There was one thing that the Hemi

Charger didn't come with – a factory warranty. Instead, there was a bright yellow sticker which stated: "This car is equipped with a 426 cu.in. engine (and other special equipment). This car is intended for use in supervised acceleration trials and is not intended for highway or general passenger car use. Accordingly, THIS VEHICLE IS SOLD 'AS IS', and the warranty coverage does not apply."

Driving a Hemi-powered Dodge Charger could undoubtedly be a very exciting experience, but the year's ultimate piece of steering must go to astronaut Neil Armstrong who, when piloting the Gemini 8 space craft, performed the first docking maneuver and described it as "Just like parking a car." Other people on the way up were Ronald Reagan who was elected as Governor of California, and The Monkees pop group who were launched into the limelight through a madcap television series. Also riding high were the hems of womens' dresses and skirts across the nation, as high fashion saw the mini skirt become all the rage.

Dodge used the success of the Charger to launch a campaign called "the Dodge Rebellion" and the new fastback sold well on the back of some heavy media promotion and race-winning results, but the '67 body looked identical and sales halved in the following year. A compl- etely new shape arrived in 1968, making the first Dodge Charger very much a child of its time.

1966 was the year that civil rights movement leader Stokely Carmichael brought the term "Black Power" into the forefront of the American political debate, but for an automotive enthusiast it was the year of "Hemi Power" and the Dodge Charger.

Right & Below: Fun in the sun. 72,000 Mustang convertibles found homes in '66. A host of options allowed prospective buyers to personalize the car into anything from a economical runabout to a ferocious street racer or a luxury cruiser.

SPECIFICATIONS

CHEVROLET CAMARO

Engine:
Cast iron - 6 Cylinders in line

Displacement:
230 cu. ins.

Bore and stroke:
3.88 x 3.25

Horsepower:
140

Body styles:
Hardtop coupe;
Convertible coupe

No. of seats:
4

Weight (lbs):
2,770 lbs - 3,025 lbs

Price:
$2,466 - $2,704

Produced:
59,000

Coming second to Ford is something that Chevrolet has never liked and, when the Mustang proved to be such a runaway success in 1964, the heat was on to find a way of redressing the balance. Chevy supporters will tell you that there were all manner of reasons why the GM division didn't have an equivalent to Ford's pony car – the Corvair Monza was selling well, they had too many different models already on offer – but the plain fact of the matter is that Ford had got there first and so it was down to Chevy to play catch-up.

Wisely, the Chevy hierarchy appreciated that arriving second in the market place meant that they had to produce more than just a Mustang clone – a new model had to be perceived as something better

Ford and Chevrolet fans will debate forever about which is best, but there is no doubt that the Camaro provided a more than adequate riposte to the Mustang and, even if it did take until 1977 to outsell the Ford, the Chevy Camaro was definitely here to stay.

Taking advantage of the example provided by Ford, Chevy abandoned the rear-engined layout of the Corvair and returned to the conventional front engine, rear-wheel-drive arrangement for their new car. Henry Haga was put in charge of the styling and, in addition to the Mustang, his influences came from a

clandestine 1962 project by Chevy design director Irwin Rybicki that used a Chevy II as the base. Certain similarities

Below: The Chevy Camaro was available with everything from an economical six cylinder up to one of the hottest small block V8s on the market. The basic version here has simple round head lights and turn signal lamps mounted in the grille. Only 2-door hardtop coupe and convertible body styles were offered, with the Camaro roof line being such that a fastback was not deemed necessary.

can also be seen with the Corvair Monza. Due to a management reshuffle, David R. Hollis took over as chief designer and, after four months intensive work, in December 1964, a full size clay model was constructed and photographed against a Mustang for comparison.

Below: With looks and performance like the '67 Corvette had, stripes were superfluous...

Above: The '69 Corvette carried strong echoes of the Mako Shark styling exercise and some truly awesome performance options. The undisputed King-of-the-Hill was the L88 set-up which comprised a 427 block with aluminum heads, a compression ratio of 12.5 : 1, extra-knobbly cams, and a massive, four-barrel carb. The transmission was up-rated to extra-heavy-duty to cope with no less than 560 bhp.

consideration, but merchandising manager Bob Lund and vice president Ed Rollert searched through Spanish and French dictionaries and picked out the word Camaro in one of them. Estes liked the name and it was announced to the Press in June '66, well in advance of the car itself being previewed. Chevy publicists said Camaro translated from French as "comrade" or "pal," but other researchers noted that in Spanish it could be interpreted as a type of shrimp or even "loose bowel movement" – but the fuss soon died down and the name became established as quintessencially Chevrolet.

Initially, the "Chevy Mustang" project was given the Experimental Project code number XP-836. Later on it got christened the "F-Car" (the "F" supposedly referring to Ford), and subsequently carried the name Panther, which many assumed would be the final model name. However, General Motors was locked in a battle with Ralph Nader and his safety crusaders during this period, so it was decided that using the Panther name was too provocative, and so a search began for an alternative. Chevrolet's head man, Elliot M. "Pete" Estes reckoned that the name should start with a "C" and, for a while, the name "Chevette" was under serious

Above: Despite its monumental performance potential, the Corvette's styling remained pure and unpretentious right through to end of the model run - a tribute to Bill Mitchell's vision.

When the Camaro was announced, on September 29, 1966, it was immediately apparent that Chevrolet's designers had taken the Mustang concept to heart and yet had added their own distinctive ideas. Where the Mustang's body lines were straight and aggressive, the Camaro's were curved and flowed ("fluidity" was a term used a lot by GM's designers) and the Chevy shape had been the subject of wind tunnel

Above: The Shelby 350GT was one of a host of specially-prepared, high-performance variations on the Mustang theme. Such cars dominated the Sports Car Club of America's Trans-American racing series.

testing to prove its superior aerodynamic performance.

But it wasn't only in the bodywork design that the Chevy differed from the Ford. The basic understructure consisted of a front subframe attached to a unitary bodyshell, instead of the complete unitized construction used on the Mustang. In many ways this configuration gave the Camaro an advantage and, because the front chassis could be isolated from the rest of the body with rubber bushings, the ride quality was improved. In addition, the design had better space utilization, improving the room allocated for rear seat passengers and the trunk capacity.

But despite these improvements, the Chevy Camaro was not without its teething problems. While the attractive 2-door coupe body could happily rival both that of the Mustang notchback and

fastback models, the convertible suffered from body flexing, door sagging and rattles - all of which required fixing. Also, the single leaf Mono-Plate rear springs used were okay with the base six cylinder engine and Powerglide automatic transmission, but the more powerful V8 cars suffered from axle tramp and all '67 Camaros would bottom out on the rear suspension with a very alarming ease.

Like the Mustang, the Camaro could be specified with any number of additional options selected from a huge list. In fact, the list was so comprehensive and so complicated that it was suggested that few people really understood all the available possibilities. Apart from the bewildering array of engines, transmissions, colors, interior trim and special packages on offer for the standard specification car, the potential Camaro owner could also select from some serious high performance options – notably the Super Sport (SS), Rally Sport (RS) and the now legendary Z-28.

Once you got into the SS and RS models (which, to add to the muddle, could also be combined together on one

car), the Camaro came with hidden head lights and a special paint stripe around the nose plus various other items. But the "bumble bee" stripe proved to be so popular that it was quickly made available on any Camaro model. Then, when the big block V8s were introduced, the SS package came as a mandatory part of the deal. Confusing? You bet!

Below: Carroll Shelby had married Ford V8 muscle to British sports suspension and a lightweight body to produce the AC Cobra - one of the most iconic sportscars of all time. By '69, U.S. customers could order the "Cobra-Jet" big block V8, with aluminum heads and semi-Hemi combustion chambers, for their very own Mustang.

Despite this apparent minefield of choice, nearly 65% of the 220,906 '67 Camaros produced were base model V8 Sport Coupes and there can be few people who would argue that this was, indeed, a pretty shrewd selection for just

Below: Pontiac's Le Mans , like the GTO, was a Tempest-based option package. top choice for performance was the 326 V8, delivering 285 bhp. Styling remained crisp and purposeful on the Pontiac range throughout the '60s.

about any form of motoring. Whether cruising down to the corner drive-thru burger joint or high speed touring cross-country on the Interstate, it was all the same and the Chevy proved a match for the Mustang in just about every department.

"Long-awaited and much-speculated, the youthful Chevrolet Camaro has arrived on the domestic automotive scene with a fine pedigree and high promise," wrote *Car Life* magazine in October 1966, continuing: "Though a follower in a field pioneered by others,

Top & Above: *The traditional Cadillac layout: front engine/rear drive was exemplified by the '67 Coupe de Ville (top). Seismic shifts were afoot, however, the first rumblings coming from the '67 Eldorado. This handsome, muscular design incorporated front-wheel drive on a Cadillac for the first time. As with the '63 Buick Riviera, it had at one time been considered as a candidate for the resurrection of the LaSalle name.*

the Camaro nonetheless seems exciting in looks and performance, is particularly well-suited to its intended market and will be sold and serviced by the world's largest dealer body." This emphasis on youth and excitement reminds us that these were indeed the heady days of the Sixties – 1967 being the so-called "Summer of Love" when everything went psychedelic and the Monterey Pop Festival heralded the hippie culture taking over San Francisco.

There were plenty of dark clouds in the purple haze, what with continuing Vietnam War protests, race riots in the Motor City of Detroit and the tragic deaths of three astronauts – Virgil Grissom, Edward White and Roger Chaffee – when their Apollo spacecraft caught fire on the launchpad at Cape Canaveral. Despite the harrowing events of this year, however, memories of '67 will, for most people, be of a highly colorful and supercharged period that welcomed the arrival of the Camaro as a small part of the more positive trends in society.

SPECIFICATIONS

SHELBY MUSTANG

Engine:
V8 - cast iron block

Displacement:
428 cu. ins.

Bore and stroke:
4.13 x 3.98

Horsepower:
335

Body styles:
Fastback coupe

No. of seats:
2-4

Weight (lbs):
2,659 lbs

Price:
c. $3,000

Produced:
42,841 (all Fastbacks)

By 1968, the United States was heavily involved in the Vietnam war. The conflict had cost billions of dollars and, subsequently, American taxpayers were saddled with a 10% rise in their taxes. Harder to swallow still, was the number of American lives lost, and there seemed no end in sight. Despite putting out peace feelers in the previous year, the North Vietnamese, together with the Vietcong, launched a massive new offensive at the end of January, during the sacred "Tet" New Year holiday, penetrating the grounds of the US embassy in Saigon. In fact, the Tet offensive was a desperate gamble for the North Vietnamese, who had suffered considerable losses in both men and equipment as a result of US bombing, particularly in the north of the country, but it paid dividends. Stung by the speed and success of the attack, and by the ever-growing peace protests at home, President Lyndon B. Johnson ordered a halt to the bombing of North Vietnam. The demoralized Johnson did not seek re-election later that year and was succeeded by Republican Richard Nixon, whose presidency was to be less than trouble-free.

Along with the relentless grind of the Vietnam

ar, there was more bad news that year: ivil rights activist Martin Luther King as assassinated, and attorney general Robert Kennedy shared his fate a short me after. The one bright piece of news as that Apollo 8 became the first pacecraft to orbit the moon, paving the way for a manned landing during the ollowing year.

In Detroit, the car makers were still aught up in the muscle car business. All he major manufacturers had at least ne horse in the race, which was fast ecoming a contest to see who could ram in the biggest engine and out-ccelerate the rest. Straight-line erformance was the main criterion and, 1 the process, handling, braking, ride, uild quality and levels of trim often left lot to be desired.

The original pony car was the Mustang, first introduced in 1965 by ord as an inexpensive-to-make, sporty ar that would appeal to young people,

and would cost less than $2,500. It was an instant success, with customers queuing up to buy them; America loved the Mustang.

The original Mustang was designed by Joe Oros, L. David Ash, and Gayle L.

Below: The Shelby Mustang was first introduced by Ford in 1965 as a low cost personal car, and it was the original pony car. In 1968 all the Detroit car makers were still competing against one another in the muscle car business, seeing who could cram in the biggest engine and out accelerate the rest in straight line performance. However, the Mustang could not only compete on that level, but had additional appeal to the customer in that there were a myriad of options on offer, which allowed each car to be personalized. The '68 model had a revised grille, with a bright inner ring around the galloping horse emblem.

265

Above: The 1968 Chrysler Dodge Charger was restyled with a sleek body to match its high performance. A 440 Magnum or 426 Hemi V8 was offered, the latter propelling the car to 60mph in under five seconds.

Right: Also new in '68 was a restyled Corvette Sting Ray, with a body reminiscent of Chevrolet's Mako Shark II show car of 1965.

Halderman of the Ford Division styling studio. Its style, with a long hood and a short deck, very quickly caught on in Detroit - and it had many imitators, that were quickly christened "pony cars" in honor of the original. The very first model was a two-seat roadster, built of fiber glass on a 90-inch wheelbase, and with a 2.0 liter V4 engine developing only 90hp. Although it was very impractical it was a pretty car, and

people flocked to see it at motor shows. The president of Ford, Lee A. Iacocca, decided that it was not suitable as a volume car, so dozens more prototypes followed, until the designers arrived at a more conventional four-seat, production model.

Part of its appeal was the massive range of options on offer, which allowed the stand model to be personalized in a great many ways. It could be anything from a neat economy car, to a nimble sporty car to a small luxury model. Transmission could be automatic, three- or four-speed manual or stick overdrive, and there were also handling packages, power steering, disc brakes and air conditioning available. A wide range of interior trims could be specified, and there were different accent trims and a selection of special moldings for the exterior.

The major problem was that, even as early as 1968, all the manufacturers were chasing a muscle car market that was already beginning to disappear. The hullabaloo that had followed the launch of the Mustang had died down and

Above: The '68 Plymouth B-Body range had smooth lines and altogether well-balanced looks. The Belvedere range comprised a Coupe, a 4-Door Sedan and a Station Wagon. In '68, of course, the CAT was optional.

emissions controls were beginning to hamper the cars, increasingly emasculating their performance. Interest was on the wane and the potential buyers were starting to look for more traditional features in a car. Although the bubble had not burst, it was beginning to deflate. This was reflected in production figures, which had dropped by nearly half, from 607,500 in '66 to 317,000 in '68.

Worthy of mention in the long list of automobiles to follow the Mustang's lead in the pursuit of ultimate, tire-shredding, road-burning, neck-breaking straight-line performance are: the Pontiac GTO, the Dodge Charger, the Plymouth Road Runner and the Oldsmobile 4-4-2. These cars represent a unique part of America's automotive heritage and have almost no equivalents anywhere else in the world. To modern eyes

they truly look like dinosaurs: huge and powerful but ultimately doomed to extinction due to dwindling space and scarce resources. While they ruled the road, however, they were magnificent: wild and untamed and reflecting a deep-seated love of freedom and resentment of restrictions that is close to the American heart.

Below: In 1968, Chrysler altered the styling of the fenders, grilles and rear deck areas, but otherwise there was little change. New roofs were incorporated in the three hardtop models and the high speed performance of the engine was improved. In total, there were now fifteen luxurious models in the range.

SPECIFICATIONS

IMPERIAL LEBARON

Engine:
V8 - cast iron block

Displacement:
440 cu. ins.

Bore and stroke:
4.32 x 3.75

Horsepower:
350

Body styles:
Hardtop coupe;
Hardtop sedan

No. of seats:
6

Weight (lbs):
4,610 lbs - 4,710 lbs

Price:
$5,898 - $6,131

Produced:
19,413

Above: The Imperial of 1969 was five inches longer than the previous year, at 229.7 inches. The LeBaron 2-door hardtop was offered with a full range of luxury options, accessories and convenience features.
According to the publicity for the car, it offered "the luxury buyer a dramatically new automobile incorporating the best of modern styling and traditional elegance."

As the Sixties came to a close, America still found itself enmeshed in the Vietnam war, although the number of US troops there was being reduced and efforts were being made towards the Vietnamization of the war by providing material and air support to the indigenous forces of South Vietnam. The anti-war rallies continued and home coming troops who had served in South East Asia often returned to find that they were looked upon with disgust by many of their peers, despite the fact that most of them had been drafted. Later in 1969 news of the massacre of innocent civilians in the village of My Lai by American troops stirred up the anti-war sentiment all the more.

It was a year of mourning, not just for the thousands who had died in Vietnam, but also for one of America's great heroes of the twentieth century. On March 28, the country was shocked by news that Dwight D. Eisenhower, former President and Commander in Chief of the Allied forces in Europe during World War II, had died.

If many Americans were not proud of what was being done in their name in Vietnam, all had reason to be proud of their country's achievements in space. Following successful orbital missions to

the moon, NASA carried out a successful landing in July, and Neil Armstrong became the first man to set foot on its dusty surface, quoting the now immortal phrase: "One small step for

Below: The Dodge Daytona Charger was the direct ancestor of the Plymouth Superbird. The projectile-shaped front end and massive tail spoiler gave it shattering track performance.

Above: Many manufacturers were still playing the pony car game in 1969. Chevrolet not only had the Camaro, as illustrated here, but also the Chevelle SS 396, a high-performance version of its standard Chevelle intermediate-sized automobile.

man; one giant leap for mankind."

The auto industry, however, took a slightly shorter step that year, with new car sales being a little below those of the previous year. It was not the easiest of times for manufacturers. With increasing pressure to improve the exhaust emissions and safety aspects of cars, production expenses increased. By this time, the industry's flirtation with the compact had just about come to an end, and the future seemed to lie with intermediate-sized cars. Some, however, continued to build big cars, among them Chrysler – a company that was rarely known for styling innovation, although they often led the field in engineering. The real luxury models in Chrysler's line-up came from the company's Imperial division which, for many years, had sought to compete with Cadillac for the prestige end of the market. For 1969, the Imperial range comprised of 2- and 4-door hardtops and a 4-door sedan. In addition, a custom-built limousine was also available to special order.

Imperial had been a name associated with Chrysler for decades but, until the

mid-fifties, it had simply been applied to the most luxurious models sold under the Chrysler badge. The company built long wheelbase sedans and limousines as well as other luxury models under the Custom Imperial and Crown Imperial

Above: A no-frills, two-door muscle coupe, the Coronet Super Bee was part of what Dodge called its "Scat Pack." Although it was a budget-priced car, it was still a roadable performance machine.

Below: The Chevrolet Camaro Z/28 was available for the street - although it was aimed squarely at the track. For 1969 it was given an extensive facelift. All the early models are coveted collectibles, but the Z became less special as time passed.

Above: *Oldsmobile 4-4-2 Holiday (hardtop) coupe. The numbers referred to 4-speed transmission, 4-barrel carburetor and 2 exhausts. From '65 it had a 400 cu. in motor as well. Performance was tremendous, with a 0-60 time of 7.5 seconds and a top speed of 125 mph.*

names. However, these were obviously Chryslers and could be associated with more mundane company products. It was not good marketing for a company that wanted to do well in the luxury market, dominated by Cadillac.

If Imperial was to make it, the image of the cars had to improve; they needed to be less obviously part of the Chrysler empire, with a mystique of their own. As

a result, in 1955, a separate Imperial division was formed and a new range of Imperials launched. Sadly, one of the new cars – the 2-door hardtop – looked very similar to the Chrysler C300, a popular high-performance automobile that had done well in competition. This undoubtedly affected the sales of the Imperial range, but even so their total sales doubled compared to the year before.

However, Imperial had become established as a maker of luxury cars, and the name became more familiar with buyers. Until the mid Sixties, many Imperials were designed by Virgil Exner, who had some quirky ideas of what made a good-looking luxury car. As with most other automobiles of the late

Fifties, Imperials grew fins that became ever-larger with each new model. Unfortunately, because the company had relatively limited resources, new models appeared less frequently than those of other manufacturers and, towards the end of each model run, the cars were beginning to look decidedly dated. This is particularly true of the '62 models which had outlandish fins at a time when all other manufacturers had dropped the idea. Lights were another of Exner's foibles. Wanting to give his designs the classic look of Thirties automobiles, he incorporated freestanding head lights and tail lights that looked as though they had been stuck on as an afterthought. If nothing else, Imperials were unique in appearance.

Exner was eventually replaced by Elwood Engel, who had worked at Ford,

Below: The '69 Chevrolet Camaro SS had a recontoured lower body, with front and rear creaselines above the wheel openings. A "V" grille was introduced, along with different rear styling

and he brought a considerable degree of Lincoln influence to the '64 Imperials, which were big slab-sided automobiles. From this point on, Imperials tended to reflect design trends within the industry, rather than setting standards of their own.

However, with falling sales, costs had to be cut so, for 1967, the Imperials used the basic Chrysler New Yorker body shell, although different front and rear end treatments gave it a distinctive appearance. It was a unibody design fitted with a 440 cu.in. V8 that developed 350 horsepower and was backed by a three-speed TorqueFlite automatic transmission; this was the same drivetrain that had been used in previous models. Imperials were back where they started, being uprated versions of existing Chrysler models. Things would stay that way until all production ceased in 1975.

Although featuring a completely new 127 inch wheelbase body, when the '69 Imperial models were unveiled, the similarity with the New Yorker was even more pronounced. The body had gently rounded sides and was referred to by Chrysler as having "fuselage styling." The drivetrain was the same as that used previously, while power steering and brakes were standard equipment. Two series of Imperial were built: Crown and LeBaron. The latter was the more luxurious of the two and was available on both hardtop models, while Crown versions of all three body styles were available.

There is no doubt that all the Imperial models were luxury cars – for Chryslers. But the company had slipped out of the market they had long wanted to be a part of. Moreover, they would never return.

Despite its obvious Chrysler parenta-

Below: Mustang Boss 429. The Boss Mustang had cool, fastback styling and serious muscle. The engine bay had to be extensively re-modelled to accommodate the big block 429 V8.

ge, the 1969 Imperial sold well comp-ared to previous years. In total, just over 22,000 examples were built; the last time sales had been above 20,000 was at the launch of the new 1964 model. Sadly, that was the highpoint for, thereafter, sales dropped quite alarm-ingly (by almost 50% in 1970 and 1971). Minor changes were made until 1974 when, again, it shared the latest New Yorker body shell. By this time, Imperial no longer existed as a separate division of Chrysler. However, the oil crisis of 1973 had sounded the death knell for big gas guzzlers and, after 1975, production of Imperials was brought to a halt.

Below: Mustang produced this Playboy Special in 1969, after Playboy *magazine had several Mustangs sprayed "Playboy Pink" for promotional purposes in '66. After receiving several enquiries, Ford offered the color as an option in '67, and again in '69. Not many were made and both versions are very collectible. All the Playboy Specials were only offered as convertibles.*

1970

SPECIFICATIONS

PLYMOUTH ROAD RUNNER SUPERBIRD

Engine:
V8 - cast iron block

Displacement:
440 cu. ins.

Bore and stroke:
4.32 x 3.75

Horsepower:
390

Body styles:
Hardtop coupe

No. of seats:
4

Weight (lbs):
3,785 lbs

Price:
$4,298

Produced:
1,920

A new decade: Henry Kissinger begins secret negotiations with his North Vietnamese counterpart as anti-war demonstrations take place across the US; the Boeing 747 enters commercial service; Midnight Cowboy wins the Academy Award for Best Picture; Gary Gabelich sets a new land speed record in Utah: 622.4 mph. - and in a State of the Union address, delivered in January 1970, President Richard M. Nixon urged the Congress to adopt legislation to protect the environment. Meanwhile...

Plymouth had gone Hollywood in '69 by adopting Warner Bros. popular cartoon character

the Road Runner as the name and symbol for a new range of low-priced, medium-sized, high-performance muscle cars that achieved instant popularity. Base price for a GTX was below $3,000 - for a car that featured a 383, 335 bhp V8 hemi with 440 heads. Performance was shattering and you even got a genuine, Road Runner "Beep! Beep!" horn. Styling had been addressed and the Plymouth range went boldly forward into 1970 with heavy-duty "fuselage" styling and a lot of vents and scoops and

Above: Introduced in 1970, the Plymouth Road Runner Superbird was developed in a wind tunnel to win NASCAR stock car races, and qualifying speeds of over 190mph were recorded at the super speedways like Daytona and Talladega. Around 1,935 road-going versions were sold, although prices were heavily discounted towards the end as demand didn't live up to Plymouth's expectations. When powered by the legendary 426 cu.in. Hemi V8 engine, this is an awesome street machine!

Above: The Ford Maverick was billed as the "first car of the '70s at 1960s prices." The Economy model was introduced on April 17 1969, exactly five years after that other popular equine Ford, the Mustang. Powered by a 170 cu.in. six cylinder, the Maverick proved to be in such demand that it remained unchanged throughout the 1970 model year too. With a 103 inch wheelbase, it wasn't really in the sub-compact class, but still sold over 450,000 units in its first full year.

humps both operative and speculative. In the mid-size range, the third-generation, '70 Barracuda could be ordered with 426 Hemi and a six-barrel 440 rated at 390 bhp. The ultimate

Road Runner - the Superbird - debuted in 1970. The Superbird was derived from the '69 Dodge Charger Daytona, employing an identical, massive, aerodynamic, front-end extension that covered the headlights and a towering rear spoiler mounted on struts above the trunk. Production models were fitted

Right: The Pontiac GTO Judge was marked by colorful striping, and had a 366bhp Ram-air V8 and three-speed manual gearbox with Hurst shifter. First introduced in '69, in 1970, it had a clumsier front end, bigger rear bumpers and pronounced bulges along the body above the wheel openings. Most collectors prefer the earlier model without these features.

with the 335 hp, 383 cu. in. V8 carrying a four-barrel carburetor and TorqueFlite automatic transmission but options included four-speed manual transmission and a 390 hp, 440 cu. in. Street Hemi with the 440 "Six Pack." Tuned, racing versions were capable of speeds in excess of 200 mph and the Superbird was campaigned with incredible success and dominated the 1970 NASCAR season. Qualifying production quotas had been increased from 500 to 1,500

and Plymouth built a total of 1,920 Superbirds. Pete Hamilton won the 1970 Daytona 500 in a Superbird, at an average speed of nearly 150 mph and Superbirds were responsible for 21 out of Chrysler's 38 Grand National wins that year. NASCAR changed the rules in 1971, bringing the Superbird's reign, and production of the car itself, to an abrupt end. The brief but glorious life of the all-conquering Superbird assured it iconic status as the muscle car to end all muscle cars and it seems fairly safe to suggest that we shall not see its like again.

The daddy of all Pony Cars - the Ford Mustang - continued from strength to strength. A fastback coupe, the Boss 302, had been added to the line in '69. The Boss was a street version of the car

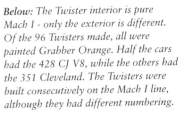

Below: The Twister interior is pure Mach I - only the exterior is different. Of the 96 Twisters made, all were painted Grabber Orange. Half the cars had the 428 CJ V8, while the others had the 351 Cleveland. The Twisters were built consecutively on the Mach I line, although they had different numbering.

that had dominated the Sports Car Club of America's Trans-American race program. The car was fitted with a 302 cu. in. "small block" V8 producing over 300 bhp and had its own, distinctive styling package. Less than 2,000 Bosses were built in '69 but more than 6,000 were produced in 1970. The price tag was $3,588. The Boss 429 cost $4,798, for which the purchaser got the "Cobra-Jet" 429 with aluminum heads and semi-hemisperical combustion chambers shoe-horned into a customized body. Ford abandoned racing in 1970, pulling out of the trans-Am, NASCAR, USAC and overseas competition. Sales were falling as the first Age of the Pony Car drew to a close; like the Titanic, powerful and magnificent, it was heading, inexorably, for the iceberg that was the oil crisis of the early '70s. Cars like the Superbee and the Boss Mustang were the last hurrah, but it's fascinating to wonder what heights might have been reached if the oil hadn't dried up and muscle hadn't gone out of style...

As things were, cars like the Maverick started to eat into Mustang sales, so what Ford lost in one market sector they gained in another. The Maverick started out, in 1970, as a 2-door compact with neat, fastback styling. Nimble rather than muscular, with 170 cu. in. 6-cylinder engine, it was a Diet Mustang, which was just what buyers were looking for, especially at a starting price of under $2,000. A determined advertising campaign pushed first-year sales to 579,000. A 4-door was added in '71, plus a more powerful 2-door, the Grabber, compete with a 302 cu. in., 210 hp, V8 option. Performance would never resemble that of the mighty Mustang but Ford were keen to stress the bloodline and the Grabber was graced with various refinements and trim options that emphasized its identity as a species of Mustang Lite. At the end of the model run in 1976, a Stallion version was introduced that mimicked the Mustang even more.

Above: The Mustang Boss was first introduced in '69, as a road-going version of the Mustangs that were doing so well in the Trans-American racing series. Although its 302 small block delivered an alleged 290bhp, estimates put it at more like 350. Only 1,934 were built in '69, and another 6,319 in '70. All of them had special striping, a front "chin" spoiler, a Mach I-style rear wing, and distinctive louvers on the rear windows.

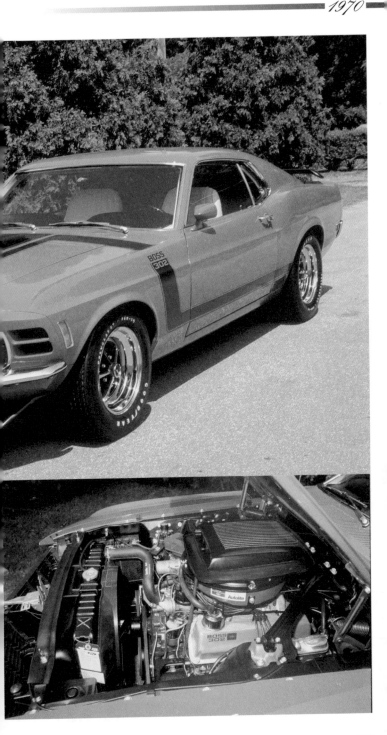

SPECIFICATIONS

**FORD PINTO
FASTBACK**

Engine:
Cast iron - 4 Cylinders
in line

Displacement:
98.6 cu. ins.

Bore and stroke:
3.19 x 3.06

Horsepower:
75

Body styles:
2 door sedan

No. of seats:
4

Weight (lbs):
1,949 lbs

Price:
$1,919

Produced:
288,606

Following the success of the Disneyland theme park in Anaheim, California, 1971 saw the opening of the much larger Disneyworld in Orlando, Florida. No doubt this was well received by kids all over the States, but young people in their late teens would probably have been more interested in the fact that henceforth, from age 18, they would be eligible to vote in all political elections.

People in the news that year included Muhammad Ali, who was cleared of draft dodging after his earlier refusal to join the army, which inevitably would have resulted in him being sent to Vietnam. The pardon allowed him to resume his successful boxing career. One person who would no receive a pardon, however, was cult leader Charles Manson, who was sentenced to death for the murder of actress Sharon Tate in 1969.

Meanwhile NASA had sent men to the moon again, but this time they had taken along a set of wheels for exploring the lunar landscape. The Lunar Rover gave the astronauts mobility, but it

was not the swoopy space vehicle of popular science fiction. Little more than a bare frame, it was fitted with a pair of seats and equipped with special wire-mesh wheels, driven by electric motors. However, it did the job, although it had to be left on the moon as the astronaut's spacecraft did not have the capacity to bring it back to earth.

Back on earth, toward the end of the year, GM recalled a record 6.7 million cars to rectify a problem with faulty engine mounts. On a more cheerful note, the styling of most Detroit cars was becoming a little more subdued, compared to previous years. However, while many of the designs were good, few of them were head-turners.

During the 1960s and 1970s, with increasingly restrictive legislation on emission control being introduced and the threat of an oil embargo, Ford remained reluctant to abandon the full-size sedan beloved of the American driver. This was very much due to the influence of Henry Ford II who, like his grandfather, was predisposed to stick with what worked rather than fix it. Eventually, Ford suffered for its reluctance to embrace change and the concept of "downsizing" and lost its lead to Chevrolet for a decade.

The Pinto debuted in 1971 as Ford's entry into the subcompact market. The larger Maverick had faired tolerably well and the Pinto's fastback styling echoed the Maverick—as the Maverick did the Mustang. The Chevrolet Vega

Below: The Pinto was Ford's 1971 entry into the small-car field. With a wheelbase of 94 inches, there was a choice of four cylinder engines with capacities of 98 cu.in. and 122 cu.in.

appeared in the same year and was a more innovative package then the Pinto. Unfortunately for Chevy, the Vega was also a lot less reliable and was easily outpaced in the sales race by Ford's little pony.

The original, L-head, 98.6 cu. ins. four cylinder engine produced 75bhp, but this was steadily improved, refined and generally beefed up until the last models could boast a base 140 cu. ins. engine producing 88bhp. An optional, 100bhp, 122 cu. ins. four was offered on early models.

Along with the power plant, the interior appointments of the car were improved considerably over the model run and a number of fun versions were produced. These included the "Woody" effect, a three-door Squire wagon and a "Cruisin'" wagon with blanked off rear windows and portholes.

Sales remained steady for the Pinto's ten year life, but it will be remembered, sadly, for a major flaw in the original design. The fuel tank had been positioned far in the rear of the car and the filler-neck design was poor. This rendered the Pinto vulnerable to fire in the event of a rear-end collision and a number of highly-publicized fatalities resulted from it. Ford, ill-advisedly, resisted the resultant lawsuits right up to the Federal Court. It did their corporate reputation no good in the process and left the Pinto with the unenviable reputation of being "the barbecue that seats four."

Below: The Cadillac Eldorado convertible of 1971 was the first open-top Eldo since '66 and thereby the first to feature front-wheel drive, which had been pioneered in the '67 Eldorado Coupe.

Above: The Oldsmobile 4-4-2 fell on hard times in the '70s, as did most other muscle cars. It was considerably tamer than it had been, because of much stricter pollution controls.

1972

SPECIFICATIONS

LINCOLN CONTINENTAL MARK IV

Engine:
V8 - cast iron block

Displacement:
460 cu. ins.

Bore and stroke:
4.36 x 3.85

Horsepower:
212

Body styles:
Hardtop coupe

No. of seats:
5

Weight (lbs):
5,362

Price:
$10,194

Produced:
57,316

Above Right: The Lincoln Continental Mark IV exhibited sharp styling from every angle. With a new, longer frame and a completely new body, it incorporated many features of the successful Mark III, including the large chromed grille, fold-away head lights and the Continental spare hump on the trunk. The Mark III had sold well, but the Mark IV did even better, outselling the rival Cadillac Eldorado for the first time.

With every move geared towards securing a second term in The White House, in many respects, 1972 was a good year for Richard Nixon. He got off to a good start by visiting communist China in February; in June he had a summit meeting with Soviet leader Brezhnev; and he was pulling American troops out of Vietnam. However, in June an event came to light that no doubt Nixon would have preferred to remain secret. It was some time before he was directly linked to the burglary of the Democratic Party's headquarters in Washington's Watergate Building and, in the meantime, he had won the sought-after second term. But when the truth came out, he had no choice but to go. Out of office and in disgrace, he retired to his home in California, but eventually he would bounce back, becoming a venerated elder statesman.

The Watergate scandal would rumble on for many months but, in September, Americans had

good reason to be proud. At the Munich Olympics, swimmer Mark Spitz picked up seven gold medals, while Bobby Fischer beat Boris Spassky to become the first American World Chess Champion.

In Detroit, Ford's Lincoln division also had reason to be proud. 1972 saw the launch of the Continental Mark IV, replacing the Mark III, which had been introduced in 1968 as a direct competitor to the Cadillac Eldorado, achieving immediate success. The luxurious 2-door coupe was originally conceived on the 117 inch wheelbase Ford Thunderbird perimeter frame. It

Above: Ford restyled its dual-purpose car-based pickup, the Ranchero, for 1972, adopting the Coke-bottle shape that was prevalent in standard automobiles at the time. As always, the Ranchero provided the comfort of a car with the load-carrying ability of a truck, but its days were numbered by the arrival of the much cheaper Japanese mini-trucks that had almost as much load space.

utilized portions of the T-bird's cowl and roof but, for the Mark IV, designer Wes Dahlberg used a new 120.4 inch perimeter frame, giving the car greater

Above & Below: For 1972, Chrysler continued with the "fuselage" styling they had introduced in 1969, as this New Yorker 2-door hardtop (above) and Brougham 4-door hardtop (below) illustrate. The smooth rounded sides accentuated the car's length, while a massive expanse of hood did the same for its width.

luxury and style.

The styling clues of the Mark III were continued, however: the classic long hood/short deck proportions; the prominent Rolls-Royce-like grille flanked by fold-away head lights; the tall, slightly rounded sides; the low roofline and Continental spare hump in the trunk lid. Because of the longer wheelbase, the rear roof pillar was wider than that of the Mark III, and Dahlberg put this to good use by incorporating an oval opera window.

In keeping with the car's luxury status, the Mark IV was richly upholstered with "loose cushion" seats, while the dashboard was designed to reduce injury in an accident. As an added safety feature, sturdy crash rails were incorporated in the doors.

Power for the Mark IV came from the same engine used in the Mark III: a 460 cu.in. big-block V8 that was rated a 212 horsepower; and the engine also used in the Continental sedan. The Mark IV also shared the sedan's drivetrain and coil-spring suspension.

It was an immediate success; the Mark III had sold well against the Eldorado, but the Mark IV outsold it and continued to do so for the next two years. The car's popularity generated intense owner loyalty, many remaining with the same owners for years, providing a degree of luxury and style that

Below: 72's Dodge Charger basked in the reflected glory of the Daytona. This 500 Hardtop coupe cost less than $3,000 in standard trim - with a 110 hp, six cylinder engine - but options included the 440 cu. ins. V8.

American manufacturers eventually ceased to offer.

The Mark IV would remain in production until 1976 but, as the years passed, exhaust emissions equipment would strangle the engine and heavy energy-absorbing bumpers would add to the car's weight, reducing performance. Even so, the Mark IV remained a winner until the end. Production peaked at 69,437 in 1973, and reached 56,110 in 1976, indicating just how popular the car was.

Below: The '72 Dodge Monaco concealed its headlights but could hardly hide its bulk.; even the 2-door coupe weighed close on 4,000 lbs. Standard power was down to 175 bhp, provided by a 360 cu. in. V8.

SPECIFICATIONS

PONTIAC FIREBIRD TRANS AM

Engine:
V8 - cast iron block

Displacement:
455 cu. ins.

Bore and stroke:
4.15 x 4.21

Horsepower:
250 (optional 310)

Body styles:
Coupe

No. of seats:
4

Weight (lbs):
3,504 lbs

Price:
$4,204

Produced:
4,802

By just about any yardstick, 1973 wasn't exactly a vintage year – although the signing of the Vietnam War ceasefire agreement on January 27 seemed to indicate that there was some cause for optimism. Unfortunately, the aftermath of the Watergate break-in was about to engulf The White House and both President Nixon and Vice President Spiro Agnew resigned following a tax evasion scandal. And, if this upheaval wasn't demoralizing enough, there was the oil crisis caused by the OPEC embargo which resulted in long queues at gas stations. The automobile industry was further hampered by the imposition of a nationwide 55mph speed limit.

Given those circumstances, it would seem

unlikely that a car born in the youth-driven Sixties – when performance was everything and fuel economy didn't matter – could even survive, let alone nearly double its sales. But the Pontiac Firebird has always been a rather special automobile and, anyway, nobody ever said there was much logic in the reasons people had for choosing which car to buy.

In many respects, it is actually quite remarkable that there was a '73 Firebird at all, given the situation in 1972. Pontiac faced problems on several fronts, the most damaging for the

Above: The Pontiac Firebird Trans Am came bedecked with spoilers, air dams, scoops and flares for '73, but in its best form – the SD-455 – it was capable of over 130mph and could handle corners well too. However, its braking capability was deemed to be rather marginal for such a high performance car. The Trans Am's giant "screaming chicken" hood decal appeared for the first time in '73 and quickly became the trademark of all Firebird models. Designer John Schinella was responsible for getting the motif approved by the GM's head of styling, Bill Mitchell.

Above: The Sting Ray had urethane plastic covers over steel bumpers to comply with federally mandated "5mph" bumpers. The extra two inches in length was more acceptable than the 35 pounds in weight. Extra insulation reduced noise as the Corvette became more of a long-distance freeway cruiser.

Above: The first major styling change to the Sting Ray came in '73 but the rear view of the Chevy didn't look much different from previous years. The famed LT1 high performance engine was dropped, and new top spec was a 454 cu.in. LS4 that produced 275bhp.

was, there is little wonder that there was considerable pressure from the GM boardroom to drop the model from the catalog altogether.

Further complications arose from the increased number of Federal safety regulations being introduced and the power-sapping emission control systems required – all of which tended to work against the pony car brigade. It was as if the fun had been taken out of driving and, as a result, many of the cars being produced lost their individuality as the design and engineering teams struggled to incorporate the new changes dictated by legislation.

It is no surprise to learn, therefore, that the '73 Firebird showed few obvious alterations from the previous year. Well, unless you look at the hood of the Trans Am that is! Nobody could possibly miss that huge "screaming chicken" decal which has since become the enduring symbol of the Firebird. The idea for the gigantic stick-on had

Firebird line being a five month-long strike by the United Auto Workers union at the Norwood, Ohio, plant where the cars were built. By the time the stoppage ended in September, the losses amounted to thousands of cars representing millions of dollars that the company could ill-afford. With the situation as it

originally come from chief designer Bill Porter and his assistant Wayne Vieira for a pair of show cars being prepared in 1970. However, GM's tyrannical head of styling, Bill Mitchell, took an instant dislike to the big bird and put a stop to it being used.

Bill Porter was promoted in '71 and in his place came young designer, John Schinella, who set about resurrecting the huge hood motif and managed to persuade Mitchell to accept it. Schinella redesigned the decal so it differed from the smaller version that had appeared on the nose of earlier cars and the Porter /Vieira design that Mitchell objected to. The name of the artist responsible for the very first rendition of the Firebird logo remains unknown, simply for the fact that it was copied from a mural on the wall at the airport of Phoenix, Arizona! But that initial design was far more traditional in execution and was

Above: In '73, full-sized cars like this Ford LTD 2-door hard top were pretty hefty animals, stretching to over 17 feet long and tipping the scales at nearly two tons. In retrospect, it's hard to believe that LTD was voted Car of the Year by Road Test *magazine, but with over 941,000 full-size Custom/Galaxie/LTD models sold in 1973, there were obviously plenty of willing customers.*

only used as a small decorative feature on the fenders and rear of '68 and '69 models.

For a model that started out in 1967 as basically a Chevrolet Camaro with a nose job and a different rear end, the Firebird quickly developed its own separate identity, partly thanks to some clever styling work – initially by Pontiac's head of design, Jack Humbert, followed by Bill Porter. Skillful engineering of the suspension and drivetrain,

and the use of Pontiac's own range of engines helped to establish this identity all the more. However, the Pontiac powerplants did face one draw back when it came to calling the model, Trans

Below: The mid-size Ford Torino was a big hit with buyers in the early '70s, while fuel prices were sky high, but as gas came down in price, the Torino gradually fell out of favor.

Am, after the race series of the same name – the V8s were all of too big a capacity to run in the championship.

The highly successful Trans Am series was organized by the Sports Car Club of America (SCCA) and, in the 1960s, it attracted a lot of media attention and factory-backed entries of Ford Mustangs, Chevy Camaros, Mercury Cougars, AMC Javelins and others. But the 303 cu.in. maximum limit on engine size presented Pontiac with a problem in that their smallest production V8 displaced 350 cu.in. In a bid to get round the regulations, Pontiac co-operated with the T/G Racing Team of Jerry Titus and Terry Godsall who entered "Canadian" Firebirds (actually Camaros with Pontiac front sheet metal) equipped with Chevy 302 cu.in. engines. After a while, Pontiac produced a special destroked version of the 400 cu.in. engine and managed to convince SCCA officials that this was going into series production, and so allowing them entry to the series. However, with this hurdle overcome, winning was to prove elusive.

As it happened, track success wasn't necessary for the Firebird Trans Am to be triumphant on the street and, after its low key introduction in '69, the model went on to evolve into a great American sports car. Bedecked with spoilers, air dams, hood scoops and flares, the Trans Am looked just like a race car should, and handled better than most of the competition too. From 1971 onwards, the only engine available was the 455 cu.in. V8 and, if by '73 its power had been strangled down to a meek-sounding 290 horsepower for the optional Super Duty version (250hp was standard), there was still sufficient "grunt" to give some seat-of-the-pants excitement when the right hand pedal was pushed to the floor in anger.

Exactly how well the people at Pontiac had preserved the Trans Am's performance in the face of the ever-increasing restrictive legislation can be judged by contemporary road test

reports. *Hot Rod* magazine cranked out a 13.54 second quarter mile at 104 mph, while *Car & Driver* were only a fraction slower at 13.75 secs and 103 mph. These were impressive numbers by any standards, and *Car & Driver* also made the point that the '73 Trans Am was actually quicker than the 1970 version with 340 horsepower on tap. It is no wonder that the SD-455 has become something of a legend among Firebird enthusiasts ever since.

And it wasn't just the car's capability to go fast in a straight line that *C&D* liked; the Trans Am was just as quick off the mark when going round corners: "...the Trans Am's second most endearing quality – next to its ability to out-accelerate anything not assisted by a rocket motor – is handling." They were

less than happy with the brakes on a car timed at 132 mph though, and suggested that the semi-metallic front brake pads from the heavy duty Police Package were a must. The report concluded: "The Firebird Trans Am is a genus of an automotive species approaching extinction. It could be the last of its kind. Just the car you need to carry you through the upcoming years of automotive sterility..." With the benefit of hindsight, perhaps it is only now that we can fully appreciate that this statement was really quite an amazing piece of prophetic writing.

The 1973 Pontiac Firebird Trans Am was virtually the final fling of the mass produced, cheap, high performance car for a couple of decades. And, even over twenty years later, it remains as an

Above & Below: '73 Cadillacs were huge and heavy and heading for a fall in the shape of the oil crisis, but well over 200,00 De Villes still found homes.

exceptional example of just how good an American sports coupe can be, no matter what obstacles are imposed by the law makers.

SPECIFICATIONS

PLYMOUTH ROAD RUNNER

Engine:
V8 - cast iron block

Displacement:
318 cu. ins.

Bore and stroke:
3.91

Horsepower:
170

Body styles:
Coupe

No. of seats:
5

Weight (lbs):
3,615 lbs

Price:
$3,545

Produced:
11,555

Above Right: Engine-wise, the top Road Runner option for 1974 was the four-barrel-equipped 440 cu.in. V8 that delivered 280 horsepower. The capacity of the engine was lettered on the hood, while bold stripes were applied to the sides and roof pillars. The 440 engine came with an automatic transmission only.

In politics, 1974 was a year of change. Watergate had finally caught up with Richard Nixon, who resigned from the Presidency on August 8. His replacement, Vice President Gerald Ford, pardoned him a month later.

Another event of that year was the kidnapping of heiress Patty Hearst, who promptly joined her kidnappers to take part in a bank robbery. There was violence in Boston over the bussing of black students; and pioneer aviator Charles Lindberg died.

There was good news on the automotive front in that OPEC had lifted their oil embargo of the United States, but sadly it came too late to save the big-bodied, big-engined, gas-guzzling American automobile that so many had come to love. Faced with stringent exhaust emissions regulations and the rising price of gasoline, Detroit had no choice but to turn its back on the type of cars it had traditionally built. Intermediate models, compacts and subcompacts with cleaner, smaller, more economical engines were the order of the day. While the majority of them would prove to be

efficient means of transportation, few would have the sort of guts, glitz and sheer personality of what had gone before. The new 1974 models heralded the dawn of another era and, for a while, things looked bleak.

The muscle cars which had appeared with the Mustang a decade before were among the casualties. Some had already ceased production, while the rest would not linger for long.

Chrysler, through its Dodge and Plymouth divisions, had been a major contender in the muscle car wars for some years, building a range of machines based on its intermediate models. These were real fire-breathing street-'n'-strip monsters: no-frills quart-er-mile machines with powerful engines, four-speed manual transmissions and beefed-up rear ends and suspensions. Engines included the awesome 425 horsepower 426 hemi V8 and the 390

horsepower 44 Six Pack engine, equipped with three two-barrel carburetors. The no-frills approach allowed Chrysler to price them for the younger market, while spectacular successes in NASCAR and drag racing helped boost sales. Included in the Dodge Scat Pack and Plymouth Rapid Transit System were the Dodge Super Bee and Charger, and the Plymouth GTX and Road Runner. But, by 1974, strangled by emissions equipment and dogged by high running costs, such cars were no longer selling well.

Typical of these Chrysler products was the Plymouth Road Runner. Based on the "fuselage-styled" Satellite body shell, it came with a 170 horsepower small-block 318 cu.in. V8 as standard, which had replaced its previous 400 cu.in. big-block engine in 1973. For the first time on the Road Runner, the engine was fitted with a two-barrel

carburetor. The normal transmission was a three-speed manual, although a four-speed and automatic were options. Also optional were 360, 400 and 440 cu.in. engines.

By now, looks were more important than power, and the car sported bold contrasting stripes that curved down from the rear roof pillars and along the waist line to the front edges of the front fenders. Its looks may have promised more than its standard drivetrain could deliver but, nevertheless, it was the last true Road Runner. In 1975, it would be based on the small Fury, and after that became merely an options package for the Volare.

A couple of familiar Dodge model names were dropped from the catalog listings during 1974. The Polara series was discontinued but the Challenger name also disappeared – although it returned in 1978 on a Japanese import version, showing the direction things were headed.

Above & Right: In 1974, Chrysler introduced a new 2-door hardtop, the New Yorker Brougham St. Regis, which featured formal fixed-position rear quarter windows for greater privacy. Inside, the individually-adjustable bench seats came in white as standard, with either gold or black accents.

Right Below: The shape of things to come. Ford's original muscle car, the Mustang, had already been transformed into its new, "more respectable" form. Mustang II was down in size, down on power and down in charisma. Some of the original styling cues were still there – the protruding grille, the side moldings and the running horse emblem – but it was not enough to give the car the raw excitement of the original. Nor were the engines: a 140 cu.in. overhead-cam four and a 171 cu.in. V6. In time, Mustang II would receive a V8 and various trim packages to make it look more aggressive but, even then, it would

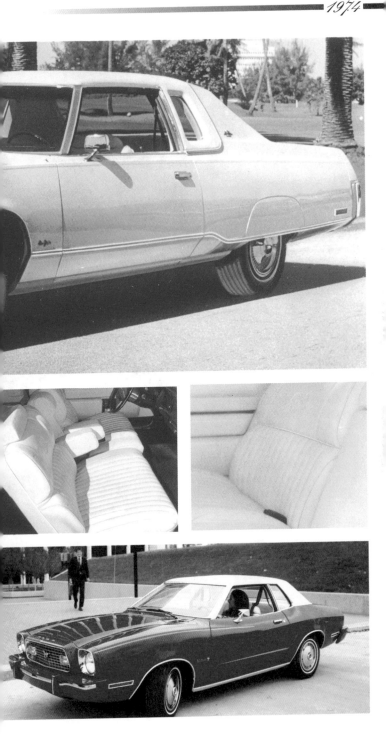

SPECIFICATIONS

AMC PACER

Engine:
Cast iron - 6 Cylinders
in line

Displacement:
232 cu. ins.

Bore and stroke:
3.75 x 3.5

Horsepower:
100

Body styles:
Hatchback sedan

No. of seats:
4

Weight (lbs):
2,995 lbs

Price:
$3,299

Produced:
72,158

If there had ever been a competition to select the most unique car of the 1970s, a leading contender for the title would have to be the AMC Pacer. And, as with the Gremlin five years earlier, the American Motors Corporation's "Philosophy of Difference" was to pay handsome dividends initially. The Pacer was the first completely new model from AMC in some years, but the car that eventually made it into production was quite different from the model that was originally planned.

With its vast areas of glass and rounded styling, the Pacer is often referred to as a goldfish bowl and even the factory press release of the time called it "a car that breaks with automotive design tradition" – something of an understatement to say the least. Leaving the Pacer's unusual appearance aside for a moment, it was the engine under that steeply sloping short hood that created the problems for the independent AMC when deciding to bring such a radical car to the marketplace. The intention at the outset of the highly innovative

project was that the Pacer should be front-wheel-drive and have a Wankel rotary engine, yet neither of these futuristic ideas made it into the finished car.

Although the Wankel was a very compact and powerful unit for its size, the problem was that the revolutionary engine couldn't achieve the sort of gas mileage figures that buyers were now looking for from smaller cars. Of course, AMC didn't have the research and development resources (or the finances) to build a rotary engine of its own from scratch, so the plan was to buy in engines from General Motors who were proposing to use the Wankel in a number of models. The oil crisis of '73 meant that GM dropped the rotary, which instigated the need for a major re-evaluation at American Motors.

They decided to take a step backward

Above: A massive "B" pillar was needed to accommodate the Pacer's unique arrangement of having the passenger door 4 inches wider than the driver's. A large rear liftgate provided easy access to nearly 30 cubic feet of carrying space with the rear seat folded down. Slot-style wheels were only available on the Pacer "X," but an extensive list of optional extras were available and it is estimated that each Pacer sold had more than $1,000 worth of extras added to the advertised price of $3,299.

and shoehorn the reliable old 232 cu.in. straight-six engine into the Pacer, at the same time reverting to a traditional rear-wheel-drive format. While the drivetrain components were readily available from the AMC parts bin, squeezing them into the Pacer required considerable re-engineering and the bulkhead had to be

completely revised. The six fitted, barely, with the rear sparkplug virtually inaccessible as it was hidden away under the cowl. Despite the retrograde running gear, some new technology survived, notably the rack and pinion steering and electronic ignition. Overdrive was offered as an optional extra.

However, it's styling that sells cars, and the Pacer's looks were guaranteed to create an enormous amount of interest. Billed as "the first wide small car," the Pacer sat on a 100 inch wheelbase (only 6 inches longer than a Volkswagen Beetle), but at 77 inches wide it was a whopping 16 inches more from side to side than the VW. In other words, the

Above: The high-performance limited-edition Chevrolet Cosworth Vega engine featured 16-valves, a DOHC cylinder head, Bendix electronic fuel injection and stainless steel exhaust headers. It developed 120 horsepower from the 122 cu.in. four banger. With close-ratio four-speed manual transmission and heavy duty suspension, the Cosworth Vega was only available in black with gold highlights and matching wheels. Priced at almost double the base model, only 2,061 Cosworth variants were sold

compact-length Pacer gave passengers the same internal space as an intermediate model like the Chevrolet

Chevelle. The concept was the brainchild of AMC stylist Richard Teague, who overcame opposition within the company to pursue his vision for the car with zealous determination.

Apart from the low beltline and obvious expanse of glass used in the design, one totally unique feature of the Pacer is the fact that the passenger door is nearly four inches longer than the driver's door! The idea behind this oddball arrangement was that it made for easier entry and exit, with door hinges that tilted outward as they opened to give even better access. A basic part of the body design was the massive "B" pillar (described as having the same characteristics as a roll bar), which was used to connect the rear subassembly and the forward unit construction section together.

Announced at the Chicago Auto Show in March 1975, the Pacer created something of a sensation. Extensive media coverage had people flocking to the AMC showrooms and 96,769 Pacers were sold – the bubble-shaped car was an outstanding hit. Sadly, although the Pacer provided a much-needed boost to American Motors' sagging sales figures, it wasn't enough to prevent the company from recording a loss of $27.5 million, and things were set to get much worse from then.

SPECIFICATIONS

**CHEVROLET
CORVETTE Z37
COUPE**

Engine:
V8 - cast iron block

Displacement:
350

Bore and stroke:
4.0 x 3.48

Horsepower:
180 - 210

Body styles:
Coupe

No. of seats:
2

Weight (lbs):
3,445 lbs

Price:
$7,605

Produced:
46,558

This being the bicentennial, marking 200 years of American independence, the fourth of July took on an extra special significance and there were countless celebrations across the country to commemorate the occasion. But, as well as all the fireworks and parades, there were also quite a few departures in 1976: Oil tycoon J. Paul Getty died, as did eccentric billionaire Howard Hughes and film director Busby Berkeley. The death of Chinese leader Mao Tse-tung in September sparked off a power struggle in that vast nation. Meanwhile, in one of the closest elections of the century,

Republican Gerald Ford was ousted from the White House when Democratic nominee Jimmy Carter was elected as President.

As far as the auto industry was concerned, there was one type of model that was due to become a thing of the past in '76 – the convertible. The demise of the ragtop had been widely predicted as a consequence of the increasingly vocal demands from consumer pressure groups for improved safety in car design

Above: *The Corvette was only available as a coupe in '76 – the convertible had been dropped the previous year due to the threat of safety legislation outlawing ragtops, although the removable roof panels did allow open-top motoring. Thankfully, the ban never happened and convertibles are still on sale. That apart, the 1976 model Vette saw only small revisions to the preceding year, but it was a fairly lackluster version of a once great sports car.*

313

and proposed federal roll-over strength regulations. Indeed, only one major manufacturer, Cadillac, still listed a convertible in their catalog, and the company declared that the 1976 Eldorado would be the last such model to be built.

This generated a huge amount of publicity and speculators clamored to buy the car, convinced it would become an instant "classic" that they would be able to sell on at a big profit. Some people did make money from buying and selling the Eldorado convertible, particularly Cadillac, who sold 14,000 of them – over 5,000 more than they produced the previous year.

If the Eldorado ragtop wasn't exactly rare in 1976, it wasn't the last convertible either. A number of specialists soon began offering to chop the roof off an Eldorado coupe and Cadillac themselves would bring the model back

in 1984. Today the convertible can be found in just about every dealership. And although the Eldorado still sat on a full-size 126 inch wheelbase, stretched to more than 18 feet 8 inches in length, tipped the scales at well over 5,000 pounds and was powered by a 500 cu.in. V8 (the largest car engine in production), there were signs that the days of the mammoth Cadillac were numbered.

The most obvious indication that things were changing at Cadillac was the arrival of the Seville, introduced mid year as a '76 model and on sale in the showrooms from May 1975. A thousand pounds lighter, 27 inches shorter and 8 inches narrower than a Sedan deVille, the Seville was designed to take on European luxury cars such as Mercedes. Despite being more expensive than the full-size Cadillacs (it was nearly $1,500 more than an Eldorado convertible) the Seville 4-door sedan

ound plenty of customers, with over 4,700 built during '76. It helped to stablish a new annual record total for he marque.

Based on the GM corporate "X" platform and using an Oldsmobile-designed 350 cu.in. V8 equipped with electronic fuel injection, the downsized Seville was a refined package that offered European-style ride and performance combined with the luxury expected in a Cadillac. Acceleration time from zero to 60mph was 11.5 seconds, and it had a top speed of 115mph, but of almost equal importance was the fuel mileage statistic of 15-17mpg. Virtually all '76 Sevilles came with a vinyl-covered padded roof because it was easier to cover up the modified Chevrolet Nova panels on the assembly line rather than spend a lot of time getting the sheet metal smooth enough to be painted.

No doubt many of the bicentennial celebration parades included a new 1976 Eldorado convertible somewhere in the lineup and they will probably continue to appear in lots of future pageants. But the reality is that the only way this Cadillac could be considered as "the last convertible" is if it is positioned at the very rear of the motorcade.

Below: Massively over-hyped and massive in almost every other sense, the Eldorado convertible was far from being "the last of the breed" as claimed by Cadillac in their advertising. Thanks to speculators trying to cash in on the model's "instant classic" status, prices zoomed to ridiculous heights. Demand boosted sales by over 50%, destroying the model's rarity value. Cadillac re-introduced a convertible in 1984, which also served to diminish the desirability of the gargantuan '76 ragtop.

SPECIFICATIONS

LINCOLN CONTINENTAL MARK V

Engine:
V8 - cast iron block

Displacement:
400 cu. ins.

Bore and stroke:
4.0 x 4.0

Horsepower:
179

Body styles:
Hardtop coupe

No. of seats:
5

Weight (lbs):
4,567 lbs

Price:
$11,396

Produced:
80,321

At first glance, if you were looking for an automotive styling or engineering revolution in '77, the last car you would consider would be the Lincoln Continental Mark V. Indeed, that initial look would probably have convinced you that the new Mark V was bigger – and therefore heavier – than ever before. But appearances can be deceptive and, although it is true that the overall length had increased by a couple of inches, the wheelbase remained unchanged at 120.4 inches the weight was actually down by around 400 pounds when compared to the Mark IV of a year earlier.

By saving that amount of weight on a full-size family sedan you might expect to see some significant improvements in performance and gas mileage. However, even after putting the gigantic Lincoln luxury 2-door cruiser on a strict diet it still showed an unhealthy appetite for fuel, struggling to better 10 miles per gallon. The reason for this was twofold. Firstly, the Mark V was still a very heavy car, and could easily top 5,000 pounds by the time it was ready to hit the road. Secondly, the standard engine had been downsized to a 400 cu.in. V8 (an enlarged version of the 351 cu.in. Ford Cleveland unit) that produced just 181bhp when fitted with all the emission control equipment required in California. The 460 cu.in. engine however, was still available as an option.

As far as the styling goes, the changes to the Continental Mark V could best be described as evolutionary rather than revolutionary. Its heritage was immediately identifiable, but designer Don

Above: The Lincoln Continental Mark V was new in 1977, although in reality there was little about the model that could be described as being different from its predecessor. At a time when most cars were getting smaller, the Mark V actually grew two inches in length. However, there were some reductions – a marked saving in weight and the base engine was now "only" 400 cu.in., though the behemoth Lincoln remained a heavyweight gas guzzler. Even so, over 80,000 drivers were not to be denied and their choice helped keep a smile on the faces of the dealers.

DeLaRossa had cleverly accentuated the angularity of the lines by replacing rounded corners with sharp edges in key places. Other noticeable Mark V exterior features included three louvers introduced behind each front wheel arch, body side moldings dropped down by a few inches and the vertically arranged taillights.

Four model variations that did carry over were those in the special edition Designer Series. Renowned fashion designers Bill Blass, Cartier, Hubert de Givency and Emilio Pucci each gave their names to a model finished in a distinctive body color and upholstery combination. The Cartier was fairly muted, using dove gray paint with a matching vinyl roof and leather interior, while the Givency came with metallic dark jade paintwork, chamois, vinyl roof and dark jade leather. The Bill Blass used midnight blue paint and chamois, and the Pucci was painted in black diamond fire with white vinyl and leather. Other items fitted as standard on the Designer Series models were the gold-finished instrument panel, dual vanity mirrors and turbine-style aluminum wheels.

But if the bulky Mark V seemed to be slightly out of step with what was happening in the world, there were still plenty of people for whom "big was beautiful" and the Lincoln dealers found no less than 80,321 customers willing to pay for this gas guzzler. Less successful, by a long way, was Lincoln's belated 1977 answer to the Cadillac Seville – the Versailles. Based on the Ford Granada/Mercury Monarch platform, the Versailles only lasted until 1980 and never came close to capturing the compact luxury market in the same way as the Seville.

Yet, even though the enormous Continental Mark V was an undoubted hit in 1977, the most worrying figure for the US auto industry was the 2.1 million imported vehicles that were flooding in to the country. This represented 20% of the sales total, and most of the foreign models were in the compact and subcompact market sectors where fuel-efficiency was more important than flashy special editions. This dominance caused Ford's small car factories to close early for the annual model changeover.

The giants on wheels might have been slow in disappearing from the freeways, but all too many giants of the entertainment world were departing and leaving huge gaps in American society that would prove impossible to fill. The biggest loss of all, and grieved around the globe, was when Elvis Presley died, aged 42, on August 16. Other icons who passed away were Bing Crosby, Charlie Chaplin and Groucho Marx.

SPECIFICATIONS

CHEVROLET CORVETTE SILVER ANNIVERSARY

Engine:
V8 - cast iron block

Displacement:
350 cu. ins.

Bore and stroke:
4.0 x 3.48

Horsepower:
210

Body styles:
Coupe

No. of seats:
2

Weight (lbs):
3,401 lbs

Price:
$10,000

Produced:
2,500

Facelifts were very much in vogue this year, along with changes of model names. Some manufacturers introduced new names on what were basically revamped versions of '77 models, while others brought back old names from the past. It was all part of an attempt to persuade the buying public that what they were looking at was something totally different from last year's model and, in most cases, it worked pretty well. Otherwise, the status quo remained very much as before. Chevrolet's production fell slightly, while Ford's increased, though not enough to topple Chevy from the number one position in the sales charts.

It was Ford's 75th Anniversary and they marked the event by introducing Diamond Jubilee editions

Above: *1978 was the Corvette's 25th birthday. This momentous event was marked by a special Silver Anniversary edition and a much-plagiarized Indy Pace Car Replica - both effectively paint & sticker jobs. The real change was the new fastback styling incorporating a huge, steeply raked, wraparound rear window.*

Left: *The Silver Anniversary Corvette was pretty much like every other '78 Corvette except for the paint job, a badge or two - and around $3,000 on the price.*

Above: This was the final year for the monster New Yorker Brougham before it was downsized, and sales of big Chryslers slumped 35% in '78. The base engine was large enough at 400 cu.in., but the old 440 cu.in. V8 was still available as an option for this luxury leviathan. Priced at nearly $8,000, it is no wonder that only 9,624 of these dinosaur 2-door coupes were sold.

of the Lincoln Mark V and Thunderbird. More pleasing to investors was the announcement of record profits in the first half of the year. The compact Fairmont was a newcomer to replace the ailing Maverick and sold extremely well, equaling the figures of the Mustang's first year. In addition, the Fiesta was shipped in from Europe to compete in the subcompact sector. However, Ford

didn't enjoy a trouble-free '78 – there were recalls for more than 4 million vehicles (including the infamous problem with exploding gas tanks on the Pinto), which damaged the company's reputation. And in June, Henry Ford II fired company president Lee Iacocca, which indirectly set in motion the resurgence of Chrysler after Iacocca took over the helm of that troubled organiz-ation in November.

Over at Chevrolet, the second genera-tion Camaro had received its third – and final – facelift, featuring a new grille and taillights with soft, integrated bum-pers in the body color. The nose-job worked, and Camaro sales leapt to over 272,000 (up from 218,000 in '77), which was very encouraging, especially as this reworking was only an interim

Above: The AMC Concord was little
more than a made-over Hornet pushed
upmarket and sold as a plush, but
economical, compact family car with
the slogan "The luxury Americans want
– The size America needs." The 2-door
sedan was the best-selling Concord
model with a base price of $3749. It
accounted for almost half of the 121,
293 units produced, over 110,000 of
which were powered by a six-cylinder
engine. Curious styling of a small
triangular side window and a thick B-
post was presumably an attempt to
disguise rather ancient Hornet body
origins.

measure pending the arrival of a
completely new model in 1982. Part of
the Camaro's success was down to its
ever-increasing list of optional extras,
which included numerous choices of
wheels and tires, power-assistance on
almost everything and even a variety of
radios. But probably the most important
option included in '78 was the T-top
with removable glass roof panels, at a
cost of $625.

The Z28 Camaro had reappeared in
'77 (having been dropped in 1974), but
the 1978 version obviously caught the
imagination of enthusiasts as sales
multiplied more than threefold. The

revised Z28 featured a hood scoop with a pointed throat highlighted black, functional louvers behind the front wheel arches, a rear spoiler and special graphics. Engine was a 350 cu.in. V8 with a four-barrel carb and dual exhaust that would put out 170 horsepower as sold in California, but 5-10bhp more in

other states. Californian Z28s could also only be purchased with an automatic transmission, but a stick-shift

Left: In keeping with its rival, the Chevy Blazer, the four-wheel-drive Ford Bronco grew by a foot in the wheelbase and was now based on the F-150 pickup chassis. The new Bronco was ten inches wider, five inches higher and over two feet longer than the original, and could seat six adults. Standard engine was a 351 cu.in. V8. Ford sold more trucks than anyone else in 1978, but was still running second to Chevrolet in the car market..

was available elsewhere.

AMC were still down at the bottom of the ladder in 12th place but, thanks to their Jeep subsidiary, did better than expected. Of the four AMC model lines, three were virtually unchanged, while the compact Hornet was turned into a more luxurious car called the Concord. It became AMC's best seller of the year but the rest of the range continued to decline and the company began negotiations with French auto-maker

tation of the Corporate Average Fuel Economy (CAFE) regulations that specified each company should achieve a set fuel economy figure across its entire model range. The standard set in '78 was 18 miles per gallon, with a target of 27.5 mpg to be reached in ten years time.

Left & Below: The Mustang King Cobra was eye-catching if nothing else. It might not appeal to everybody's taste, but as a "limited edition" it didn't have to: exclusivity was the name of the game.

Below: Is it a pony? Is it a python? The Mustang King Cobra was one of a bewildering range of option packages on offer. These off-the-shelf customs sometimes actually featured enhanced performance equipment and sometimes were exercises in paint and decal engineering. However, they anticipated the "personalization" of the the mass-produced automobile which has now become a powerful marketing tool.

Renault with a view to arranging a co-operation deal. This agreement would culminate in Renault becoming a major stockholder in AMC by the end of 1979.

One thing that affected all manuf-acturers in 1978 was the implemen-

1979

SPECIFICATIONS

**FORD MUSTANG
PACE CAR**

Engine:
V8 - cast iron block

Displacement:
302 cu. ins.

Bore and stroke:
4.0 x 3.0

Horsepower:
140

Body styles:
Coupe

No. of seats:
4

Weight (lbs):
2,588 lbs

Price:
$5,000+

Produced:
6,000

The year started with President Jimmy Carter announcing "a crisis of confidence" in a half hour television address to the nation during which he unveiled a six-point plan to combat America's wasteful consumption of oil. His statement was precipitated by the Organisation of Petroleum Exporting Countries (OPEC) increasing the price of a barrel of oil by almost 25% in three months. Carter's conservation program was designed to reduce oil imports and speed up the development of alternative methods of producing energy, with

Below: The third-generation of Ford Mustang arrived in 1979 and the new shape proved to be an immediate hit, boosting model sales by over 80%. Pace cars used for the Indy 500 race used highly modified 302 cu.in. V8 engines, but replicas sold to the public could have either a turbo four-cylinder or a 5-liter V8. Front air dam with integral foglamps, non-functional rear-facing hood scoop and sunroof were standard features on Pace Car models, together with a special paint scheme, but the factory left lettering decals to be affixed by the dealer or the customer.

the target of saving 4.5 million barrels of oil a day by the end of the next decade.

Unfortunately, one of the possible alternative sources of energy – nuclear power – suffered a major setback following a disaster at the Three Mile Island facility in Pennsylvania. The accident, caused by a faulty cooling system, released radioactive gases and further reinforced the protests by

Above: A rear spoiler was another item fitted to the Pace Car replica. The third generation Mustang was available as what Ford called a 2-door sedan or a 3-door hatchback in '79; a convertible didn't arrive until the '83 model. Almost 2.5 million Mustangs were sold between 1979 and 1992, with only minor changes made to the front and rear of the body.

antinuclear campaigners.

In addition to the energy problems, President Carter was also facing difficulties in the financial sector, with soaring inflation and wildly fluctuating interest rates adding to his worries. The consumer price index jumped by 13.3%, the biggest rise for 33 years, and many Wall Street investors lost money as trading leapt to record levels. U.S. Steel closed ten factories, laying off 13,000 workers in the process. The struggling company had been forced to rationalize its operations in the face of fierce competition from overseas and the hefty $1.8 billion expenditure needed to bring plants into line with clean-air regulations.

It wasn't all bad news for Carter, though. He managed to broker a peace deal in the Middle East, bringing the leaders of Egypt and Israel together to sign a treaty at the White House. Carter also signed the SALT II agreement with the USSR to limit strategic missiles.

As far as the automobile industry was concerned, the big story of the year was the decision by Congress to approve a loan of $1.5 billion to rescue the Chrysler Corporation from bankruptcy. Although there were plenty of commentators in Detroit and the media elsewhere who were happy to let Chrysler die, they reckoned without the dedication and determination of the charismatic Lee Iacocca who had taken charge of the company a year earlier. Thanks to his efforts, a deal was thrashed out with the unions for wage cuts and deferred payments to pension funds in order to safeguard the jobs of 150,000 employees, and this agreement helped to secure the government aid.

Iacocca also initiated a morale-boosting campaign using the slogan "We Can Do It!" that not only created confidence throughout Chrysler's workforce – leading to noticeably improved build quality in production – but also gave customers the belief that he would restore the fortunes of the ailing company.

Meanwhile, on the other side of Motor City in Dearborn, Iacocca's old company Ford were launching the third-generation of Mustang. The bare bones of the concept for this version were actually laid down prior to the arrival of the Mustang II in '74, and began as an attempt to come up with a "world car" – in other words, a design that could be built in Ford factories around the world, with only small variations needed to take care of local requirements. As it turned out, the problems associated with the idea proved insurmountable at that time, but some of the original principles set out for a compact, fuel-

Above: A restyled front end came along for the Pontiac Firebird in '79, with two large grilles set low down in the bumper and quad recessed rectangular headlamps positioned above. The Red Bird trim package was an attractive option that included two-tone red paint and custom interior. Pontiac enjoyed one of its best years ever, building nearly a million cars over the 12 months.

efficient car, remained.

As they had done previously, Ford gave the task of producing design proposals for the new Mustang to a number of styling studios – three in the USA and Ghia in Italy (owned by Ford and headed by Don DeLa Rossa). Certain fixed parameters were issued to the design teams, including wheelbase, overall length, width, and so on, and using these limits they each had to come up with drawings and models for wind tunnel testing. As a result of this work a number of full-size mockups were generated for consideration by the Ford hierarchy. The design chosen was that produced by Jack Telnack's group at the company's North American Light Car and Truck Design department. Telnack had earlier spent some time at Ford Europe and his experience of designing smaller cars was to prove invaluable. From the outset, Telnack's team (which included Fritz Mayhew, David Rees and Gary Haas) looked at ways of making the new Mustang as aerodynamic as possible. This was rather than creating a stylish shape and then modifying it in the wind tunnel to make it more efficient as had been done in the past. The result was a drag coefficient of 0.44 for the 3-door fastback and 0.46 for the 2-door notchback – not terribly impressive by modern standards, but a major step forward in 1979.

Like almost any trend-setting design, the success of the Mustang came about from the stylists breaking the rules. The car's slim, wedge-shaped front end was accentuated by the rake of the hood – a feature Telnack's team achieved by ignoring one of the so-called "hard points," the height of the cowl. To get the effect they wanted, the cowl was raised an inch above the dimension for the Fairmont/Zephyr platform that was being used as the basis for the new model. Despite protests from the production engineers, the cost of manufacturing the special items brought about by this change was quickly approved. The integrated spoiler under the front bumper and a small lip on the rear deck-lid were aerodynamic aids that also added to the overall effect.

The new Mustang came with the usual choice of engines, starting with a 2.3-liter four cylinder putting out 88bhp, a turbo version that produced 140bhp, a 109bhp 170 cu.in. V6 and the 302 cu.in V8 that produced 140 horsepower. Later in the model year, problems in obtaining sufficient quantities of the German-built V6 saw the return of the old 200 cu.in. inline six. Prices started at $4,494 for a 2-door coupe with a four-cylinder engine, with a 3-door hatchback listed at $4,828. You could also get Ghia and Cobra versions.

That the Mustang's new shape proved to be extremely popular is evident by the

Above: *The Jeep Cherokee got a new grille with rectangular headlamps and a more substantial-looking front bumper, the first changes made to the model since it appeared five years earlier. Apart from these alterations, the boxy wagon remained much as before. After a couple of years of increasing sales, poor economic conditions saw the popularity of big four-wheel-drive vehicles taking a dive and production had to be cut back at the Toledo factory.*

fact that production went up from around 180,000 in '78 to over 332,000 this year, elevating the model to number 7 in the 1979 sales charts (up from number 22 the previous year). Another acknowledgement of the Mustang's significance came when it was chosen as the Official Pace Car for the Indianapolis 500 – Ford built something like 6,000 replicas.

But possibly the most significant thing about the third-generation Mustang was that it went on to establish itself as one

f the most potent drag strip performers f the 1980s. The V8 was briefly disco-tinued, but quickly made a comeback, nd throughout the following decade a whole new industry grew up providing arts for enthusiasts who wanted their Mustang to go quicker. The '79 Musta-g might not have created the same sort f sensation as was seen in '64, but if immy Carter was looking for someth-ng that could give America confidence n the future, maybe he should have visited his local Ford dealership.

Below: Full-sized Chryslers became a thing of the past, while the Cordoba was promoted as "the contemporary classic." The first use of the 300 nameplate since 1971, the Cordoba 300 package included bucket seats, blacked-out grille, special trim, a 195 horsepower 360 cu.in. V8 and uprated suspension. Adding over $2,000 to the base price of around $6,000, it's no wonder only 3,811 of the Spinnaker White-painted 300 models were sold.

SPECIFICATIONS

CADILLAC SEVILLE

Engine:
V8 Diesel - cast iron block

Displacement:
350 cu. ins.

Bore and stroke:
4.06 x 3.39

Horsepower:
105

Body styles:
4 door sedan

No. of seats:
5

Weight (lbs):
3,911 lbs

Price:
$20,477

Produced:
39,344

If 1979 was a bad year, 1980 was even worse. mixture of an economy in recession and inflatio wreaked havoc across the whole auto industr Ford were the worst affected, outsold 2 to 1 b Chevrolet and recording a $1.54 billion los Henry Ford II resigned as chairman and, for th first time in the company's history, there was n longer a member of the Ford family in charg Someone else who wouldn't be in charge for muc longer was President Jimmy Carter, his popularit undermined by the financial crisis. Republica Ronald Reagan enjoyed a landslide victory i November, making Carter the first electe President to lose an election since Franklin D Roosevelt defeated Herbert Hoover in 1932 coincidentally at the beginning of the Grea Depression.

The designers and planners working in th Motor City couldn't help but be influenced b

Below: The restyled 1980 Seville was one of the last projects overseen by GM styling chief Bill Mitchell before he retired in 1977. The use of bustle-back design harked back to the razor-edged Rolls-Royces produced by Hooper and Vanden Plas in the 1950s. Although its distinctive appearance was not wholeheartedly welcomed at first, the Seville quickly established itself as a quintessential Cadillac.

hat was going on around them, but the ew models they had produced were reated well in advance and a couple of utomotive gems arrived on the scene in 980. Wayne Cady's dramatic restyling f the Cadillac Seville was initially not o everyone's taste, but the bustle-back ear deck endowed the car with haracter and marked it out as a special nodel that was instantly recognizable as oming from the luxury marque.

Below: The front view of Seville is probably the least interesting, but it still retains all the elements of a classic Cadillac design. Sadly, the assertion in the sales catalog that "Through the years, Cadillac has earned for itself an exclusive place... a solitary niche...in the pantheon of the world's truly fine automobiles" was rather let down by the troublesome 350 cu.in. diesel engine fitted as standard.

Unfortunately, under that distinctive Seville bodywork there was one particular problem for Cadillac – and it involved the engine.

For the first time ever, a diesel engine was standard in a Cadillac, but the 350 cu.in. V8 fitted into the Seville proved to be a rather troublesome unit. Not only that, it took 19 seconds for the diesel-powered Seville to lumber to 60mph – some 8.5 seconds slower than the '75 model. With the normal 6-liter (368 cu.in.) gasoline engine in place, the front-wheel-drive Seville was in a class of its own, but a number of price increases during the year saw the basic cost of the model escalate by over a thousand dollars and, by the summer, it had reached a whopping $21,000. Reflecting the difficult economic times, Cadillac's overall sales slumped by 30%.

It was a far cry from the heady days of the Seville's first introduction in 1975, when the new car was compared favorably, to the Rolls-Royce Camargue and the Mercedes Benz 450 SE. Performance was what impressed reviewers particularly, leading to it being pronounced by one to be the best Cadillac since the '49. The ride was described as "glass smooth," and the handling as "quick, precise and predictable," with "hardly any lean in sharp turns." Speed and silence were the defining features of what was hailed as the definitive American luxury car, more than able to take on the world's best before the decision to fit a diesel engine...

At the other end of the scale, AMC carried out another of their "mix and match" juggling acts and, by combining the body and chassis of the Concord with a four-wheel-drive system from the Jeep, came up with the Eagle. This unique 4x4 car established a hitherto

Production of cars across the industry was hit badly, the total figure of 6.4 million units being some two million less than in 1979, and over 3.2 million down on the record set in '73. Truck manufacturing was similarly devastated – at under 1.6 million, it was little better than half of the '79 figure.

Left: With much publicity, the new front-wheel-drive Buick Skylark made its debut as a 1980 model in the spring of '79. Shorter than its predecessor of the same name by 19 inches, it shared the X-body with the Chevrolet Citation, Pontiac Phoenix and Oldsmobile Omega. Powered by either a Pontiac "Iron Duke" 2.5-liter four cylinder or a Chevy-built 2.8-liter V6, the Skylark reached 100,000 sales in its first year but, in common with all the X-body variants, it suffered from a number of safety recalls.

Below: The Eagle station wagon was the most popular version of the AMC 4x4 (2- and 4-door sedans were also available). A venerable 258 cu.in. six cylinder was the only engine on offer, together with automatic transmission and full-time four-wheel-drive. The Eagle body stood about three inches higher than the Concord on which it was based, with plastic wheel arch flares and 15-inch wheels also unique to the 4x4 model.

ntapped market niche at very little ooling cost but, despite extensive overage in the media, it failed to sell as well as AMC predicted. In addition, the quirky Pacer had had its day and was dropped to cut costs. Even so, by the end of the year AMC's losses amounted to a staggering $197,525,000.

In December 1980, Lee Iacocca announced to the press that "1981 belongs to Chrysler, because no other American car company is better equipped to meet the new market requirements of the eighties than the New Chrysler Corporation." His confidence was partly based on the fact that Chrysler was the only auto manufacturer to record an increase in sales during that month compared to the same period in 1979. The rise might have been a very small 2.6% but, put against the 6.2% loss of sales by GM and the even worse 12.6% drop for Ford, the gain was significant.

The flagships of the new Chrysler fleet leading this revival were the front-wheel-drive K-cars – the Plymouth Reliant and Dodge Aries. But it wasn't just the arrival of a couple of new models that turned the tide. It was also due to Iacocca

novative marketing programs that had earlier cleared thousands of old models from stock and then continued by making people aware that things were on the mend at Chrysler. In July '80, a promotional campaign had been launched with the slogan "K-cars are coming" and this was repeated nationwide in newspaper adverts and on radio and television.

Closer to the October launch date, another catch-phrase was adopted: "America is not going to be pushed around any more." Together with the prominent use of the emotive red, white and blue colors, this new slogan sent out a dual message. The first part empha-

Below: Chrysler wasn't only selling economy cars in 1981 – the luxury Imperial was another new model introduced that year. Frank Sinatra featured in a television commercial and a number of press adverts interviewing Lee Iacocca about the company's products. With its bustle-back styling and vertical grille, the Imperial drew immediate comparisons with the Cadillac Seville, but priced at $18,300 only 7,225 of these limited-edition Chryslers were sold. The Imperial used a fuel-injected 318 cu.in. V8 and had only one optional extra – a powered moonroof priced at £1,044. Everything else was included as standard.

sized the fact that the K-cars were ultra-modern front-wheel-drive models and pulled the vehicle along, rather than pushing it as in the traditional arrangement that drove the rear wheels. The second was meant to demonstrate Chrysler's commitment to building small cars in America and that the company was not going to hand over this important market sector to foreign imports without a fight.

Today, the K-cars' specification looks like pretty basic stuff. The shape was almost utilitarian, with very squarish styling, and the 2.2-liter overhead camshaft Trans4 engine (rated at 84

horsepower) was the first four cylinder built by Chrysler for nearly half century. But the Plymouth Reliant wa two feet shorter and almost half a to lighter than the Volare model replaced. Its EPA figure of 25mpg fc city driving was probably the mo important statistic of all. The Relia

Below: Based on the Chevy Cavalier an Buick Skyhawk J-cars, the Cimarron, introduced in 1982 was definitely not one of Cadillac's more inspired projects It was intended to compete against up-scale, European imports such as the BMW 320i, Audi 5000 and Saab 900 .

Above: One advantage the Chrysler K-car had over compact rivals from General Motors was having a station wagon in the lineup, though the Reliant wagon was only available in the Custom and Special Edition series. The Plymouth Reliant had a small 99.6 inch wheelbase but squared-off styling made it look like a much bigger car. In fact, the Reliant was two feet shorter and half a ton lighter than the Volare model it replaced.

Below: Despite the air conditioning and genuine leather seats, the four-cylinder Cimarron didn't appeal to buyers of upmarket imports and was out of step with the tastes of traditional Cadillac owners. While it may not have been a bad car, the Cimarron was definitely the wrong car.

also had another advantage over GM's X-body rivals in that there was a station wagon in the lineup, over 50,000 of which were sold in the first year alone. Sales of Reliant coupes and sedans added up to just over 100,000 units, and when you add in the 155,000 Dodge Aries models that were also produced, it highlights the huge impact that the K-cars made on the fortunes of Chrysler.

Ford, on the other hand, were in dire straits. Output fell to around a million units – the worst annual total for the company since 1958 – and the company was nearly overtaken by Oldsmobile for second place in the sales charts. Losses amounted to $1.06 billion, and about the only bright spot in this very gloomy period was the arrival of the front wheel-drive Escort compact model. Developed as an "international size" car, the Escort was built in five different countries with small variations to suit local regulations. In the USA it immed

Below: In a reaction to the Energy Crisis Cadillac introduced a diesel engine as standard on the Seville in 1908, where it proved unreliable and unpopular. Gasoline engines came fitted with a "variable-displacement" engine that cut the number of operating cylinders down from 8 to 6 to 4 as driving conditions allowed. The combination of V8 power and four-cylinder economy was a dream in theory; in practice it was a nightmare.

ately proved to be a winner, easily outselling its ill-fated Pinto predecessor. Escort sales for '81 topped 284,000 units and the smaller-sized Granada model (actually a re-styled Fairmont) also did well. The problem for the company was that the remainder of the

Above: The elegantly styled Eldorado would shortly benefit from a lightweight aluminum, fuel-injected 250 cu. in. V8.

range suffered badly – Mustang sales dropped by a third and Thunderbird numbers halved.

1982

SPECIFICATIONS

CHEVROLET CAMARO Z28

Engine:
V8 - cast iron block

Displacement:
305 cu. ins.

Bore and stroke:
3.74 x 3.48

Horsepower:
145

Body styles:
Coupe

No. of seats:
4

Weight (lbs):
2,870 lbs

Price:
$9,700

Produced:
63,500

The recession was finally beginning to bottom out, but there were still some hard times ahead before any noticeable improvements in prosperity would be apparent. In February, President Ronald Reagan announced that the deficit in the forthcoming fiscal year would amount to a staggering $91.5 billion and proposed a program of increased taxation and severe reductions in federal spending. By the end of the year the deficit had risen to over $110 billion, the unemployment rate was 10.8% industry was working at two-thirds of full capacity.

Below: Chevrolet produced six thousand replicas of the Camaro Z28 1982 Indianapolis 500 Pace Car, with each Chevy dealer given the opportunity to order one of the "Commemorative Edition" models. They were finished in silver and blue, with Indy 500 graphics, sport mirrors and the red highlights on the five-spoke aluminum wheels, but didn't have roof-mounted lights or checkered flags on the back. "Commemorative Edition" Camaros could be specified with either a carbureted or fuel injected 5.0-liter V8, and manual or automatic transmission, and they were all built at the Van Nuys, California assembly plant in March and April of '82.

nd the number of people classified as being below the poverty line had risen to he highest level since 1967. Interest ates still remained high, yet housing onstruction and car sales began to how signs of a slight recovery.

One auto company to disappear was De Lorean. Set up in Northern Ireland with substantial UK government grants by the former General Motors executive ohn De Lorean, the company built a futuristic gull-wing sports car. However, the DeLorean's design, produced in (theoretical) collaboration with Colin Chapman, of world champion race car constructors Lotus, had catastrophic

Below: Mustang engine options for '82 ranged from a 140 cu. in. 4 Cylinder to a 302 cu. in. V8 - with a difference of around 70 horsepower. A turbocharged Four was to follow.

flaws: the front end was so light that the hood had to be weighted with lead and it was discovered that paint would not adhere to the stainless-steel panel work. On top of that, the rear-mounted Volvo power plant was incapable of delivering the level of performance that the car's appearance implied.

Despite further massive injections of British tax-payers' cash, courtesy of Margaret Thatcher's Conservative government, annual production and sales of the model never came close to the 20,000 units forecast. After De Lorean went out of business, many questions were raised about mismanagement of the business, but most remain unanswered. The car was immortalized as Michael J. Fox's time machine in the movie Back to the Future.

The economic recession was being felt around the world and set against this somber background, the arrival of the third-generation Chevrolet Camaro was

hardly likely to raise much attention outside the automotive press, but the new model did create a few headlines. Selected as *Motor Trend* magazine's Car of the Year, the Camaro enjoyed a great first year, selling a very impressive 189,747 units despite only being introduced in February '82. And, for the third time, the Camaro was chosen as the Indianapolis 500 Pace Car, with 6,360 replicas of the Z28 being sold to the public.

Above: From time to time, there have been all sorts of styling oddities used by designers, but one of the most superfluous must be the way part of the rear quarter panel was incorporated into the door on the Chrysler LeBaron. Surprisingly, this curious feature was to remain in use for several years on various Chrysler models. In common with many other smaller cars on the market, the downsized '82 LeBaron was powered by a four-cylinder engine.

With an increasing trend towards the use of front-wheel-drive on new models in the '80s it might seem peculiar that the Camaro remained with the traditional front-engine, rear-wheel-drive configuration. A change to front-wheel-drive was considered, but the engineers decided that if the V8 engine was to be retained (and there were plenty of good reasons for keeping the V8) then the only sensible solution was to keep things as they were. That didn't mean that there weren't many changes made to the third-generation. Far from it. The '82 Camaro was almost ten inches shorter than the '81, had a seven-inch shorter wheelbase and was 2.8 inches narrower. A 500 pound weight reduction and fuel economy stipulations saw a four-cylinder engine offered in the Camaro for the first time – the 155

Below: A year short of the Corvette's 30th birthday, a "Collector's Edition" was offered, with special trim, a lift-up rear window and a price tag of $22,538 - more than $4,000 over the price of the standard model.

cu.in. Iron Duke from Pontiac. Other engines available were a 173 cu.in. V6 of 102 horsepower, and a couple of 305 cu.in. (5.0-liter) V8s. The standard Z28 V8 engine came with a single four-barrel carburetor and put out 145 horses, while the optional fuel injected version was rated at 165hp.

The Camaro was offered in three basic models: the economy Sport Coupe, the luxurious Berlinetta and the high performance Z28. Each was trimmed differently, the Z28 being easily identifiable by having no grille openings above the bumper line and extra air dams on the front and sides. The third-generation Camaro proved to be so successful initially that it stayed pretty much unchanged (apart from juggling with option lists and minor alterations to model specifications) through to

Above: Emission Control caught up with the Corvette in 1981, but the following year, for the first time since 1965, Fuel-Injection was offered. For the first time since 1955, there was no manual gearbox option. '82 was the final fling of the fifteen year-old, fifth generation 'Vette.

1992. But it was the years to 1987 that were most successful, with 1.1 million Camaros sold in total. Thereafter, only 412,000 were purchased in the final five years.

These later years saw the Camaro produced solely at the Van Nuys, California assembly plant following the closure of the Norwood, Ohio factory in '87. In '92 the Van Nuys facility closed and Camaro production transferred to Canada.

1983

SPECIFICATIONS

**FORD THUNDER-
BIRD TURBO COUPE**

Engine:
Cast iron - 4 Cylinders
in line

Displacement:
140 cu. ins.

Bore and stroke:
3.78 x 3.13 -
Turbocharged

Horsepower:
145

Body styles:
Coupe

No. of seats:
4

Weight (lbs):
3,100 lbs

Price:
$11,790

Produced:
122,000 (all models)

To most people, this year marked the return of the convertible. Of course, to all intents and purposes, the convertible had never gone anywhere at all – although the major auto-makers had dropped the model from their lineups in the '70s there were always a number of specialist companies who would custom-build a ragtop from almost any make or model if the price was right. Quite a few cars also came with removable roof panels which, if not exactly true convertibles, at least retained the idea of driving with the wind in your hair. When the impending safety legislation that was supposed to outlaw the convertible failed to materialize, a couple of manufacturers almost simultaneously decided they would bring back the ragtop.

Apart from the fact that they both had classic fold-down tops, the two offerings were about as

Below: The new 10th generation Thunderbird had modern aero styling that was, according to the Ford catalog. "Conceived for today with an eye on tomorrow." The wheelbase was reduced by 4 inches (to 104 inches) and the choice of engines was of either a 232 cu.in. (3.8-liter) V6 or the fuel injected 302 cu.in. (5.0-liter) V8. A turbocharged 2-3-liter four also became available during the year. Thanks to the redesign, total T-Bird sales jumped threefold to nearly 122,000.

ar apart in the automotive spectrum as t is possible to get. The Ford Mustang convertible marked a return to the sporty, front-engine, rear-drive, ultimate fun car ethos of the Sixties, whereas the Chrysler LeBaron Town & Country Convertible was truthfully described in advertisements as "...like no other car on the road today." The front-wheel-drive, "woody"-styled Town & Country actually harked back to a Chrysler model of the late 1940s and was

Below: Ford was another marque to bring back the convertible, but the Mustang was converted from a coupe by Cars & Concepts, not built on the assembly line at Dearborn. Available with either a V6 or V8 engine, the price of a Mustang ragtop increased sharply during year and was up by a whopping 25% in a few months. A restyled front end improved the aerodynamics, but otherwise the Mustang remained very much as before.

intended as an out-and-out luxury car.

While the Mustang convertible may have been listed as an "official" Ford model, it was actually built by an outside company. After assembly at Dearborn, completed notchback coupes were shipped to Cars & Concepts of Brighton, Michigan, for conversion and installation of interior trim. Sold as either a GLX with a 3.8-liter V6 engine or a GT with the 302 cu.in. (5.0-liter) V8, the ragtop 'Stang also featured a glass backlight, roll-down quarter windows and a power top. Factory price for a GLX convertible began the year at a touch under ten thousand dollars, but jumped to $12,467 after a few months.

The Town & Country wasn't the only LeBaron convertible introduced in '83. There was also a base model and a luxury Mark Cross version, but it was with the "woody" that Chrysler said it was "re-introducing an American classic." Unlike the original, however, the '83 had a fake white ash wooden frame on the body and a 2.2-liter four cylinder engine under the hood plu Torqueflite automatic transmission. The power convertible top came with zip down window and weather-seal sides and there was also a tailored top boot The LeBaron Town & Country convertible carried a factory price o $15,595 and promised buyers that "No indulgence has been overlooked." While that statement was a rather ambitious one, the car was undoubtedly unique to America.

Sales of the two ragtops were directly opposite to the fortunes of the respective companies. When Chrysler re-introduced the convertible they forecast sales of

round 3,000 units and hoped to break even, but it was the publicity that would be generated by the ragtop that was the attraction. By the end of the '83 model year, a total of 9.891 LeBaron convertibles had been sold – 5,441 were Mark Cross versions and 1,520 had the Town & Country package installed.

Mustang sales for '83 were 23,438, and while Ford hung on to second spot in the sales charts, they slipped to fourth in terms of production numbers behind Oldsmobile and Buick – the first time Ford hadn't been in the top two since 1905. Ford had the best-selling car in the country with the compact Escort and launched an exciting new Thunderbird, but it was still losing money.

Chrysler, on the other hand, had increased its market share and was making substantial profits – so substantial that Lee Iacocca was able to pay back its government loan in full, seven years early. A proposal for a merger between Chrysler and Ford was made in 1981, but rejected out of hand by the Ford management, who must have had second thoughts about that decision on more than one occasion during this period.

Below: "Chrysler brings back the romance of the past with the luxury and technology of the present in the Town & Country Convertible," said the advertisements. The "woody" look was a re-creation of the famous wood-frame exterior used in the late 1940s, but the plush '83 ragtop had a 94 horsepower, 2.2-liter, overhead cam four-cylinder engine under the hood and not a 114 bhp, 250 cu.in L-head six.

SPECIFICATIONS

PONTIAC FIERO SE

Engine:
Cast iron - 4 Cylinders
in line

Displacement:
151 cu. ins.

Bore and stroke:
4.0 x 3.0

Horsepower:
92

Body styles:
Coupe

No. of seats:
2

Weight (lbs):
2,465 lbs

Price:
$9,599

Produced:
67,671

*Right: The Fiero SE was
the top of the range
version and came with
special WS6 performance
handling package and rear
deck luggage rack as
standard. It also had
P215/80R13 tires and a
padded Formula steering
wheel. Despite costing
$1,500 more than the base
model, the SE was the top-
selling Fiero in '84.*

As long as examples of the Fiero survive, people will continue to argue whether the Pontiac two-seater was a classic in the making that got prematurely killed off by the accountants or merely an expensive failure that was put on sale before it was fully developed. The truth probably lie somewhere in the middle of these two extremes.

There had, in actual fact, been ideas for a Pontiac sports car bouncing around the division's engineering and styling departments since the early '60s but, apart from a couple of concept cars on the auto show circuit, nothing had come of these proposals. One example of this was back in 1966. As a response to the runaway success of the Ford Mustang, John DeLorean tried to win approval from his GM masters for a two-seater Pontiac for the 1967 model year, but he had to be satisfied with the Firebird – basically a restyled Chevy Camaro with a Pontiac engine.

Although the genesis of the Fiero dates back to around '75, credit for providing the required impetus to get the project moving goes to Bob Stempel, who became Pontiac's general manager in 1978. Stempel's reasoning wasn't based upon producing a mid-engined, high performance sports model but rather a fuel-efficient commuter car to

combat the projected escalation of gas
prices and likely disappearance of
models like the Firebird as a consequence of future government legislation.
This resulted in an immediate conflict as
to exactly how the Fiero should turn
out.

Another problem was the lack of

*Above: On its debut, the Fiero 2M4 (the
designation stood for two-seat mid-
engine, four cylinder) seemed to put
some real meaning into the Pontiac
slogan "We Build Excitement."
Unfortunately, lack of development and
disappointing performance meant that
the excitement soon died out.*

finance. Stempel had left Pontiac in 1980, to be replaced by William E. Hoglund. Immediately after taking over, Hoglund was informed that there would be very limited funds made available for the Fiero project. The whole auto industry was suffering during the early '80s, with record losses being recorded all round, and these were not the best conditions for trying to get sufficient money allocated to develop a completely new type of car.

Hoglund wasn't to be deterred and set about cutting costs to the bone. The engineering work was subcontracted out to Entech Engineering (under the control of Pontiac's project head Huldi Aldikacti), with a directive to use as many existing components as possible, and pressure was applied to parts

Below: There was no 1983 model (Chevy decided to skip a year) but a completely redesigned Corvette arrived in '84. Lower by 1.1 inch, shorter by 8.8 inches and sitting on a 2 inch shorter wheelbase, the Jerry Palmer-styled coupe was also 2 inches wider than its predecessor and 250 pounds lighter. Powered by a 205 horsepower, 350 cu.in. V8 with Cross-Fire fuel injection and electronic spark control, the aerodynamic new 'Vette would reach 140mph – a significant improvement over the '82 model. Corvette chief engineer Dave McLellan described the car as "absolutely superior to any production vehicle in its part of the market" and though sales figures hit 51,547, they sank to under 40,000 the following year.

Right: Based on the Ranger pickup, the Ford Bronco II was 19 inches shorter and 9 inches narrower than the full-size Bronco. The 4x4 light utility vehicle came with a 2.8-liter V6 engine built in Germany and a choice of either four- or five-speed manual and three-speed automatic transmissions. Aimed chiefly at women drivers for shopping or transporting children, the Bronco II was launched in March '83 as an '84 model and in direct competition to the Chevy S-10 Blazer, though it only sold about half as many as the small bow-tie off-roader.

suppliers to reduce prices wherever possible. The end result was, predictably, that far too many compromises had to be made and the Fiero suffered badly as a consequence. The underpinnings of the car read like a list cobbled together from the corporate GM parts catalogue: the drivetrain consisted of the four-cylinder engine/ transmission unit used in the front-wheel-drive X-body quartet (Chevrolet Citation/Pontiac,

Phoenix/ Oldsmobile, Omega/Buick, Skylark) and the front suspension was mainly taken from the Chevy Chevette.

Although the designers made space for a V6 engine right from the outset (it was added in '85), the '84 Fiero arrived in the showrooms with a 92 horsepower, 2.5-liter "Iron Duke" four-cylinder mated to either a four-speed manual or three-speed automatic transaxle mounted midships. Although placing the

Below: Lincoln described the all-new Continental Mark VII as "the most airflow-efficient luxury car built in America" and at over a foot shorter and nearly 400 pounds lighter than the Mark VI it was certainly a step in the right direction. European-style aero headlamps were opposed by federal government to begin with, but Ford won approval for them after a two-year battle. A turbocharged six cylinder diesel engine was offered as an alternative to the standard 5.0-liter V8 for the first time, and Lincoln sales rose by 31%.

Above: While most manufacturers were busy announcing new models, at least one car looked exactly the same as it had for years. First produced in 1965 by industrial designer Brooks Stevens, and despite the fact that it only had modern Chevrolet running gear, the Excalibur (based on the 1920s Mercedes SSK) quickly became a status symbol. Thereafter, the Excalibur Automobile Corporation, based in Milwaukee, Wisconsin, produced, on average, around 250 cars a year and stayed under Stevens family control until bankruptcy in 1986 forced the sale of the company.

engine in such a position creates the optimum weight distribution – and therefore excellent roadholding – the Fiero's modest power output meant that it was always going to be found rather wanting when it came down to performance.

While a 0 to 60mph time of around 11 seconds and a top speed of just over 100mph would be outstanding figures for a utilitarian commuter car, they were totally out of keeping with a sports car that looked like a miniature Ferrari. And that was possibly the Fiero's biggest problem – it simply couldn't deliver what its appearance promised. The story of the swoopy body started out at one of GM's Advanced Studios headed by Ron Hill, and the styling was finished off by a team of designers under the leadership of John Schinella at the Pontiac II Studio that included Jack Folden, Bob Menking and John Snell.

Schinella was later quoted as saying:

"Maybe we made it look too good, because people were expecting more out of it than what it was. If it had looked a little dumber, maybe they wouldn't have had so many high expectations that it was hot." Visually the Fiero bears a slight resemblance to the Bertone-designed Fiat X1/9 and also the Toyota

MR2 (both mid-engined), but while it could almost match the performance of the Italian car the Pontiac fell a long way short of matching the Japanese one.

But if the Fiero's shape and configuration seemed vaguely similar to other cars, the body's construction was very unusual indeed. Instead of a conventional unitary body of welded steel, the Pontiac's panels were molded from Enduraflex, an impact-resistant plastic, and attached to a space-frame chassis. The strength of the car was contained in this frame and it could be safely driven around without any bodywork at all. In theory, this method of construction not only made accident damage repairs a lot easier, but also allowed annual body styling alterations to be carried out at a minimum cost.

As part of the original justification for the Fiero, Stempel and Hoglund had estimated that Pontiac would sell between 50,000 and 60,000 units a year. This was considered wildly over-optimistic by many in the hierarchy of General Motors – especially as the long-established Corvette was only averaging around 40,000 annual sales and that no other two-seater had got anywhere near these sort of figures. But it turned out that everyone was wrong. At the end of its first year the Fiero production total

was an incredible 136,940.

A runaway success then? Yes, as far a the '84 sales figures go, but there were some problems that needed to be addressed. Firstly, an alarming numbe of reports were received about engin fires breaking out in the early four cylinder cars, leading to a major recall i '87 for remedial work. Then there were the questions concerning the lack o performance. This was partially solve with the introduction of the 2.8-liter V6 but it was still saddled with four-speed manual trans because the five-speed offered with the four-cylinder engin couldn't take the torque of the six. I was this sort of poor planning that together with an equally ineffective marketing strategy, handicapped the Fiero's development and ultimately led to its demise.

Sales dropped dramatically by almos 50% in '85, and continued to fall in each subsequent year. Increased competition from imports in this specialized marke sector and major rises in insurance premiums were a couple of the factors in this decline, but customer preferences were also changing. At first Pontiac argued for a major revamp of the Fiero, and then looked at other price-cutting ways to keep the model going. Eventually, however, mounting losses

After hearing of the announcement on March 1 1988 about the decision to pull the plug on the Fiero, Bob Stempel told journalists: "What you see here is the reality of what's happening in North America – when the market goes away for a particular product, that's the end."

In 1984, of course, nobody knew that the Fiero was destined for such a short life. That it enhanced the image of Pontiac in the short term is unquestionable, but whether the two-seater could have gone on to be a lasting success is another matter entirely. The Toyota MR2 is still in production, but the US market represents only a fraction of the car's worldwide sales, and that international appeal is something that the Pontiac Fiero was never really given the chance to match.

...orced the inevitable and the company ...topped production of the Fiero model.

Top & Above: Mustang's flirtation with ...he Turbocharger was short-lived; the Turbo GT - a hold-card against the ...hreatened gasoline shortage - was ...eleted from the line in '85.

Below: The open-air Eldorado returned in 84 with the Biarritz Convertible. At $32,105, this was the most expensive American production convertible to date.

359

SPECIFICATIONS

BUICK GRAND NATIONAL

Engine:
V6 - cast iron block

Displacement:
231 cu. ins.

Bore and stroke:
3.80 x 3.40

Horsepower:
200

Body styles:
Coupe

No. of seats:
5

Weight (lbs):
3,500 lbs

Price:
$13,315

Produced:
2,100

As the year began, things were looking up in the auto industry. Gasoline prices had stabilized at the lowest level for some time and consumers were starting to look at bigger cars once again. Fuel economy was no longer the prime selling point and, rather than the subcompact models, people wanted compacts and intermediates instead. In general, this change in the market was good news for the "Big Three" and they would turn in record profits as a result. But independent AMC had based their forward planning on the continuing demand for small, four cylinder cars, and were left without any new models to compete in these areas. Labor problems, changes in the top executives that saw Renault personnel take full charge of the company, reductions in car sales and a loss of $12 million meant '85 was a pretty awful year for AMC. In total contrast, Jeep division sales improved to almost 193,000 – a new record. But this wasn't enough and rumors began to circulate about the closure of the Kenosha, Wisconsin, plant or a tie-up with Chrysler.

At this time Buick's image to the youth market was in the process of being revamped thanks mainly to the Grand National. Initially brought out in '82 as a Regal with a fancy paint job, T-roof and alloy wheels, the Grand National took its

spiration from the Buick NASCAR racecars of the same name. Performance-wise, though, the mechanically stock road version was less than exciting. After a very limited production run of only 215, the model was dropped for '83. When the Grand National came back in '84 it was a completely different animal, thanks to a 200 horsepower, turbocharged and fuel injected 3.8-liter V6 that cut the zero to 60mph time from over 15 seconds in '82 to less than nine seconds.

The Grand National's exterior appearance had also been radically altered, with the color scheme now all-black and devoid of any fancy decoration on the bodywork. It was sold as an option package on the Regal T Type and, as well as the paintwork, the Grand National specification included special alloy wheels and spoilers. It added $1,282 to the $12,118 factory price tag.

Apart from the black grille getting seven thin vertical bright metal bars, the '85 Grand National stayed virtually unchanged. True, the base price for the Regal T Type went up by some five hundred dollars, but the cost of the Grand National option package was substantially reduced so the overall effect was of very little change. Precisely how many of the 5,401 T Types produced in '84 were fitted with the Grand National package in '84 isn't clear, but in 1985 (when Regal T Type production totaled 4,169) a figure of 2,102 has been quoted.

The Grand National continued unaltered until the end of '87, by which

Below: Buick boosted its youthful image by promoting the Regal T Type Grand National. Powered by a potent 3.8-litre turbocharged V6, the all-black coupe almost represented a return to the muscle car era of the '60s and enthusiasts were saddened when production was terminated in 1987. A top speed of approximately 120mph and a 0-60mph time of under 9 seconds made the Grand National highly desirable when new, and it is still sought-after today.

time it was the last rear-wheel-drive Buick being made. The final flourish was a run of 500 GNX models – with engine, suspension and body modifications carried out by McLaren Engines and ASC Inc – that were sold at highly inflated prices. Back in '85, the Grand National television ad featured the rock song "Bad to the Bone" by George Thorogood and the Destroyers – an apt description for a car with a harsh ride and that could lay rubber in any gear!

Above: The SVO Mustang was an attempt by Ford to provide a more sophisticated (European style) version of the car, but despite all the innovations and an uprated 175 horsepower, turbocharged 2.3-litre four cylinder engine, it proved too expensive for traditional Mustang buyers. And in any case, they preferred a V8 under the hood! Intended as a "BMW killer" the SVO Mustang could accelerate to 60mph in 7.5 seconds and top 134mph

The year saw a brand new marque arrive on the scene when, after a three-year gestation period, General Motors added the first nameplate to the family since Chevrolet joined in 1918. – the Saturn Corporation. It was set up as a wholly owned subsidiary company and Saturn models were planned to be smaller and lighter than the GM J-cars (Chevy Cavalier, Pontiac Sunbird). The first offerings were a 4-door sedan and a 2-door coupe. Up to 20,000 people would eventually be employed by the company and five billion dollars was earmarked to build the Saturn assembly plant in Tennessee.

At the other end of the scale, bankruptcy proceedings were filed against the Avanti Motor Corporation of South Bend, Indiana, who were still building a couple of hundred cars a year based on the old Studebaker Avanti design. The New Avanti Motor Corp was formed a year later, with the company moving to Youngstown, Ohio in late '87.

Below: The Saturn prototype was unveiled by General Motors in 1985, who put five billion dollars into setting up the wholly owned subsidiary to compete with Japanese imports. Saturn Corporation constructed a brand new high-tech factory in Tennessee to build cars, using state-of-the-art manufacturing techniques. The first Saturns did not go on sale until October 1990, as '91 models.

1986

SPECIFICATIONS

FORD TAURUS

Engine:
Cast iron - 4 Cylinders
in line

Displacement:
153 cu. ins.

Bore and stroke:
3.70 x 3.60

Horsepower:
88

Body styles:
4 door sedan; Station
wagon

No. of seats:
5

Weight (lbs):
2,878 lbs - 3,306 lbs

Price:
$9,650 - $13,900

Produced:
236,000 (all models)

This year the price of crude oil fell to under $1
a barrel (good for motorists, not so good for
the oil companies) and America's second large
steel company, LTV, filed for bankruptc
However, the news wasn't all bad. Auto sales wer
still pretty strong and tax reforms reduced rate
but probably the most symbolic event that gave a
Americans hope for the future was the Fourth o
July celebrations to mark the Statue of Liberty
100th birthday.

As far as the auto industry was concerned, ther
were two items of note in '86 to accompany th
encouraging sales figures. The first was a new piec

*Below: The Ford Taurus was a new (if slightly late
midsize arrival – a European-style, front-wheel-
drive model that had no connection to the LTD
model it was replacing. At 106 inches, the Taurus
wheelbase was a fraction of an inch longer than
the LTD, but was over eight inches shorter in
overall length. The lack of a conventional grille on
the front end was seen as major departure of
aerodynamic design. Although seemingly similar in
appearance, the Mercury Sable had no common
body panels, but it did share drive-train, running
gear and most of its equipment with the Taurus.*

Above: The Taurus station wagon had different rear suspension to the sedan in order to provide more cargo space. The unusual liftgate was sharply angled in at the top, and other features included fold-down rear seat split 60/40, dual lights inside the cargo area and tie downs. Power brakes and steering were standard equipment on all Taurus models, along with gas-filled shocks, steel-belted radial tires and AM radio. The extensive options list had everything from rear-facing third seat to cast aluminum wheels.

of equipment that had to be incorporated into the design of every new car – the central high-mounted stoplamp. There was also a revision to the CAFE standard, which was reduced to 26mpg after Ford and General Motors claimed that the previous 27.5mpg figure would kill off big cars.

Ford's replacement for the rear-wheel-

Above: The Ford Aerostar was introduced in the summer of 1985 as an '86 model, and had traditional rear-wheel-drive. Basically a scaled-down van with a steeply-sloped front, the heavy (3500 pound) Aerostar sat on a longer 119 inch wheelbase in comparison to other mini-vans. Base engine was a 2.3-liter four, with a 2.8-liter V6 available at extra cost. This was replaced by a 3.0-liter V6 later in the year.

Right: The Jeep Wrangler looked like a CJ-7 with rectangular headlamps, but it was a different vehicle altogether. Sturdier roll cage, smoother ride (thanks to the use of Cherokee suspension components) and several other improvements saw AMC describe the Wrangler as being "all-new," although it did, in actual fact, share quite a few body parts and engines with the CJ-7. However, poor sales figures of 30,000 units weren't enough to offset the expensive retooling costs.

drive LTD was the midsize, front-wheel-drive Taurus, but there was nothing in the styling of the new model to link it to its predecessor. In a way this was hardly surprising, because the Taurus owed its origins to the Fords designed and built in Europe. The aerodynamic front of the Taurus was especially distinctive because of the lack of a grille. In place of this identifying feature was a solid panel painted in the body color, with a small Ford badge set in an oval opening positioned centrally between the headlamps. A wide air-intake slot was set low down, in the bottom half of the bumper.

The Taurus was initially offered in three series: L, GL or LX (the sporty MT5 came later), in either 4-door sedan or station wagon models. A new engine, developed from the High Swirl Combustion (HSC) Tempo 2.3-liter four cylinder unit, came as standard. The Taurus HSC engine measured 2.5 liters, and produced 88 bhp at 4,600rpm. Some early models came with a 3.0-liter V6, and this engine became an optional

choice as the year progressed, although it was standard on GL and LX station wagons. Four cylinder Taurus models came with a three-speed automatic or five-speed manual transaxle, but the V6 versions used a four-speed overdrive automatic. Manufacturing delays meant that the Taurus (and its companion, the Mercury Sable) was introduced later than usual, but Ford recorded figures of 178,737 sedans and 57,625 station wagons coming off the assembly lines. (Mercury numbers were 71,707 sedans and 23,931 wagons.) The Taurus would continue in this form for a decade before it received its first major redesign and it was a model that always sold well for Ford.

Over at troubled AMC, sales were down yet again. Even the introduction of the new Jeep Wrangler to replace the CJ-7 (production of that model ceased in January) failed to reverse AMC's decline as the Wrangler didn't do any

better than the earlier version. Th situation couldn't last and, late in '8 Lee Iacocca began secret negotiation with Renault for Chrysler to buy o their share in AMC. The end of "Th Last Independent" was only month away.

Right & Below: Ford's Mustang GT f 1986 featured the same radiator grille in '85, but was now also offered with choice of automatic or a five-spee manual gearbox. The main change wa the adoption of port fuel injection an lower compression for a single 302 V8 rated at 200 bhp. Ford also no offered a longer anti-corrosio warranty, increased sound-deadening and a convenient single-key lock system

SPECIFICATIONS

FORD THUNDER-BIRD V8

Engine:
V8 - cast iron block

Displacement:
302 cu. ins.

Bore and stroke:
4.0 x 3.0

Horsepower:
150

Body styles:
Coupe

No. of seats:
5

Weight (lbs):
3,300 lbs

Price:
$15,000

Produced:
128,135 (all models)

In March it was revealed that Chrysler were definitely going to buy American Motor Corporation. The news broke at about the same time that Renault launched their new Medallion model. The arrival of an unremarkable imported compact car was understandably overshadowed by the Chrysler takeover and the Renault quietly disappeared without trace. The stockmarket was not impressed by the deal either and, despite Lee Iacocca's assurances that the merger would strengthen both companies, some observers reckoned he was making a huge mistake. The total purchase price worked out at $1.1 billion but, as Iacocca explained, the assets acquired – the high margin Jeep brand, an AMC dealership network of 1,400 showrooms and the modern Bramalea assembly plant that was gearing up to build the all-

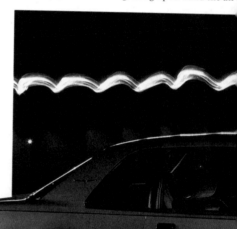

ew Renault Premier intermediate model – represented excellent value for money.

Another asset gained by Chrysler was he new 4.0-liter in-line six cylinder ngine that had just been introduced by eep. Developed from the old AMC six ylinder, the 173 horsepower 4.0-liter vas a real winner and soon became the avorite choice of Jeep buyers. It has emained so ever since. In the fall of '87, \MC was renamed as the Jeep/Eagle Division of Chrysler Corporation and ll the cars that had previously sold inder the AMC or Renault name were ebadged as Eagles. The final chapter on he last of the independent auto manufacturers came to a close on December 14 when production of the Eagle 4x4 station wagon (the last of the true AMC models) ended.

Gasoline prices remained low in '87 and performance cars were making

Below: The Ford Thunderbird was fully restyled, but underpinnings remained much as before. The Turbo Coupe was top of the range and its body design featured a grille-less nose and functional hood scoops. The turbocharged 140 cu.in. (2.3-liter) four cylinder engine churned out 190 horsepower thanks to use of an intercooler and propelled the Turbo Coupe to a top speed of 131mph.

something of a comeback with the restyled Ford Thunderbird winning *Motor Trend*'s Car of the Year title. The Ford Motor Company also enjoyed increased profits and higher market share, but mourned the passing of Henry Ford II on September 29.

Although the Thunderbird's sleeker skin was new, the platform underneath remained as before. The top of the range Turbo Coupe Thunderbird was easily distinguishable from the base and luxury LX models because it had adopted the grille-less look. However, just to confuse things, the Sport model also had the same style of front end, but

not the functional hood scoops, and wa powered by the 5.0-liter V8. Turb Coupe T-Birds came equipped wi antilock disc brakes all round ar Automatic Ride Control. The use of a intercooler boosted the output of th Turbo Coupe's 140 cu.in. four-cylind engine to 190bhp, but this was reduce to 150 horsepower when automat transmission was fitted. Otherwise, th 140bhp, 232 cu.in. V6 was standard c base and LX models, with the 15 horsepower, 302 cu.in. (5.0-liter) V available as an option. Prices range from $12,972 for a base model coupe u to $16,805 for the Turbo Coupe, wit

just over 128,000 Thunderbirds produced.

Appearance-wise nothing had changed on the Corvette for '87, but there were 35 more horses on tap from the 350 cu.in. engine than in '84. This translated into a top speed of 150mph and a 0-60mph time of 6.5 seconds. On the other hand, the concealed headlamps of the Chrysler LeBaron Turbo GTC were a definite departure from the styling trends in use elsewhere (and something of a retrograde step), although the 140 horsepower, 135 cu.in. turbocharged four cylinder was potent enough to push the coupe to 120mph.

That such levels of performance could be achieved with relatively small V8

Below: The Corvette convertible was in its second year after being reintroduced (the ragtop had been dropped in 1975) and over 10,000 cars were sold – the most since 1969. Visually, the '87 Corvette was the same as the '86 model, and small increases in horsepower and fuel economy from the 350 cu.in. (5.7-liter) V8 were hardly noticeable by driver. Corvettes have long been one of the most stolen cars in the USA and a new key system was introduced in '87 as a deterrent.

engines or turbocharged four cylinder units demonstrates how far automotive technology had come in two decades. And things would get even better.

For the Reagan administration, however, things couldn't get very much worse. US oil tankers came under attack in the Persian Gulf, which was followed by the Irangate scandal in July.

In October, the Wall Street stock market suffered its worst day ever, falling 508 points. President Reagan also imposed higher duties on Japanese electronic goods to try and stem the flood of imports coming from that country, but by this time automotive companies like Honda, Isuzu, Mazda and Mitsubishi were already opening factories in the Midwest.

Right: The Chrysler LeBaron Turbo GTC's concealed headlights harked back to the styling of another era, but in all other aspects the car was right up to the minute: a turbocharger, four cylinder engine and front-wheel-drive. The LeBaron 2-door coupe and convertible models were completely restyled but sedan versions retained much of previous year's looks.

Below: Not all cars were getting modern aerodynamic styling. The luxury Lincoln Town Car kept its traditional lines and upright stance. Town Car performance talk was all about the new Ford JBL audio system (with 12 speakers and 140 watts) plus optional compact disc player rather than acceleration or top speed.

SPECIFICATIONS

PONTIAC GRAND PRIX

Engine:
V6 - cast iron block

Displacement:
173 cu. ins.

Bore and stroke:
3.5 x 3.0

Horsepower:
130

Body styles:
Coupe

No. of seats:
5

Weight (lbs):
3,100 lbs

Price:
$12,539 - $15,249

Produced:
86,357

Pontiac started using the slogan "We Build Excitement" in 1983, as a means of focusing attention on the sporting nature of the cars it produced. But a new slogan didn't automatically mean that all cars carrying a Pontiac badge were exciting. In 1988, for example, there was the return of the LeMans model name after an absence of seven years, but this car was now a subcompact built in Korea by Daewoo and little more than a mildly reworked Opel Kadett. This year also marked the end of the line for the Fiero but the top-of-the-range Bonneville SSE remained, wearing

Below: The Pontiac Grand Prix was given the accolade of Car of the Year by Motor Trend *magazine in 1988, and sales of the model more than doubled. The top of the line SE came with special front-end styling and other features, but with a price of over $15,250 it was least popular of the Grand Prix range with 19,888 produced. The 2-door coupe's drag coefficient of .299 made it one of the most aerodynamic production cars available in the world.*

showy plumage but hiding some impressive technical advances including anti-lock brakes. Sales of the new Bonneville range reached 124,000 in the first year of production, even without the advantage of the coupe styling of the Delta and LeSabre.

The introduction of the all-new fourth-generation Grand Prix created quite a bit of excitement – especially when the model picked up the

Above: The last of the breed – Fiero GT. Just when it seemed as if Pontiac had finally refined the Fiero into a serious performance car with the 2.8-liter V6, five-speed transmission and revised suspension, the announcement came that the plug was being pulled on the two-seater. While the Fiero undeniably provided some of the "excitement" Pontiac desired, it didn't generate enough dollars to make profits.

prestigious Motor Trend Car of the Year award. The front-wheel-drive 2-door coupe (the only body style available) came in three trim levels: base, LE and SE. One of the most aerodynamically efficient production cars then around, the Grand Prix had flush fitting windows and headlamps, door handles recessed in the B-pillars and hidden windshield wipers. These refinements paid dividends as they all added up to give a drag coefficient (cd) of just .299. The wheelbase, at 107.6 inches, was half

Above: The restyled Chevrolet Cavalier was also smoother all round. In additio to what the Chevy publicity called the "very stylish" RS 2-door coupe, there were 4-door sedans, station wagons and a "posh" convertible on offer with a choice of four-cylinder or V6 engines.

Below: 1988 was the year of the Corvette's 35th birthday. A Special Edition model was produced, painted t recall the original white bathtub of 1953.

Above: Re-profiled cams and new head ports kept the venerable L83 Corvette V8 competitive pending the imminent arrival of the ZR1

an inch less than before but the overall length had come down by six inches and there was also a weight reduction of around 200 pounds.

Below: Some owners of the Special Edition Corvette, however - like Mr. Tom Bell - preferred more basic trim options to go with their basic-state-of-tune 245 horsepower.

The standard Grand Prix engine was Pontiac's 2.8-liter multi-port fuel injected, 130 horsepower V6 coupled to a four-speed automatic overdrive transaxle. The top of the range SE came with different front-end styling that included integral foglamps and there were also special taillamps and side body moldings. Another feature of the SE was the use of a five-speed manual transaxle with overdrive in place of the automatic. Prices for the base Grand Prix started at just over $12,500, with the LE priced at $13,200 and the SE at $15,250. Production of the '88 Grand Prix totaled 86,357 units, more than twice the number sold the previous year.

There was no doubt that it a very successful debut indeed. Overall, Pontiac sales went up only slightly, but the small increase was enough to put them back into third place in the charts for the first time since 1969. This saw them taking over from fellow GM division Oldsmobile, who were now starting to suffer rather badly in the production stakes.

In the meantime, Chevrolet had a restyled Cavalier plus new Beretta and Corsica models to promote. The sales catalog described the Cavalier's facelift in glowing terms: "You'll love the surprising new look that extends fro[m] Cavalier's new grille and hood, along i[ts] body-side molding, around its wheel[s] all the way to its new rear bumper." Th[e] Cavalier model range also got the fu[ll] treatment: "...the coupe, sedan an[d] wagon; very stylish RS coupe and seda[n,] aggressive Z24 coupe and pos[t?] convertible."

Right: The Saleen touch is evident i[n] the carefully detailed, custom-porte[d,] tuned and balanced 302 V8 motor tha[t] occupies the engine bay of this 198[8] Mustang[.]

Above & Right: Steve Saleen began his business with specially-prepared customs - like this '88 Mustang - in 1983 . Painstaking attention to detail and the use of race-quality parts could improve performance and handling almost beyond recognition.

Right: Since 1994, Steve Saleen's company has produced DOT and NHTSA certified, high performance Mustangs, licensed for sale in 50 States. His ability to produce a better car for the street comes directly from his experience on the track.

CHEVROLET CORVETTE ZR-1

Engine:
V8 - aluminum block

Displacement:
350 cu. ins.

Bore and stroke:
3.90 x 3.66

Horsepower:
385

Body styles:
Hatchback coupe

No. of seats:
2

Weight (lbs):
3,465 lbs

Price:
$58,995

Produced:
3,049

Producing "grunt" from a V8 engine has never been a problem for US motor manufacturers and, ever since the early 1950s, this tire-shredding horsepower had come from cubic inches. At the height of the muscle car era in the late 1960s, the race for an ever greater power output usually meant an increased engine capacity – it really was that simple. While putting such monster powerplants in relatively inexpensive automobiles with fairly soft suspension and running on skinny biased-belted tires was exciting in a straight line, the combination couldn't be said to do much for controled cornering at high speed.

As was stated earlier, the original Chevrolet Corvette came about because design chief Harley Earl wanted to show that he could produce a car that would rank alongside the best sports cars from Europe. The 1953 model wasn't up to that standard, but over the years the 'Vette evolved and

Right: The front-end body styling of the Corvette ZR-1 was the same as the standard 'Vette and dated back to the introduction of the 1984 model.

mproved immeasurably. Even so, it wasn't until the arrival of the ZR-1 version in 1989 that the Corvette truly became the first American sports car to beat the Europeans at their own game.

Below: Although it carried the Corvette name on the cam covers, the LT5's 350 cu.in. V8 was actually developed in England by Lotus from a stillborn engine project.

And this was done not with brute horsepower from mega cubic inches, but thanks to modern technology and state-of-the-art chassis design.

It was General Motors' acquisition of Lotus – the famous British sports car and Formula One grand prix racing company – as a research and development facility in 1986 that sparked off the transformation. Prior to the takeover, Chevy engineers had been working on an ambitious project intended to make the Corvette one of the fastest production sports cars in the world.

Above: If you've built a Corvette that can compete with the best sports cars from Europe, why not take them on in their own back yard? The ZR-1 was introduced at 1989 Geneva Motor Show in Switzerland and subsequently won rave reviews from journalists who road tested the car on a route through southern France.

They intended to achieve that aim with either a twin turbocharged or 600bhp naturally aspirated V8. Once the Lotus expertise became available "within the

Above: The rear of the ZR-1 was three inches wider than the '89 Corvette; extra width was needed to accommodate the 17 x 11 inch wheels and P315/35ZR17 tires. The flared body required new doors, rear quarters, rockers, rear facia and upper panel. Rectangular taillights were originally an exclusive feature of the ZR-1, but became part of standard Corvette design a couple of years later.

family," so to speak, approval came from GM management for work to begin on a brand-new small-block engine.

Although it had the same 350 cu.in. capacity as the long-running Chevy small-block V8, the ZR-1's LT5 engine that resulted from the transatlantic hookup was different in just about every other detail. Deriving from a 4-liter Lotus V8 that never went into production, the LT5 featured four valves per cylinder with dual overhead camshafts in each head. Block and heads were

aluminum, and the compression ratio was a healthy 11:1. If the origination of the LT5 came from overseas, the actual production of the engine was handled deep in America's heartland at Mercury Marine of Stillwater, Oklahoma, a company most people would associate with the famous "Mercruiser" boat engines. The LT5 came equipped with a computer-controled, multiple-throttle induction fuel injection system that closed off eight of the 16 inlet ports when the engine was cold or at small throttle openings; this optimized gas mileage and low-end smoothness. Then, when the secondary ports opened at 3500rpm, an impressive amount of power was delivered to the road.

How impressive exactly? Try 380 horsepower and 375 lbs/ft of torque for

Above: In an attempt to compete with the rising sales of imported cars, General Motors introduced a new brand name to the US market – Geo. Operating within the Chevrolet organization, Geo models were mainly rebadged versions of existing Japanese cars. Shown are three of the 1989 Geo range. The Prizm (front) was built by New United Motor Manufacturing Inc., in Fremont, California (a joint GM-Toyota venture). The Metro (center) and Tracker (rear) were produced by Suzuki in Japan.

starters, plus the glorious accompaniment of the hightech V8 howl that wound up to a maximum of 7,200rpm. Translated into performance terms, the result was a zero to 60mph time of 4.3

transmission was strictly for cruising – geared to give 41.6mph per 1,000rpm – as the ZR-1 could pull 7,200rpm, in sixth it would be doing almost 300mph! One unusual facet of the gear selection mechanism was a fuel-saving device that obliged the driver to change into fourth directly from first when using a light touch on the throttle.

Among all the '80s technology, however, was one piece of engineering on the ZR-1 that harked back to the Corvette's earlier days. The all-independent suspension still used transverse leaf springs, albeit made of glass-fiber composite material rather than steel, but something of an anachronism nevertheless. The standard Z51 Performance Handling Package included heavy-duty springs and stabilizer bars, uprated disc brakes and a cooler for the power rack and pinion steering. Selective Ride Control was a feature previously seen on

Below: *Another example of an American/Japanese hybrid was the Ford Probe. Assembled at the plant in Flat Rock, Michigan, the front-wheel-drive Probe used a Mazda platform and a 2.2-liter four cylinder engine with multi-port electronic fuel injection. The LX model shown had an air-drag coefficient of 0.304, which was at that time the most aerodynamic production car that Ford had ever designed.*

seconds, with 100mph coming in 10 seconds and an ultimate top speed of 180mph attainable in fifth. Top ratio in the ZF-designed six-speed manual

Lotus Formula One cars that allowed the driver to choose "Touring," "Sport," or "Performance" modes using a switch mounted on the console. The Sport setting was roughly equivalent to the normal '89 Corvette set-up, with Touring set as the soft option and Performance for the racers. Within each of the three bands there were six different shock absorber damping levels, electric motors automatically adjusting to give a firmer ride as the car's speed increased.

The final pieces in the handling jigsaw were a Bosch ABS II antilock braking system and the widest tires ever fitted to a US automobile (at that time): P315/35ZR-17 Goodyear Eagle unidirectionals at the rear, with P275/4-0ZR-17s on the front. Covering those vast expanses of rubber required some subtle flaring of the composite bodywork which began at the doors and extended rearward to the then unique convex panel with its four rectangular taillamps. As you can imagine, ZR-1 owners were not best pleased therefore when the 1991 facelift of the Corvette incorporated "their" rear quad light into the standard model.

The basic design for the ZR-1 goes as far back as 1978, when, under the direction of Jerry Palmer, the stylists at Chevrolet Studio Three in Warren, Michigan, began working on the new fourth-generation Corvette for its introduction in 1984. However, the credit for the ZR-1 body rests mainly with John Cafaro, studio chief in charge of the new Corvette project, who was also responsible for the Chevy Beretta that came out of Studio Three.

Above: It had been a difficult decade, but Ford was confident in the continuing popularity of its pony car at the end of the 'eighties. The company was investing some $200,000,000 on upgrading its Dearborn assembly plant.

The body of the ZR-1 was three inches wider than that of the regular '89 Corvette and an inch longer overall. The horizontal breakline that ran around the car served a dual purpose. Not only was it a styling feature intended to impart an imperceptible rake to the body, but it also acted as a part line between the major body sections, thereby eliminating unnecessary seams. The clamshell hood was also the largest single urethane molding in the automotive industry.

But the man who had steered the Corvette's fortunes since taking over as Chief Engineer from the legendary Zora Arkus-Duntov in 1975 was Dave McLellan. At the start of his tenure, McLellan was faced with a situation where higher gas prices, lower speed limits and tightened emission controls were all seemingly working against a performance car like the 'Vette. But despite everything, he maintained the Corvette's performance image and actually managed to enhance it.

At the launch of the ZR-1, McLellan stated his philosophy for the Corvette: "I guess the best way I would describe it is that between Jerry Palmer, John Cafaro, the interior people and the engineering team, we've really invented a car for ourselves. It's a car that's the ultimate expression of what we would like to drive around. That's the only way I know to do the Corvette. You can't do it for somebody else. You've got to do it for yourself. Then you literally say to your customers, 'We've got this car that we're excited about. And if you'd like to buy one, we'll make you one.'" He summed up by saying: "ZR-1 is Corvette. Only more so!"

The price of wanting more came to something like $50,000 – over $10,000 more than a standard L98 Corvette – but it was a price that plenty of people were prepared to pay in 1989.

Below: The '88/89 Mustangs went European in their styling, eventually to the extent of renaming the 302 V8 as "5.0 Liter." The muscle that it generated remained true to the all-American tradition, however.

SPECIFICATIONS

OLDSMOBILE SILHOUETTE

Engine:
Aluminum - V6

Displacement:
207 cu. ins

Bore and stroke:
3.50 x 3.27

Horsepower:
185

Body styles:
All purpose vehicle

No. of seats:
6-7

Weight (lbs):
3,948 lbs

Price:
c. $27,650

Produced:
-

This year heralded the arrival of a ne[w] Chevrolet, Pontiac and Oldsmobile. In automo[t]ive terms at least, the announcements that Chev[y] were going to sell the Lumina APV, Pontiac woul[d] offer a similar vehicle called the Trans Sport an[d] Olds had their equivalent called the Silhouett[e] could quite justifiably be regarded as some sort [of] a milestone. The launch of a couple of All Purpos[e] Vehicles by General Motors was merely a reactio[n] to market forces, with the continued success of th[e] Plymouth Voyager and Dodge Caravan model[s] something Chevy, Pontiac and Oldsmobile dealer[s] needed to combat.

But the idea of marques like Oldsmobile an[d] Pontiac producing a multipurpose vehicle wasn[t] met with universal approval. A Chevrolet dealer a[t] one GM convention was totally against the whol[e] idea stating, in effect, that "Chevrolet dealers ar[e] the only ones who know how to sell family cars[.] Pontiac dealers are more used to handling sportin[g] or performance models." Maybe he was facin[g] tough competition from a Pontiac dealershi[p] across the street. The breaking down of suc[h] traditional marketing attitudes was an ongoin[g] process that gathered speed in the 1990s and no[w] it is seen as quite acceptable for any ca[r]

Above: The Pontiac Trans
Sport had its origins in a 1986
show car of the same name and
carried over many of the concept
van's styling features. The right rear
door, was originally a swing-up gullwing
design, but was found to be too
impractical in garages and tight parking
spaces. The production version used a
conventional sliding door. Pontiac's
press release compared the Trans Sport's
appearance to a shuttlecraft from the
starship Enterprise on the Star Trek TV
series, saying: "It's Pontiac's space
vehicle for the '90s."

Below: The Silhouette was Oldsmobile's
entry into the burgeoning market sector
for people carriers or minivans. Based
on the same platform as the Chevrolet
Lumina APV and Pontiac Trans Sport,
and produced in the same Tarrytown,
New York, assembly plant, the
Silhouette was an unsuccessful attempt
to reverse sagging Oldsmobile sales.

manufacturer to produce any style of vehicle, from a two-seater sports car to a rugged 4x4.

While Trans Sport represented Pontiac's move into a new sector (as did the Oldsmobile Silhouette), it was only one model. Chevy's Lumina range consisted of a 4-door sedan and 2-door coupe models as well as the APV. The Lumina name had actually been introduced by Chevrolet in the spring of '89 (as 1990 models) to replace the Monte Carlo and Celebrity sedans, and it's interesting to note that the higher specification versions were known as the Lumina Euro – perhaps suggesting a desire to impart something of an imported car status to the name.

By way of contrast, the launch of the 1990 Lumina 4-door sedan was about a American as mom's apple pie – it wa tied in with opening of the new Disney MGM Studios theme park in Florida. I addition to having the Lumina designa

Below: *The Chevrolet Lumina Euro Sedan was the top model in the range and came with a 135 horsepower, 3.1-liter V6 engine, giving a 0-60mph acceleration time of 10 seconds. The standard Lumina came with a 2.5-liter four cylinder engine and was three seconds slower to 60, but nearly $2,000 cheaper than the Euro recommended $13,776 price. Introduced in the spring of 1989 as a 1990 model, it was then the largest front-wheel-drive car ever to wear the Chevy badge.*

ed as the official car of the tourist attraction, Chevy also used Disney animation and cartoon characters in television commercials and the theme

Above: NASCAR *Chevrolet drivers like Dale Earnhardt quickly switched to the slippery Lumina in 1989, which replaced the Monte Carlo SS.*

park served as the setting for Lumina magazine advertisements. This was said to be the first time that the famous Disney figures had been incorporated into an automotive advertising campaign, and Chevrolet's general marketing manager was delighted with the result. "When you think Disney, you think family," he said. "And we're aiming to sell the Lumina sedan to meet the needs of growing families – making the partnership between Disney and Chevrolet a sure hit."

Chevy weren't about to let the Lumina's fortunes rest solely on the appeal of cute cartoons though, and immediately introduced the model as the official factory stock car racer in the NASCAR Winston Cup series, replacing the Monte Carlo SS. Leading drivers who switched to the more compact, sleeker bodystyle of the Lumina coupe included Dale Earnhardt, Darrell Waltrip, Ken Schrader and Geoff Bodine. Although NASCAR regulations allowed a model

to be used in competition as soon as the production car appeared in dealer showrooms, there were a couple of anomalies about the 1990 Lumina making its debut in the Winston 500 at Talladega on May 7, 1989.

To begin with, the 2-door coupe version wasn't actually due to go on sale until much later that year. The other thing was that the Luminas were all front-wheel-drive models, whereas the race cars remained rear-wheel-drive.

Below: The much-awaited - and much delayed - Chrysler TC was the company's first ever production two-seater. The 4 cylinder, 16 valve, turbocharged 2.2 liter engine was developed by Maserati and produced 200 bhp. There was a 160 bhp, single-cam, automatic transmission version too. Equipment was lavish and and the styling was elegant and restrained, but Chrysler customers seemed indifferent to its charms.

he fact that the NASCAR entrants used
'8 engines and the biggest unit you
ould get in the production car was a
.1-liter V6 was another slight differe-
ce that didn't seem to bother anyone
oo much.

The Lumina APV went into produc-
ion at the Tarrytown, New York, plant
during the summer (the sedan and coupe

Below: *The 1990 Cadillac Eldorado was
classified as a personal luxury coupe.
Changes to the exterior consisted of
minor refinements such as a new front
bumper and a redesigned body-side.
Equipped with a 4.5-liter, fuel injected,
180bhp V8 (up from 155bhp in '89), all
1990 Cadillacs had their top speed
limited to 115mph.*

were built at Oshawa, Ontario, in Canada) for release in the fall. It comes as little surprise to learn that both the Trans Sport and Silhouette were also assembled at Tarrytown. So how did three different GM divisions market what was essentially the same vehicle?

Chevrolet played heavily on their heritage of providing family transportation for 80 years and described the Lumina APV as "a trend-setting, multipurpose minivan." Pontiac couldn't quite decide whether the Trans Sport was a multipurpose vehicle or a minivan and tried to associate the newcomer with a concept car of the same name that was shown at the 1986 Detroit Auto Show.

Meantime, Oldsmobile had the Silhoue tte down as a multipurpose passenge van.

"Lumina APV combines versatilit with distinctive styling and smooth rid and handling," read the Chevrolet pres release. "Trans Sport owners can arriv fashionably at the most exclusive socia gatherings or restaurants in a manner n

Below: *T-Bird for the 'nineties: anti-lock braking; Automatic Ride Control; air-conditioning; tinted glass and an overdrive automatic transmission system. All this - and more - in a handsome, almost European-looking, coupe styling package that debuted in '89.*

Above: The Thunderbird Super Coupe featured a supercharged, intercooled V6 that developed 210 bhp and drove through a five-speed manual gearbox.

minivan can match" proclaimed Pontiac's PR department. "The Silhouette looks like no other vehicle on the American road. It's also built like no car or truck gone before using state-of-the-art materials and manufacturing processes," said the Oldsmobile news release.

It clearly wasn't an easy task finding alternative ways of presenting similar products in what one Pontiac release obliquely referred to as "...the mundane world of motorized boxes." And, in an ever-changing world, Pontiac were obviously wary of the response from their customers, posing the question "Why is a company best known for its exciting, driver-orientated cars going into the van market?" The answer, of course, was simple – to tap into a rapidly growing market sector, boost sales and make more profits. A corporate motive that remains a constant, whatever else might change.

Above: Overdrive automatic transmission had replaced the old three-speed 'box in the '87 Thunderbird. All-round disc brakes now came as standard too.

SPECIFICATIONS

FORD EXPLORER CURRENT)

Engine:
V6 - Cast iron with aluminum heads

Displacement:
281 cu. ins.

Bore and stroke:
3,55 x 3.54

Horsepower:
239

Engine Electronics:
EEC-V Electronic engine controls with Integrated EDIS

Body styles:
2/4 door Utility/ATV

No. of seats:
7

Price (base):
$24,020

This year saw the demise of the Ford Bronco II which was replaced by the Explorer. Apart from the hood and stone shield, all the Explorer bodywork was new and used car design techniques to improve the boxy 4x4's aerodynamics. And although it was definitely shaped more like a truck than a car, Ford reckoned the compact utility Explorer was capable of blurring the distinction between the two types of vehicle. In this vein, Ford

Division general manager Thomas J. Wagner was quoted as saying: "Explorer offers some of the same comforts you would expect to find in cars – right down to the lighted vanity mirrors, optional compact disc player and leather seats. But when you need a truck, Explorer is there, with part-time four-wheel-drive, trailer towing, plenty of

Below: The Explorer replaced the Bronco II and the new model immediately increased Ford sales in the compact utility vehicle sector of the market. 2-door versions sat on a shorter 102.1 inch wheelbase, could accommodate four passengers and had a maximum load capacity of 69.4 cubic feet with the rear seat folded down.

cargo space and built-in ruggedness."

There were three 2-door Explorer models (102.1 inch wheelbase) and three 4-door versions (111.9 inch wheelbase) in four series: base XL, Sport, XLT and Eddie Bauer. The Explorer Sport came as a 2-door only, while the XLT was available just as a 4-door. The sole engine available was the 155 horsepower, 4.0-liter V6 with multiple-port electronic fuel injection, but there was a choice of either five-speed manual or four-speed automatic transmissions (both with overdrive), limited slip axle, manual locking hubs and other goodies, for those who intended to do some serious off-road driving. The Eddie Bauer models, on the other hand, came with a whole stack of special trim items and creature comforts, not the least of which were a couple of designer bags for garments and such.

The factory price of an Eddie Bauer 4-door Explorer was almost $22,000, as against under $17,000 for a 2-door XL (which was still two times the cost of the cheapest Escort), but the Explorer's arrival boosted sales of Ford's compact utility vehicles by a huge margin. Indeed, the Explorer proved so successful that during the month of March 1991 it reached number seven in

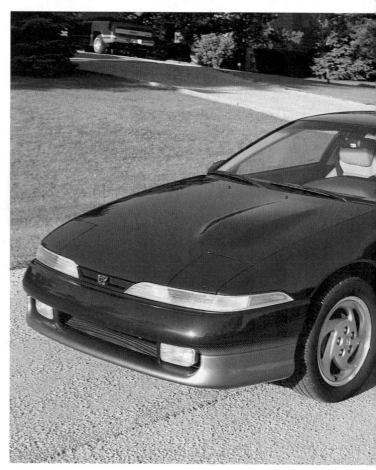

Above: *In an attempt to halt a worrying decline in sales, Oldsmobile added the Bravada 4x4 to its lineup. However, the sport utility was manufactured by GM's Truck and Bus Operations and based on the Chevrolet Blazer. But it was the drivetrain that really set it apart from the Chevy. The 4.3-liter Vortex V6 engine was coupled to a four-speed automatic transmission and a SmartTrack system consisting of full-time four-wheel-drive and antilock brakes.*

Left: *The Eagle Talon came about as part of the joint venture between Chrysler and Mitsubishi. Although the Talon was assembled in Normal, Illinois, other Eagle models were either built in Japan or the former AMC factory in Ontario, Canada. The Talon 2-door coupe was equipped with a 2.0-liter four cylinder unit producing 135 horsepower as standard, but a 195hp turbo version was also available, along with an all-wheel-drive model. Jeep/Eagle used the slogan "Expect the Best" and the Talon did collect a number of awards.*

401

the list of best-selling vehicles in the USA. The popularity of the Explorer and similar utility models like the Aerostar promoted the demise of the full-size, rear-wheel-drive station wagon at Ford, as production of the LTD Crown Victoria came to an end. The Thunderbird got a V8 back under the hood, and the Taurus SHO, with its 220bhp Yamaha V6, established itself as a refined example of the '90s muscle car. For the 10th year in a row, Ford's F-Series pickup trucks remained their top-selling vehicle, but despite all this, the company still posted a record loss of $2.3 billion. Development of the Explorer continued. The later model had off-road ability - and agility - comparable to the Jeep Grand Cherokee and was available in a number of trim levels with an extensive option list.

Driving impressions were excelle the new base V6 and the optional, a alloy 281 cid V8 both giving increas performance and considerable refiner ent. The Explorer was soon establishe as one of the leaders in this increasing crowded market sector.

Below: The Chevrolet Lumina Euro Sedan was the top model in the range and came with a 135 horsepower, 3.1-liter V6 engine, giving a 0-60mph acceleration time of 10 seconds. The standard Lumina came with a 2.5-liter four cylinder engine and was three seconds slower to 60, but nearly $2,00(cheaper than the Euro's recommended $13,776 price. Introduced in the spring of 1989 as a 1990 model, it was then th largest front-wheel-drive car ever to wear the Chevy badge.

Above: Styling of the '87 Cadillac Allante was by Pininfarina, who built the bodies on to modified Eldorado platforms. The car was great-looking and sharp handling, but nobody wanted to buy it. Sales were embarrassingly slow, even when the model was fitted with the fabulous North Star V8, traction control and active suspension. The Allante was abandoned in 1993, no doubt to become a much sought-after collector's car.

Below: The Mercury Capri had a pre-owned name and the floorpan from the Mazda 323. The car had four-wheel discs and turbocharging on the XR2 version, but American sportscar buyers didn't buy it.

SPECIFICATIONS

1992 DODGE VIPER

Engine:
V10 - All Aluminum

Displacement:
488 cu. ins.

Bore and stroke:
4.00 x 3.88

Horsepower:
400

Body styles:
Roadster

No. of seats:
2

Weight (lbs):
3,476 lbs

Price:
$50,000

Produced:
162

In some ways, the evolution of the Dodge Viper could be said to have run parallel to the Chevrolet Corvette ZR-1 of 1989, and the on-the road performance of the two cars is also pretty close. But while GM went looking in England for some technical expertise from Lotus, Chrysler homed in on Italy and Lamborghini for their European connection.

The other major difference is, of course, that while the ZR-1 was a development of an existing production model, the Viper was a totally new vehicle and came from a manufacturer that had never previously been associated with a sports car. And, unlike the Corvette variant, the genesis of the Dodge was a concept car that was built to create publicity on the auto show circuit rather than a serious corporate decision to enter a very specialist market sector.

With a name like Viper there was no doubt where the inspiration for this awesome two-seater

ad come from – the 'sixties Shelby
obra. Another American/British
ybrid, the Cobra was the brainchild of
exan racecar driver and constructor
arroll Shelby, who married the muscle
f Ford V8 engines to the chassis and
odies produced by AC Cars of Thames
itton in Surrey, near London, England,
o create an all-time classic that has been
loned many times over.

As well as providing the inspiration,
Carroll Shelby himself was involved at
he early beginnings of the Viper idea,

*elow: The Viper name and concept
arks back to the Shelby Cobra sports
ar and the design of the badge reflects
his heritage. Just like its historic
orbear, the Dodge snake was full of
enom and lightning fast!*

*Below: The awesome Dodge Viper
RT/10 was a "back-to-basics" exercise
bringing the '60s sports car bang up to
date. Demand was such that a long
waiting list for cars developed after
some initial production problems were
experienced with the composite body,
and this saw Vipers changing hands for
double the original $55,000 price. This
stunning supercar could accelerate from
zero to 60mph in 4.5 seconds and go on
to top 165mph.*

but the throbbing heart of this car was its 400 horsepower 8-liter (488 cu.in.) V-10 engine. And the story behind this amazing powerplant goes back to the latter half of 1987, when American Motors Corporation was bought by Chrysler and turned into the Jeep/Eagle division. One result of this amalgamation was the creation of the Jeep & Truck Engineering Department, which was given the task of revamping the Dodge Ram full-size pickup truck range. A prime requirement in this process was the need to provide a larger capacity engine to compete with the big block V8s on offer from Ford and Chevy.

It was apparent that the existing 5.9-liter (360 cu.in.) small-block Chrysler V8 couldn't be stretched any further [so] the notion of building a V-10 by simp[ly] adding two cylinders to the end of t[he] block was discussed. At the behest [of] Chrysler President Bob Lutz, just su[ch] an exercise was carried out and, much [to] the consternation of those experts wh[o] said the V-10 would produce unbearab[le] vibration, the experimental engi[ne] performed remarkably well. There wa[s] still a great deal of development wor[k] needed before the V-10 would be read[y] for everyday use, but more prototype V[-] 10 engines were tested and one of thes[e] was used in the Viper show car tha[t] caused such a sensation when [it] appeared for the first time at the Nort[h] American International Auto Show i[n] Detroit in January 1989.

This gave rise to the myth that the [Vi]per was powered by nothing more [th]an a truck engine. This was far from [th]e truth. Bernard Robertson (then Vice [Pr]esident of Jeep & Truck Engineering): [']As the Viper program evolved, we [ne]eded numerous changes to package [th]e V-10, which led to the low profile [cr]oss ram intake with dual throttle

[B]elow: The Viper is a pure minimalist [t]wo-seater, with crude sidescreens [in]stead of wind-up windows and a ["]build-it-yourself" type of top that was [la]st seen on early '60s British sports [ca]rs. But the Viper wasn't intended to be [f]or mundane daily transportation – it's a [fu]n car and one that should be left in the [g]arage when it rains.

Above: *In keeping with its muscular, masculine image, the Viper's interior was totally devoid of frills. Steering, and brakes were power assisted but there were no power-windows - there were no windows! The hood was a crude, clip-on affair, with separate side-curtains, harking back to the original, '53 Corvette.*

bodies, unique cast steel exhaust manifolds and revised oil pan, front end accessory drive system, etc. We also needed a significant weight reduction and were enticed by the 150 pounds or so achievable with aluminum versus cast iron. Because Lamborghini are experts in aluminum and have captive casting facilities, I personally delivered the iron block truck engine blueprints to Mauro Forghieri in March 1989 and arranged for the first five sets of aluminum blocks and heads to come from Italy."

"Lamborghini also proposed some innovative changes to the cooling system and crankshaft balance, which we adopted," he added.

"During the development process, we increased the compression ratio, lightened the pistons, increased the valvetrain critical speed, changed the valve sizes and strengthened the rods and crank, all to achieve 400bhp in

Viper configuration. Consequently, t only remaining components shared wi the truck engine are some nuts and bo and minor valvetrain pieces, althou the bore, stroke and architecture rema common."

"As you can see, there is a stro family connection between the tv versions of the V-10 engine, althou each is optimized for its particul application. Both were developed Jeep & Truck Engineering and both a built at our Mound Road engine plant Detroit. Lamborghini played a valuab supporting role and their aluminu design and casting expertise probab saved us six months."

But if the V-10 gave the Viper venom, the curvaceous bodywo undeniably added to the car's immedia appeal. The design concept aros following a series of meetings early 1988 which, at various times, involve

o or more of Carroll Shelby, Bob utz, Francois Castaing (Vice President Vehicle Engineering), Tom Gale (Vice esident of Product Design) and nowned Chrysler President Lee cocca. Once the idea for a balls-out orts car had been aired, it didn't take ale longer than a couple of weeks to rogress from his "back of an envelope" ketches to a sheaf of styling drawings. ith approval granted, the next stage as to make a full-size clay mockup and om there, the original show car soon llowed.

Although all the people involved in e Viper project at Dodge and Chrysler ere highly enthusiastic about the car, it unlikely that many of them believed at e outset that it would ever be put into olume production. After all, it was othing more than a "back to basics" ront-engined, rear-wheel-drive, two-eat sportster without a top – a no-frills,

high-performance fantasy machine from an auto manufacturer that had experienced a torrid time over the previous ten years.

But the Viper struck a chord in the hearts of American drivers like few other show cars before or since. Yes, it was impractical. Yes, its 8-liter engine and 166mph top speed were out of step with 1990s concerns about the environment and safety. But it didn't matter. Every red-blooded person who saw the Viper wanted one. Deposit checks and orders were mailed to Chrysler's head

Below: The Taurus was proof positive of Ford's continuing commitment to building cars for the US market that shared styling and engineering with models produced by the company in Europe. The 1992 Taurus represented the first major redesign since the model's launch in December 1985.

office in Highland Park, dealers were inundated with enquiries whenever the Viper appeared and the media gave it rave reviews. Chrysler had, unwittingly perhaps, tapped into a rich vein of customer demand. Eventually, in May 1990, Lee Iacocca announced that the Viper would go into production in early 1992.

Turning a show car into something that can be used out on the highway isn't a simple task. Yet surprisingly few changes were needed to the original Viper body design in order to make it work. Engineering was more complicated but, even so, the original ethos of

the Viper remains. It is not a practic car, there are no side windows and no a conditioning, it is noisy and you g buffeted by the wind at high speed– bu the fact remains it is fun!

When the 1992 Vipers went on sa you could have any color you like providing you wanted red (black becam available in '93 and other colors subs quently followed). But the demand fo

Below: Pontiac's Firebird for '92 came as a hatchback coupe or a convertible with engine options that ran to a 350 cu. in. V8 giving 240 bhp.

...he $50,000 car was almost insatiable ...nd it still remains popular today.

Looking back, it can be said that the ...iper helped enormously in transfo-...ming the image of Chrysler. In much the ...ame fashion as the Chevy Bel Air of ...955 altered forever the American ...ublic's perception of GM's cheapest ...rand name, the Viper showed the ...orld that a revitalized Chrysler Corpo-...ation was changing into an innovative ...nd imaginative organization that was ...repared to take chances. It has certai-...ly paid off, big time.

Above: The Pontiac Firebird continues in production, most popular in Trans-Am spec, as part of the defiant Second Age of the Muscle Car, its sleek lines formed by the computer and the wind tunnel.

Below: The Caprice was big and heavy, and old-fashioned, and even after the '91 restyle it still looked it. Its popularity with the public was soon on the wane, despite the introduction of a short-lived "muscle" version of the LTZ.

SPECIFICATIONS

1993 CADILLAC ALLANTE

Engine:
V8 - all aluminum

Displacement:
279 cu. ins.

Bore and stroke:
3.66 x 3.31

Horsepower:
295

Body styles:
Convertible coupe

No. of seats:
4

Weight (lbs)
3,776 lbs

Price:
$61,675

Produced:
4,670

The idea of having an exotic car body designed in Europe and then installing an American V8 engine into it isn't a new one. It wasn't new when Cadillac introduced the Allanté in the late summer of '86 as a 1987 model. What was different about the Cadillac ultra-luxury two-seater was the fact that the bodies were handbuilt in Turin, Italy, by Pininfarina and then flown across the Atlantic – six at a time – in a Boeing 747 freighter known as the

Below: Although the price of the Allanté had risen to over $60,000 by 1993, its Northstar V8 and other improvements over the years meant that Cadillac's two-seater was now capable of beating Jaguar and Mercedes models in the same class. Regretably, just as they seemed to have got it right, Cadillac decided to axe the Allanté. The problem that proved impossible to overcome was its image of being an under-performing luxury cruiser.

irbridge." Some of the body mponents actually made the eight-our flight in both directions, because e Allanté was based on an Eldorado nderbody and these were shipped out Italy (along with various other parts) r modification.

After Pininfarina's craftsmen short-ned the Eldorado platform slightly and sembled the Allanté body onto it, the nished unit was fully painted and immed before being sent to Detroit for mpletion. In a relatively small corner

Below: Cadillac's first all-new engine for a decade, the 4.6-liter Northstar V8 is one of the truly great automotive powerplants. Featuring dual overhead camshafts on each cylinder head and 32 valves, with a compression ratio of 10.3:1, the Northstar produced 290bhp at 5,600rpm and 290 pounds per sq. foot of torque at 4,400rpm. Redlined at 6,500rpm, the computer-controlled sequential port fuel injection would automatically cut off fuel delivery at 6,700rpm.

of the GM Hamtramck assembly plant the front-wheel-drive powertrain and suspension were added to produce an unusual combination of Italian style and US muscle. Unfortunately, although the understated (for a Cadillac) looks were generally well received, the performance

of the Allanté never quite lived up potential customers' expectations.

The interior, with its hugely intrusi rectangular central console set into t dash was also criticized, as was t amount of plastic used on as $50,0(automobile. And the disappointing 4.

ter V8 only produced 170bhp, which gave the '87 Allanté a 0-60mph time of 9.5 seconds and a top speed of around 120mph. While those figures aren't too bad, a Road & Track comparison test with a Mercedes-Benz 560SL showed the German sportster to be two seconds

Below: Cab-forward styling, a wider stance and new engines were introduced on the revised '93 Ford Probe. The body and interior were designed by Ford's studio team headed by Jack Telnack, while Mazda supplied the engineering input.

quicker to 60mph and more than 15mph faster.

Allanté sales in the first year amounted to only 3,363 cars, and the figure dropped to 2,569 in '88. A bigger 200 horsepower engine was fitted for '89 and this, together with the uprated suspension, helped the performance aspect, with various improvements to the interior being another step in the right direction. An antilock braking system was introduced in 1990 but, positive though these changes were, Allanté couldn't seem to shake off its image as being a luxury cruiser rather

Right: *The Buick Park Avenue sedan Buick's sales were down to around ha of their mid-'eighties levels. The born again Roadmaster of '91 had picked u a few purchasers, perhaps attracted b the nostalgia factor. By '93 the Par Avenue was a range of 1 with a "Ultra" options package*

Below: *One of Buick's Great Names from Flint was the Riviera. It had not been revised to any great extent for five years. 1993 sales were way down, but 1994/5 would see a completely new model.*

than an exclusive, high-performance machine. Sales hovered around the 3,000 mark for most years, but fell disastrously to 624 in '92.

The 1993 Allanté was by far the best yet, thanks to the arrival of the fabulous Cadillac Northstar V8. This 4.6-liter all-aluminum engine, with double-overhead camshafts for each cylinder bank and 32 valves, pumped out a mighty 290bhp, turning the Allanté into the quickest and fastest Cadillac ever tested by Road &

Track. Zero to 60mph was achieved i 6.7 seconds, while the top speed ha jumped to 145mph. In recognition of t Allanté's elevation to performance ca status, the Cadillac was chosen as th Pace Car for the Indianapolis 500 and was said to have undertaken the role i completely standard form (apart fro additional safety equipment, like the ro bar). But it still wasn't enough. Deman remained depressingly low and the '9 model was decreed to be the last aft

pproximately 3,500 were built – it was sad ending. The Allanté, particularly tted with the North Star V8, was a otential winner, not only in the omestic market, but across the world - f only the price had been right.

1993 was also celebrated as the entenary of the gasoline-powered American automobile. It was on September 21 1893 that Frank Duryea ook his buggy for its first test drive on ublic roads in Springfield, Massachu-setts. Steam-powered contraptions had been around for much longer of course, but the Duryea is usually regarded as the forefather of the modern car.

Below: The Blazer's looks are square-jawed and purposeful, and its abilities live up to their promise. Fitted with the V6 Vortec engine, this is a vehicle that is capable of climbing over more than kerb-stones and has a towing capacity of 5,000 lbs.

SPECIFICATIONS

1994 FORD MUSTANG

Engine:
V6 - Cast iron block & head

Displacement:
232 cu. ins.

Bore and stroke:
3.80 x 3.40

Horsepower:
145

Body styles:
Coupe; Convertible coupe

No. of seats:
4

Weight (lbs):
3,065 lbs - 3,245 lbs

Price:
$13,365 - $20,160

Produced:
33,525

Right: The Mustang got its first major redesign since 1979, bringing back traditional styling elements like the running horse grille badge. The GT in theforeground is fitted with optional 17 in. alloy wheels. The full heritage of Ford's pony car is shown here, including 1965 models. The 1994 Mustang would never match the first year sales of 30 years earlier, but the new version was well received.

After 15 years and 2.5 million cars, For decided to introduce a brand-new Mustan and dealers nationwide were inundated wit people wanting to see it on the official launch dat of December 9, 1993. Although the styling change

vere immediately apparent, the designers had cleverly combined the modern aero look with the traditional "running horse" identification features n a great package. However, just as important as the bodywork were the changes that had been engineered in the running gear to update the Mustang's performance.

Based on a much revised version of

Above: While the Mustang's exterior was completely revamped, the Fox-4 platform it was based on dated back some years. Engineering alterations were made to the steering and suspension for '94 to improve road holding and ride. The base coupe model illustrated had a 3.8-liter V6 engine.

Right: The Aurora was the new flagship model for Oldsmobile and lined up against luxury imports like Lexus and Infiniti. Using a 4.0-liter, 250bhp derivative of the Cadillac Northstar V8, the Aurora was part of an effort to reverse troubled fortunes at the Oldsmobile division. Although the Aurora won much approval and sold well, Oldsmobile continued to lose money.

Below: '94 Corvettes in O-ZR1 form had 5 bhp over even the Viper...

he well-proven "Fox" platform that had served the previous decade and a half of Mustangs so well, the Fox-4 featured a slightly longer wheelbase (by three-quarters of an inch) and a wider track (increased by 3.7 inches on the standard model and 5.6 inches on the GT), together with improved steering and suspension geometry. The aim was to iron out the shortcomings of the earlier model – primarily in the high-speed handling and tire wear – and 85% of the '94 Mustang platform was either modified or new. The addition of a rear sway bar as standard also helped to eliminate the "tail happy" tendency experienced with the third-generation

Above: A Ford V8 had powered the legendary AC Cobra, but the meanest varmint around these days was the ten-cylinder Dodge Viper mill, producing 400 bhp in standard tune, with plenty of room for improvement on that figure.

'Stang, and the overall effect was to create superior handling as well as improved ride quality.

The 79 Mustang had quickly established a reputation for itself as an affordable high performance car and

Above: The Pontiac Firebird had some impressive equipment including anti-lock brakes. The Trans-am V8 version produced 275 bhp and drove thru a six-speed manual gearbox - a four-speed automatic was optional.

Above: Chevrolet's massive Suburban wagon was surprisingly popular with urban dwellers who liked the sense of security that its 5,000 lb. bulk imparted.

Below: The Suburban's base motor is the Vortec 5300 V8. With aluminum heads on a cast iron block, it displaces 325 cu. ins and produces 285 bhp.

throughout its life was regarded as excellent value for money. Ford weren't about to change this philosophy of providing "the best bang for a buck," but they did make some alterations to its range of engines. It may be hard to believe that any enthusiast regretted the passing of the 2.3-liter four banger, especially as it was replaced with the 145 horse, 3.8-liter V6 as used in the Thunderbird Super Coupe. However, the news that production of the 5.0-liter HO V8 was to cease because of rationalization at the Cleveland engine building plant was disappointing.

In its place came the Thunderbird version of the V8 (designated the MN-12) with a new low-profile fuel injection system that produced a maximum of 215 horsepower at 4,200rpm. So equipped, a Mustang GT could gallop from zero to 60mph in 6.7 seconds and reach 140mph in the stretch. For those more interested in quarter horses, on the drag strip a '94 Mustang could traverse the 440 yards in 14.8 seconds and reach 93mph at the finishing line. Once again, the numbers were impressive and once again the Mustang was chosen as the Pace Car for the Indy 500 – it was 1979 all over again.

The actual car used to lead the pa[...] around the famous Indianapolis ov[...] was a Cobra convertible, harking ba[...] to the ragtop Mustang used for the 19[...] race. A thousand Cobra Pace C[...] Replica convertibles were built by For[...] as well as 5,000 Cobra coupes, but t[...] Indy 500 decals only came on the so[...] top models.

The 2-door coupe and convertib[...] models were available from the outs[...] (the 3-door fastback now eliminate[...] from the range), but later in the year[...] convertible/hardtop version also appea[...]

d. Similar in concept to the detachable hardtop offered on the original 1955 Thunderbird, the Mustang version weighed in at only 84 pounds and was rollover certified. The ragtop also came with a dome light and a special rear window defogger, as well as its very own storage dolly.

Car and truck sales increased across the industry in '94, with a total of 15 million vehicles streaming off the assembly lines. Over 137,000 of these were new Mustangs. But the automotive event that grabbed the most media attention of the year was the high-speed police pursuit of former football star O.J. Simpson along the highways of California, which was shown live on TV. whether this affected Ford Bronco sales either way has never been revealed.

Below: The '94 Dodge Viper's uncompomising styling is matched by its raw performance. The mighty, all-alloy 488 cu. in. V10 motor produces 400 bhp but has been tuned to double that.

Below: The Viper's beauty is like that of a predatory animal; it is something to be admired and feared - and treated with great respect.

Below: Stark and functional - the Viper lacks creature comforts but it can get past 60 mph from a standing start in under 5 seconds or cruise on the highway, with the engine turning at 1,200 rpm.

SPECIFICATIONS

1995 BUICK RIVIERA

Engine:
V6 - Cast iron block & head

Displacement:
231 cu. ins.

Bore and stroke:
3.80 x 3.40

Horsepower:
205

Body styles:
Coupe

No. of seats:
4

Weight (lbs):
3,748 lbs

Price:
$27,632

Produced:
41,422

Opinions about automotive styling are a very subjective matter, something that Buick acknowledged in their Press release for the new 1995 model Riviera. But perhaps not unnaturally the statement went on to say: "...we think you will find this car to be beautiful." Depending on your point of view, that might seem rather presumptuous, although there was no doubt that the Riviera certainly looked striking. Whether it will ever attain the status of a "modern classic" in th

Right: Exterior design chief Bill Porter with the 1995 Buick Riviera that his studio team produced. The elliptic body styling only came about after months of trying to adapt the lines of a concept car proved impractical, and designers tried sticking paper sketches onto a clay model.

ame manner as the 1963 Riviera emains to be seen.

It is the job of any public relations eam to hype the company product, and motive phrases like "highly energized urfaces" and "a hint of mystery" were cattered throughout the Buick media naterial describing the luxury coupe's tyling. However, Riviera exterior lesign chief William L. Porter was rather more prosaic with his observations, saying: "Essentially, the body is a big ellipse resting on wheels. The theme is reflected in both the front and the rear, in the elliptical grille and elliptical taillamps." He continued by calling the Riviera's shape "muscular, well-balanced and modern – and free from cues that quickly go out of style."

The process of arriving at the finished

shape for the Riviera was not a straightforward one. The initial plans were to adapt the styling of the Buick Lucerne concept car but, after several months of trying, the changes needed to make the Lucerne's design features fit into the dimensional framework of the Riviera proved to be unworkable and the team had to look elsewhere for a solution. The answer came when Porter's assistant, Andy Hanzel, and a designer named Eric Clough went into work one Saturday and tried taping one of Clough's sketches of a grille onto a clay model.

Although the faceless, aerodynamic model was only a roughed-in clay without a specific theme, the front-end drawing transformed its appearance and

Above: The Chrysler Cirrus was voted Car of the Year by Motor Trend *magazine and introduced the company's innovative cab-forward design into the compact sedan range. The Cirrus was intended to win back younger families who had been buying imported cars instead of domestic models.*

gave the stylists the inspiration they were looking for. Chuck Jordan, then design president, walked through the studio, saw the model, liked it and encouraged them to keep going. Hanzel and Clough began by using tape to mark out shapes on the clay model and the whole thing came together very quickly. A sort of creative frenzy took hold of the entire Riviera team and within a few

weeks the design had swept through to its final form.

But while body styling can be created by individual improvisations, the engineering and manufacturing of a car requires team-work. This aspect of the new Riviera was developed at the Engineering and Development Center of

Below: Taillights and the rear end also carried the characteristic styling curves of the Riviera that were used on the front. Buick marketing described the car as a personal luxury coupe and aimed to attract a new generation of buyers by undercutting the prices of competitive models.

the Cadillac/Luxury Car Engineering and Manufacturing Division located at Flint, Michigan. The modern approach of using a network of overlapping teams within a single unit is in direct contrast to the old days when projects of this type were run by the "over the wall" method. Put simply, one department would finish its part of the development process, then throw the end result "over the wall" to the next department. Revisions were constant – which in itself added to the

cost – and delays were inevitable. An by the time the line workers wh actually had to build the car saw th model, it was too late to make eve minor changes that would make th thing easier to assemble.

The final link in the chain came wit the Riviera's optional 3800 supercha rged V6 engine. While the standar 3.8-liter V6 unit would use its 205 hors epower to get from zero to 60mph in 9. seconds, the 225hp supercharged vers

n cut acceleration time to 60mph down o 8.5 seconds. This level of performance was aimed at a new generation of purchasers, who market research had indicated were the potential buyers of a luxury car like the Riviera coupe.

Did the Buick team come up with "a home run" with the Riviera, as designer Bill Porter suggested in an interview when the car was introduced? It's too early to say for sure. Will the recession years of the early 1990s hold the same nostalgia for people in 30 years time as the '60s do today? It seems unlikely, but maybe enough '95 Rivieras will be around in 2025 to prove differently.

Below: The Ford Windstar defines the minivan concept of car comfort with truck carrying capacity. It is a little larger than either the Dodge Grand Caravan or the Plymouth Grand Voyager, as well as being pleasant and easy to drive.

SPECIFICATIONS

1996 DODGE CARAVAN 3.0

Engine:
V6 - Cast iron block
with aluminum head

Displacement:
181.4 cu. ins.

Bore and stroke:
3.59 x 2.99

Horsepower:
161

Body styles:
Minivan

No. of seats:
5

Weight (lbs):
3,500 lbs - 4,000 lbs

Price:
c.$20,000

Produced:
-

Although Chrysler had been the leading player in the minivan market ever since it introduced the front-wheel-drive Plymouth Voyager and Dodge Caravan in 1984, the opposition was getting stronger year by year as other manufacturers brought out their own versions of the multipurpose vehicle. In order to maintain their dominant position as the number one seller in this lucrative sector, the Chrysler team realized that they had to come up with something new for '96. The answer was revealed at the 1995 North American International Auto Show held in Detroit.

In addition to the Dodge Caravan and Grand

Right: *A new badge was chosen by Chrysler in '96, the design based on the original "gold seal" emblem used by founder Walter P. Chrysler in 1924. The famous Pentastar logo was retained to represent the Chrysler Corporation as a whole, but all Chrysler-branded cars would henceforth carry the new badge.*

Below: Chrysler president Bob Lutz (left) with chairman Robert Eaton and the leapfrogging Dodge Caravan that made its debut at the '95 Detroit show.

Caravan, Plymouth Voyager and Grand Voyager, and Chrysler Town & Country luxury minivan models on display, there were also the Chrysler Voyager and Grand Voyager versions to be sold overseas. But the star of the presentation hosted by Chrysler president Bob Lutz and chairman Robert Eaton was a bright red Dodge Caravan that was connected to a hidden mechanical arm to make it jump into the air. With the aid of a Kermit the frog look-a-like and some humorous poetry, the point was made that, with this new model, Chrysler were

leapfrogging ahead of the competitio once again. The stylish, more curvac eous lines of the cab-forward desig marked a definite advancement of th minivan concept, while at the same tim clearly retaining the Chrysler corpora identity.

But as well as the modern styling there were a couple of innovativ touches announced on the new models The first surprise was the option of left-side sliding door, making it possibl to have sliding doors on both sides Then there were the patented "Eas

Above: *It was the end of the line for the Buick Roadmaster Estate Wagon, and it carried the Collector's Edition designation for its final year. A 260 horsepower, 5.7-liter V8 was standard, combined with four-speed automatic transmission, but a new generation of multipurpose vehicles was supplanting these full-size, rear-wheel-drive wagons. Once production of these models was phased out, the Arlington, Texas, assembly plant where they were built was converted to truck manufacturing.*

Left: *Plymouth's Grand Voyager was one of a family of new minivans introduced by Chrysler as '96 models. It sat on a 119.3 inch wheelbase (six inches longer than the normal Voyager/ Caravan) and could carry seven passengers plus their luggage. Modern aerodynamic styling and an optional left-side sliding door were part of Chrysler's initiative to keep the number one slot in this valuable market sector. All-wheel-drive was also available on the long wheelbase versions, though this didn't arrive until later in the year.*

Out" roller seats and first-for-minivan features such as dual zone climate control, memory seats and mirrors. An all-new 150 horsepower, 2.4-liter, 16 valve, dual overhead camshaft four cylinder engine was one of the powertrains available, the others being a 3.0-liter SOHC V6, a 3.3-liter V6 and a 3.8-liter V6. A 2.5-liter turbo diesel four cylinder would be offered in those vehicles sold outside the USA. Transmission options were a three-speed manual or a four-speed automatic (only on V6 models).

Another surprise at the Detroit show was the 1996 Ford Taurus and Mercury Sable models, the first complete redesign

of the pair since their introduction te years previously. Although the sleeke Taurus seemed rather smaller tha before, it was actually slightly large with an extra two inches in th wheelbase, and 5.4 inches longe overall. The width had increased by 2. inches, and a new 3.0-liter, 24 valve "Cleveland" V6 engine rated at 18 horsepower was now on offer, as well a an improved version of the original bas 3.0-liter V6.

Both Taurus and Sable followed th trend of the cab-forward styling schoo but subtle alterations to the front and rear were used to try and give th Mercury a different appearance to it

Right: The first major redesign since 1986 saw the Ford Taurus adopt a prominent oval theme in its styling, which wasn't universally approved. That didn't stop the car from selling very well. To begin with there were only two trim levels offered – GL and LX – but a base G and the high-performance SHO model were added midway through the year. The station wagon also made a comeback as part of the Taurus line.

Above: The Mustang got the new "modular" 281 cu. in. Ford V8 for '96. The Cobra option package pushed output to 305 bhp, putting the Mustang back at the front of the pack once more.

stablemate from Ford. Later in '96, a further example of the growing globalization of the industry became evident when Ford announced that it had bought a controlling interest in Japanese auto-maker Mazda.

While all manufacturers were busy looking ahead and trying to come up with an edge over their rivals, there were still a few who were prepared to cater to customers with more traditional demands. It's true that Buick produced their fair share of futuristic concept cars and radical new models, but in 1996 you could still buy an old-fashioned, full-size Roadmaster Estate Wagon – and it even had the fake wooden panels stuck on the

sides! But this was to be the last year fo the rear-wheel-drive Roadmaster seda and wagon and the models were give the Collector's Edition designation.

Right: Viper on tour. These cars hav raised the profile of the American auto mobile abroad to an incredible exten

Below: *A closed, GTS coupe version of the Viper was introduced for 1996, retailing at a cool $66,000. erformance, incredible from the outset, steadily increased. Its high profile has doubtless helped to boost sales of bread & butter U.S. vehicles in European markets and beyond.*

SPECIFICATIONS

1997 OLDSMOBILE INTRIGUE

Engine:
V8 - All Aluminum

Displacement:
244 cu. ins.

Bore and stroke:
3.43 x 3.31

Horsepower:
250

Body styles:
4 door sedan

No. of seats:
5

Weight (lbs):
3,967 lbs

Price:
$35,735

Produced:
25,309

Oldsmobile celebrated its centenary in '97 (the first American automobile manufacturer to do so) and thousands of vintage and classic Oldsmobile owners took their cars to Lansing, Michigan, to take part in the historic festivities in August. The week-long 100th birthday celebration was one of the largest automotive gatherings ever staged and, apart from all the cars, there was a whole host of commemorative merchandise on sale, plus a chance for a sneak look at some possible future models.

Much more important than anniversaries, however, was Oldsmobile's fluctuating fortunes. Going into the 1980s, Oldsmobile were riding high in the charts and regularly grabbed the number

elow: Oldsmobile celebrated its 100th
irthday on August 21, becoming the
*rst American auto-maker to do so.
*art of the "Centennial Plan" to revive
agging fortunes involved a whole new
eneration of cars, the first of which
*vas the 1998 Intrigue that went on sale
*n '97. The midsize sedan was powered
*y the 3800 Series II V6 and used the
*Hydra-Matic 4T65E four-speed
utomatic transaxle. The Intrigue came
ully equipped with air conditioning,
ntilock brakes and traction control.
*The GL model added extra sport and
uxury items.

Above: A new Oldsmobile logo was
introduced in 1995. It formed the focal
point of an image change at the start of
the marque's second century.

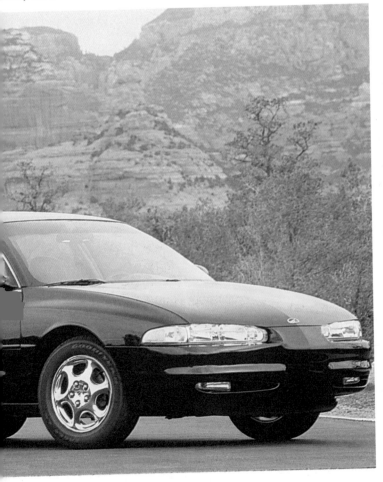

three spot behind Ford and Chevrolet; annual production frequently topped one million units. Even as late as 1986, almost 1.2 million cars were rolling off the assembly lines, but then a catastrophic decline set in and ten years later only 363,000 new vehicles carried the Oldsmobile name. And when 250 Olds employees from the marketing and operations departments were transferred to the GM Renaissance Center in Detroit there was talk of Lansing losing its Oldsmobile factories altogether.

Happily this didn't happen. Although current Oldsmobile models are produced at a number of locations in addition to the marque's hometown – in Ohio, Kansas and Georgia – the revival is underway. The credit for the turnaround must go to the ten year "Centennial Plan" worked out in 1995 under the direction of general manager John Rock. The plan was to establish a clear positive image and identity for Olds through a new generation of cars and better buying and ownership experience. Part of the identity revolution came in the form of a brand new logo to replace the so-called "chicken track" Rocket badge.

The new 1997 Cutlass formed part of the Centennial Plan strategy and replaced the ageing Ciera. Built on the GM "P90" front-wheel-drive platform, the Cutlass got its performance from the highly regarded 3100 V6 that delivered

160 horsepower. A couple of months later came the revamped Silhouette and the 1998 Intrigue model went on sale in the spring of '97 – things were looking up for the start of Oldsmobile's second century.

No such problems for the folks over at Chrysler, besides which they were far too busy designing and producing fun machines like the Plymouth Prowler. If the Dodge Viper had been regarded as an outrageous project, then the Prowler was totally unbelievable. When the Prowler show car first appeared in 1993, nobody would have bet that a giant auto-maker like Chrysler would be willing to even consider putting the futuristic-looking street rod into produc-

tion – let alone go ahead and do it.

The story of the Prowler goes back to May 1990 and a brainstorming session at Chrysler's Pacifica Design, a small

Below: The Plymouth Prowler caused a sensation when it first appeared as a concept car in 1993, but nobody believed that four years later it would be in full production. Powered by a 3.5-liter V6, the street rod used aerospace-grade aluminum in its construction to reduce weight and was seen by Chrysler engineers as something of a test bed for new material technology. Of course, most buyers weren't concerned with the technology – they just loved the Prowler's wild looks.

studio near San Diego, California. From that meeting, the proposal for a concept car which would combine retro styling with state-of-the-art technology quickly developed. The design team visited local hot rod shows in order to experience this automotive subculture at first hand and, in the summer of '91, work began on a full-sized glass-fiber model. Once the design was finalized, a fully operational car was put together and introduced at the Detroit auto show in January 1993.

Reaction to the Prowler was fantastic.

Above: The Dodge Viper, now in GTS Coupe form, was being recognized as one of the World's great Grand Touring cars. Having been selected as the Official Pace Car for the '96 Indy 500, the Viper's competition success was to include the Le Mans 24 Hour race

Judged the hit of the show by an enthusiastic automotive media, the response from the public was equally demonstrative and, within a very short space of time, Chrysler set up a study group to investigate the feasibility of manufa-

cturing and selling the Prowler. Once a serious business plan had been worked out – which involved deciding the method of assembly and sourcing of components – the vehicle regulatory requirements had to be taken into account. It is one thing to build a single concept car for static display at shows, quite another to produce a car for use on the highway.

Some of the elements of the Prowler were already in full production – the 3.5-liter, 24 valve V6 engine, for instance, came from Chrysler's full-size sedans – but many more had to be completely redeveloped. The wheelbase of the production Prowler was stretched by 1.5 inches compared to the original concept car and the body widened by

three inches for engineering reasons. Practical modifications included the headlamps requiring a new design to make them street legal. The four-speed automatic transaxle was mounted in the rear to help even out the weight distribution but, in keeping with the hot rod theme, it used the AutoStick feature which let the driver shift gears without

Above & Below: Racing versions of the Viper are yet more spartan than the production cars, but the excitement they provide to both driver and spectator is surely worth the discomfort. Extensive use of carbon-fiber in the car's construction results in greatly increased strength and safety as well as optimum lightness in the structure.

using a clutch, simply by tapping the gear lever. Some of the parts raided from other Chrysler models include the steering mechanism, front and rear springs and air conditioning and ventilation systems. The steering wheel was borrowed from the Jeep Grand Cherokee and even the interior door handles came from the Viper (which were turned upside down on the Prowler). The body was all aluminum (with steel reinforcements) and there was extensive use of aluminum, magnesium and other advanced lightweight materials throughout the Plymouth roadster.

When word got out that Chrysler were serious about putting the Prowler on sale, the demand was overwhelming. Over 100,000 inquiries were received via telephone calls, letters and e-mails, with interest coming from every age and type of driver and not just the die-hard street rod enthusiast. The Prowler went into production in mid-1997 at the Conner Avenue assembly plant in Detroit, the same factory where the Dodge Viper was being built. Annual output was set for around 5,000 Prowlers and originally they were only available in purple, although yellow became available subsequently. Supply being so restricted, and with no possibility of production increasing, it is no wonder

Below: The fifth-generation Corvette was a complete redesign and, although the external dimensions were virtually unchanged, the wheelbase had been extended by 8.25 inches to provide more space for occupants and their luggage. A 5.7-liter V8 gave the Corvette a top speed of 173mph, and antilock brakes, traction control and dual airbags were standard. A new powertrain configuration had a rear transaxle with the option of either four-speed automatic or six-speed manual transmission.

hat Prowlers were soon changing hands n the open market for more than double he original $40,000 price.

The retro styling theme was also in vidence at Jeep, with the new Wrangler - codenamed TJ – reverting to round eadlamps. It gave the 4x4 a much more raditional look that was welcomed by ficionados. Despite its appearance, the Wrangler had completely revamped

Above: The 30th Anniversary edition of the Camaro, the Z28 SS was created by Chevrolet in conjunction with SLP Engineering. Loaded with special features and limited to a production run of 1,000 units, it was launched with a paint job of white on orange.

body panels (apart from the doors and tailgate) and the suspension was changed to coil springs. Capable of seri-ous off-road work straight off the show-room floor, the Wrangler could also exceed 105mph on the freeway when equipped with the 4.0-liter in-line six cylinder unit. The other engine available was a 2.5-liter in-line four, and there was the choice of either five-speed over-drive manual or three-speed automatic transmissions. The three models in the Wrangler lineup were SE, Sport and Sahara. And while it may be something of a contradiction to talk about an aerodynamic Jeep, the new Wrangler did include a few ideas to cut down on wind noise and soft top flapping, with the windshield raked at an angle of four degrees.

With Pontiac delving into their back catalog to revive the "Wide Track" and "Ram Air" designations on their Firebird and Grand Prix models, the arrival of the 173mph fifth-generation Corvette, and a limited edition 30th Anniversary Camaro Z28 SS from Chevrolet, things on the automotive front were looking pretty exciting in '97.

SPECIFICATIONS

**FORD SVT
CONTOUR**

Engine:
V6 - All aluminum

Displacement:
155 cu. ins.

Bore and stroke:
3.21 x 3.08

Horsepower:
195

Body styles:
4 door sedan

No. of seats:
5

Weight (lbs):
2,811 lbs - 3,068 lbs

Price:
$14,460 - $22,405

Produced:
217,000

There was a great deal of newsworthy activity the auto industry, starting with the annoncement in May that Daimler-Benz and Chrysle were to merge which stunned many industry obsevers. The amalgamation – estimated to be wor some $92 billion – was the world's largest ev industrial merger. Called Daimler-Chrysler, th new company was jointly led by Juergen Schremp and Robert Eaton at first, but the merger was, reality, a takeover. And when Eaton subsequent retired, control reverted to the Daimler hierarch With this tie-up, Daimler-Chrysler became the fif largest auto-maker in the world.

Even prior to the establishment of the conne

Below: Ford's SVT Contour had subtle styling touches to distinguish it from regular models, including a unique front fascia with round foglamps and a different grille. Special badging an 16 inch cast aluminum five-spoke wheels with 205/55ZR-16 tires completed the exterior appearance package, but it was the 195 horsepower 2.5-liter Duratec V6, upgraded brakes and suspension that gave the SVT Contour sedan its sports car performance. Top speed was 143mph.

ion with Daimler, Chrysler were in the process of rationalizing its car business. The end of the Eagle brand came on February 5 when the last Eagle Talon sports coupe rolled off the Normal, Illinois, assembly line – the Eagle Vision sedan had been quietly dropped from the lineup earlier on.

There was also upheaval in other parts of Motor City. General Motors

Above: For its final model year in 1998 the Buick Skylark was only sold to fleet customers. Standard equipment on the 4-door sedan (the only model produced) included traction control, antilock brakes, power windows and dual air bags. The Skylark's powertrain was a 3.1-liter V6 producing 155hp with a four-speed automatic overdrive transaxle.

were busy gathering together all its divisional headquarters at the Renaissance Center in downtown Detroit, but meantime Ford's Lincoln-Mercury division was relocating to the west coast. The new home of Lincoln-Mercury was in Irvine, California, the same place that Mazda had its American offices and this fuelled speculation that there was another merger in the offing. Ford swiftly denied the rumors.

Another offshoot of Ford was also moving fast in 1998 – at 143mph! But in this instance Ford's Special Vehicle Team (SVT) was doing it in their first front-wheel-drive offering, the Ford SVT Con-

tour. A high-performance sports seda the SVT Contour combined Europea bred handling with a 195 horsepow V6 engine, some distinctive stylin features and a value-oriented price make a formidable package. The outp of the 2.5-liter Duratec V6 was uprate by modifying the fuel injection, cams

Below: The Team ORECA Dodge Vipe GTS-R driven by Justin Bell, David Donohue and Luca Drudi, won the GT Class in the world famous Le Mans 24 Hour Race in June. The car completed 317 laps of the 8.4-mile circuit without any problems.

Above: The five passenger Oldsmobile Intrigue sedan was offered in three trim levels, Standard, GL and GLS. Built in Fairfax, Kansas, it was powered by a Series 2, 3800 V6 engine.

afts and exhaust system, to give the SVT Contour a 0 to 60mph time of 7.9 seconds; the standing quarter-mile could be completed in 15.7 seconds. Sales of the model were dealt with exclusively through 726 SVT-certified Ford dealers, with production estimated at 5,000 units a year.

It was Buick's 95th birthday in 1998, and a limited edition 25th Anniversary Regal model went on sale. However, this was also to be the last year for the Skylark, a name with a heritage that stretched all the way back to 1953. It started out as a 50th Anniversary convertible on a Roadmaster chassis, with a smaller Skylark ragtop following in '54, but the name was then dropped until 1962. It remained in the Buick lineup for the following ten years. After a short period off the production line it was revived again as a compact in 1975 and was a fixture in the Buick catalog until this year. The 1998 Skylark was only produced as a 4-door sedan and just sold to fleet operators – a sad end for a name that started out on such a highly desirable automobile.

SPECIFICATIONS

PONTIAC GRAND AM GT COUPE

Engine:
V6 - cast iron block/alu-
minum head

Displacement:
207 cu. ins.

Bore and stroke:
3.63 x 3.31

Horsepower:
170

Body styles:
2 door coupe; 4 door
sedan

No. of seats:
5

Weight (lbs):
3,066 lbs - 3,116 lbs

Price:
$19,070 - $19,470

Produced:
-

Improving the design of a highly successful
well-known model is never an easy task, a
quite a few manufacturers over the years have be
led astray by the ideas proposed by stylists. For t
final year of the 20th century Pontiac seemed
have achieved a couple of hits, but at the same ti
there were also those cars that didn't quite make
to the major league. The good news was in the mi
year launch of the new-generation Grand Am. Th
was the model that had been Pontiac's volur
leader since 1992, ranking in the top ten list of t
most popular cars in the US and selling more tha
200,000 units every year. And, for the previous fi
years, the Grand Am had led the compact secto
for most retail registrations.

Pontiac related the design of the new Grand A
to an athlete, talking about its "lean shape" an

*Below: The new-generation Pontiac Grand Am G
Coupe seemed as if it had the looks and
performance to continue sales success, with a
longer wheelbase and wider track, designed to
improve handling and increase passenger room
and luggage space. Thanks to a 175hp 3400 V6
engine, the GT could sprint to 60mph in under
eight seconds and was said by Pontiac to have
"low-speed vigor, midrange muscle, and
high-end energy."*

ell-toned curves," but the practical
ects of the changes that had taken
ce revolved around the 107 inch
eelbase being 3.6 inches longer than
model it replaced, with a slight
uction in the overall length. The
ck width increased by 3.3 inches and

*Above: The Ram Air name harks back
to the late 1960s Pontiac muscle cars,
but the functional induction system on
the '99 Grand Am GT feeds cool air to
a large volume filter housing – boosting
output of the 3.35-liter V6 by five
horsepower.*

the overall width at the center of the car had only grown by 1.5 inches. The effect was a "wheel-at-each-corner" appearance that also helped to provide extra passenger and cargo space. While the Grand Am model lineup consisted of 2-door coupes and 4-door sedans in both SE and GT versions, the most attractive model in the range was the GT Coupe.

Backing up the aggressive styling with performance was taken care of by the 3400 V6 engine. In the GT models this produced 175 horsepower at 5,200rpm (thanks to the Ram Air induction system and modified exhaust), enough to propel the Grand Am to 60mph in less than eight seconds. Antilock four-wheel disc brakes, uprated suspension and speed-sensitive power-assisted rack and pinion steering, as well as 7x16 inch five-spoke aluminum wheels and road-hugging Goodyear Eagle RSA P225/50R-16 tires with directional tread pattern, ensured that the handling also

Above: Although the optional WS6 Ram Air package gives a very unbalanced look to the sleek front of the Firebird Formula, this styling shortcoming was offset by the gain in performance. Renewing a relationship that began back in 1962, a Hurst shifter was available with the six-speed manual transmission. But it wasn't all retro. Firebirds also featured antilock four-wheel disk brakes and electronic traction control.

scored high marks.

The Grand Am GT wasn't the only model on which Pontiac placed the Ram Air set-up in '99. But, while the functional twin-port openings that were used to funnel cool air into a large volume filter housing looked fine on the front of the compact, and perfectly acceptable as small hood scoops on the Firebird Trans Am, the Firebird Formula's WS6 Ram Air option seemed

worthwhile.

Unfortunately, the Firebird was not enjoying the same sort of sales success as the Grand Am, although the legendary Pontiac muscle car that arrived in 1967 would survive until at least the 2000 model year. The best ever year for the Firebird was 1979, when over 211,000 came off the production line, but by 1990 the figure had dropped to less than a tenth of that total. In 1994 the number was up to almost 46,500, but a steady year-on-year decline followed, with 1997 sales of only 30,459. Fortunately, the '98 had slightly better figures, with 33,578 Firebirds leaving the St. Therese assembly plant near Quebec in Canada.

Numbers figured highly at Cadillac, when they were forced to publicly

Below: The Suburban name goes back to 1935 when Chevrolet introduced the Suburban Carryall truck. Over the years it developed into an all-purpose vehicle, and the 1999 GMC Suburban represented the ultimate full-size sport utility 4x4, accommodating up to nine people. Steady annual sales of around 40,000 showed there was still a market for these big wagons. Vortec 7.4-liter gasoline or 6.5-liter turbo diesel V8 engines were optional and came with four-speed automatic transmission.

lmost grotesque. The dual extra ports nd large humps detracted from the lean frontal styling of the Firebird, but s the Ram Air helped boost the power f the 5.7-liter V8 to 320 horsepower, he tradeoff may have been considered

concede that they had massaged sales figures in order to stay ahead of Lincoln. 1999 also saw the end of the line for a couple of venerable Oldsmobile model names, as the Eighty-Eight and Cutlass were struck out. They followed the Ninety-Eight, Toronado, Ciera and the mother of all station wagons, the Custom Cruiser, into retirement. The Chrysler Corporation caused a sensation in the auto world with the announcement that they were to merge with the venerable German manufacturing giant Daimler-Benz - a name as old a the automobile. So was born, in th closing hours of the millenniur Daimler-Chrysler. It was the end o almost a century of rivalry and domi ance between the three great, domest giants of the American automobile indu stry: General Motors, Ford and th Chrysler Corp. One of the first ne products to be unveiled for the U. market looked back to the glory days c Chrysler with the return of the 30 series, abandoned in 1965 at the 300I

Now, finally, nearly 35 years later, the 00M had arrived, powered by an all-aluminum V6 that delivered over 250 orsepower

The Lincoln Mk VIII was dropped at he end of 1998, having lasted from '93, eaving the Continental and the Town Car as the Linc. line-up.

Things weren't all about deletions at Oldsmobile. The Alero replaced the Achieva. It was a completely new oncept series: a compact coupe and edan, produced at Olds' Lansing, Michigan factory, with an advanced, 2.4 liter, four-cylinder engine that combined 150 bhp output with Low Emission Vehicle status.

Below: The Mercury Cougar, like so many new automobiles, is not as identifiably All-American as earlier models. Global markets and the influence of computer design tend to come up with what has been described as the "World Car" look.

2000

SPECIFICATIONS

**FORD
THUNDERBIRD**

Engine:
V8 - All aluminum

Displacement:
281 cu. ins

Bore and stroke:
3.60 x 3.60

Horsepower:
252

Body styles:
Convertible coupe

No. of seats:
2

Weight (lbs):
3,775 lbs

Price:
$36,390

Produced:
-

The dawn of a New Millennium is an event that few people - in historical terms - will witness for obvious reasons. It is one of those strange moments that serves to focus the mind and encourage us to take stock; to think about what has gone before and what may be to come. The future is always the great unknown and so we tend, at such times, to seek comfort in the past, to wax lyrical about that warm and wonderful, half remembered, half-imagined, time-gone-by that probably never was. We yearn for an age when life was safer and simpler. For some reason, that golden Age is often imagined to be the nineteen fifties.

Ford introduced the Thunderbird as a "Personal" car in 1955. The first run of '55–'57

Below: Retro styling has proved popular in recent times. The new Ford Thunderbird is due out in 2000 and is based on the same platform as the Lincoln LS. It was a concept car exhibited at the 1999 Detroit show and won many accolades. Clever use of styling cues from the original 1955 Thunderbird and modern body design could make this an instant classic.

Thunderbirds - was ever a name so evocative of power and freedom? - epitomized everything that we imagine the 'fifties to have been: colorful, carefree, youthful and exciting. It's easy to forget that 1955 was the year Martin Luther King formed the Montgomery

Above: The knife-edged Evoq concept car was said to be a forerunner of future Cadillacs. With a supercharged 405bhp, 4.2-liter Northstar V8 and rear-wheel-drive, anything like the Evoq going into production would be a major departure from models currently offered.

Improvement Association in Alabama, and that association launched a boycott of Montgomery's buses as a protest against racial segregation on the city's transportation. The Warsaw Pact was formed, West Germany was admitted to NATO - this was the time of the Cold War. Americans were fearful of the threat of the Soviet nuclear arsenal. Is it any wonder that they indulged in a little "Personal" fantasy?

Below: The shape of things to come. The Dodge Intrepid ESX2 has a 1.5 liter diesel engine and battery power to give fuel economy of 70 miles per gallon and a driving range of 420 miles. Called a "mybrid" (in other words, a mild hybrid) by engineers, the experimental vehicle uses a five-speed, electronically shifted manual transmission and a body molded from plastic panels to reduce weight.

So, as we stood on the threshold of the twenty-first century, not knowing what lay in store for us, we took comfort from the past and hankered after symbols of security. Ford, in an inspired move, provided the means of escape, as they did in '55. After 42 years in production, the Thunderbird had been dropped at the end of 1997 and a link with the glorious past was severed.

Below: The Saleen S7 was launched in mid-2000 and had rave reviews, but it struggled to get into production or to make the sales needed for a long life. The original inspiration came from Steve Saleen, who had already made his name as a much-respected tuner of Ford Mustangs. Much of the development and chassis engineering was completed by Ray Mallock Racing in the UK.

By November 2001, the T-Bird was not just back but was Car-of-the-Year. Not only had the Thunderbird returned, but it looked like it did first time around: there was even a porthole. All is again well with the world. In the 50 year period of the *Motor Trend* Car-of-the-Year award, the Thunderbird has taken the honors four times - a tally double that of its nearest competitor. The magazine's Editorial Editor, Kevin Smith, summed it all up perfectly, "The all-new Thunderbird celebrated Ford's heritage of innovation and reaffirms our goal to build the best cars on the planet - car that evoke passion and touch people' hearts and souls."

For the record, the new Thunderbird utilizes a traditional front-engine-rear drive layout and is powered by a 3.9 lite V8 with 4 valves per cylinder. Computer-controlled, electronic fuel-injection replaces the original T-bird's four-barrel carb and output is rated at 252 agains the 202. 5-speed automatic transmission replaces a stick-shift or optional Ford O-Matic. Like so many contemporary automobiles - and a few in the 'fifties

e new Thunderbird shares a platform
ith a number of other models. It has
omponents in common with the
incoln LS and the S-Type Jaguar,
cluding the basic engine design. Like
s illustrious predecessor, the Thunde-
bird remains a cruiser rather than a
cer, delivering silky smooth perform-
nce with a minimum of sound and
ury and rides like a magic carpet.
n uncertain times, it's appealing to
nagine climbing behind the wheel of
Thunderbird - a '55 or an '02 - and
riving off into the sunset.

Above: Could the car be replaced by the
"Personal Transit Module?" Corbin
Motors Inc. of Hollister, California,
think that their electric-powered
Sparrow three-wheeler could be ideal
for commuters. The composite-bodied
single-seater has a top speed of 65mph
and a range of 40-60 miles between
recharging.

Left: Launched in '99, the Chrysler PT
Cruiser was called "too cool to
categorize" and has created an unprecedented demand. Extra production
capacity was needed to meet orders and
some 180,000 units are expected to roll
off the assembly lines each year.

SPECIFICATIONS

OLDSMOBILE AURORA

Engine:
V8 - All aluminum

Displacement:
244 cu. ins.

Bore and stroke:
3.43 x 3.31

Horsepower:
250

Body styles:
4 door sedan

No. of seats:
6

Weight (lbs):
3,967 lbs

Price:
$36,229

Produced:
-

Stanley Kubrick's vision of 2001 saw PanAm space cruisers waltzing around a permanent moon base. In the 'sixties, anything was possible... It is obvious that the future of the American automobile is going to be just as varied and interesting as its past. While it is impossible to predict exactly what will happen in the years ahead, there are some changes that are already in motion – even so, the full effect of these alterations can only be guessed at.

However, one thing is for certain. After the 2001 model year, Plymouth will be no more. DaimlerChrysler announced that the name first introduced in July 1928 (on 1929 models) is being dropped, and the two models currently bearing the Plymouth badge – Neon and Prowler – will be the last. It is expected that the Dodge version of the Neon will continue as before, but the fate of the limited-production Prowler hot rod is less certain, although a change of name to the Chrysler Prowler seems a possibility. The merger/takeover that created DaimlerChrysler has also resulted in a number of designers who were responsible for the

ecent dramatic upsurge in Dodge Plymouth/ Chrysler creativity leaving the company. Quite a few have apparntly gone to work for the various divisins at General Motors, so this might erald the beginning of a bold new era or Chevvy/ Pontiac/ Oldsmobile/Buick Cadillac and their products.

One name from the past that could be naking a comeback is Avanti. The 1962 Studebaker design that survived in different guises until 1991 is being revived by a couple of businessmen who have set up he Avanti Motor Corporation in a small actory in Villa Rica, Georgia. Plans are to produce about 300 cars a year, with hardtop and convertible versions due to be offered. Carrying a price tag of less than $100,000, the first of the new Avantis was scheduled for the end of 2000.

Carroll Shelby's company is also building his brand of exciting sports cars on a limited basis. Shelby American Inc of Las Vegas, Nevada, has sold over 125 of the Shelby 427 S/C Cobra since restarting manufacture in 1996 and the first batch of the new high-tech Series 1 was completed during the last months of 1999. Designed as a latter-generation Cobra with a modern twist, the Series 1 looks like it will continue the Shelby tradition well into the new century.

In the mass market, the main engine-

Below: The Aurora was the new flagship model for Oldsmobile and lined up against luxury imports like Lexus and Infiniti. Using a 4.0-liter, 250bhp derivative of the Cadillac Northstar V8, the Aurora was part of an effort to reverse troubled fortunes at the Oldsmobile division. Although the Aurora won much approval and sold well, Oldsmobile continued to lose money.

SPECIFICATIONS

**CHRYSLER LHS
SEDAN**

Engine:
V6 - all aluminum

Displacement:
215 cu. ins.

Bore and stroke:
3.78 x 3.19

Horsepower:
253

Body styles:
4 door sedan

No. of seats:
5

Weight (lbs):
3,689

Price:
$28,700

Produced:
-

ering changes will probably revolve around the use of alternative fuels, with various hybrid vehicles being developed. Only time will tell whether these combinations of gasoline-powered engines and electric, hydrogen or other forms of propulsion will ever totally replace the internal combustion power plant. In the short term at least, gasoline would still seem to be the most practical automotive fuel. Technology such as satellite navigation systems, voice-activated controls, in-car Internet capabilities and so forth are also just around the corner.

Car styling will always change, and never totally predictably. There has been a recent trend for the "retro" look, with the Chrysler PT Cruiser and Ford Thunderbird concept car leading the way in this area, but there have also been some very "knife-edge" styled cars exhibited by major auto makers. Maybe this is the way forward for the next generation.

The auto industry is now an integrated global business with many rival multinational companies engaged in joint ventures that only a few years ago would have seemed impossible. But while the shapes will change, the engines and onboard equipment will become ever more sophisticated and some long-established names may disappear, the one constant will be the need for an efficient means of personal transportation.

Right: The Chrysler LHS Sedan bridges the gap between the old Chrysler Corporation and Daimler-Chrysler. Heading the line, it is in the grand Chrysler tradition: a powerful, luxury sedan. The LHS shares many components with the newly revived 300 series.

And in this respect the American automobile is just as much part of the fabric of everyday life today as it has been at any time since 1919. Similarly, the desire for dream machines shows no sign of diminishing as the popularity of automobiles like the Prowler and the Viper and the products of a number of small, independent manufacturers illustrate.

SPECIFICATIONS

PANOZ ESPERANTE

Engine:
V8 – light alloy block

Displacement:
280 cu. ins.

Bore and stroke:
3.55 x 3.54 ins.

Horsepower:
320

Body styles:
2 door convertible road-
ster

No. of seats:
2

Weight (lbs):
3,263 lbs

Price:
-

Produced:
-

The Esperante is produced by the Panoz Auto Development Company, under the direction of millionaire race-car enthusiast Don Panoz, in Atlanta, Georgia. Don's dream was to create a true sports car in the European tradition, built by Americans, to be driven by Americans, using all American components. At the heart of the Esperante, therefore, are Ford Mustang components, sheathed in a sleek, hand-crafted, aluminum body of classic proportions. The Esperante has none of the brashness and naked aggression of the Dodge Viper, but is, instead, elegant and understated. Don Panoz was adamant that his car should combine track level performance with family sedan practicality. The former was achieved by completing and competing the car prior to its sale to the public. The latter was assured by the use of proprietary Ford parts, including switch-gear and instruments. An Esperante owner could visit his local Ford dealer and get parts and service - at Ford rates. This set-up was designed to appeal to

Right & Above Right :
The Panoz Esperante is a
supremely elegant blend
of American engineering
know-how and classic,
European styling.

rospective purchasers of such cars as he Porsche 911, Mercedes Benz SL eries and the Jaguar XK8. Giving a top peed in excess of 150 mph and a 0-60 time of five seconds, the Esperante offers greater exclusivity, easier maintenance and, in all probability, greater reliability due to the lack of stress on its

SPECIFICATIONS

LINCOLN NAVIGATOR

Engine:
V8 - cast iron block
with aluminum head

Displacement:
330 cu. ins.

Bore and stroke:
3.55 x 4.17

Horsepower:
300

Body styles:
4 door ATV

No. of seats:
7

Weight (lbs):
5,760 lbs - 5,994lbs

Price:
-

Produced:
-

heavyweight mechanical components, than most of its competitors. The inimitable burble of a big V8 plus excellent rear-drive handling characteristics (the motor is effectively centrally mounted) should also prove appealing to the domestic driver and it is hoped to market the car in Europe in 2003.

Lincoln have entered the burgeoning luxury All-Terrain Vehicle sector with a splash. The Navigator is available in either rear drive or four-wheel drive configurations making it suitable for customers who require serious off-road/foul weather capability and those looking for spacious, long-distance touring/towing features. It is remarkable that this option has not been offered more widely as few drivers of AVT's regularly – if ever – require

Right: The Lincoln Navigator represents the ultimate in dual-purpose All Terrain Vehicles - for the time being.

ll all-wheel drive capability. Many, as we know, restrict their off-road activity to climbing the kerb outside the local elementary school or convenience store. The Navigator's potential, however, is massive. The 32 valve V8 features electronic engine management and has a fail-safe cooling system. Transmission is via a four-speed, electronic auto box, which has a selectable overdrive facility. The "Control Trac" (copyright) 4 x 4 system offers four drive modes and is also electronically controlled. The 4-channel ABS braking system includes electronic Brake Distribution and a

panic assist feature. Maximum Trailer weight for the rear-drive set-up is 8,500 lbs. The safety of the occupants is taken care of via anti-intrusion door beams, dual-stage airbags and Lincoln's "Safety Canopy" (copyright) system with side-curtain airbags and roll-over sensors plus the "Advancetrac" (copyright) vehicle stability enhancement system. Interiors are concommitant with Lincoln's image: leather trimmed seats with adjustment memory; CD stereo and back-seat video entertainment systems; adjustable pedals with memory feature; satellite navigation and a host of other features and options. Lincoln have come up with what they obviously intend to be "The Last Word" in the ATV sector - and it will be very interesting to see what all its competitors can come up with, in answer to its comprehensive features.

The Mosler is the product of a collaboration between engineer Rod Trenne and designer Warren Mosler. Beginning in 1998, their brief was to produce an all-American, mid-engined supercar that would meet all US regulations. This is a bold approach as Americans have always favored the traditional front-engine/rear-drive lay-out of cars like the Corvette and, more recently, the Dodge Viper. With the exception of the Corvette power plant – specially balanced and tuned – every element of the car has been designed from scratch, using advanced computer techniques. Trenne's chassis is highly sophisticated but eminently effective, consisting of honey-comb aluminum and glass-fiber components. The body panels are formed from carbon-fiber, the whole providing an extremely low kerb weight – and a massive power-to-weight ratio. The highly aerodynamic body-ork features "butterfly" doors, reminis-cent of the Lamborghini Countach/ Diablo and the McLaren F1, and is a thing of purposeful beauty. Despite the numerous European styling references is, somehow, instantly recognizable as an American automobile – the LaSalle

SPECIFICATIONS

MOSLER MT 900S

Engine:
V8 – cast aluminum
block

Displacement:
346 cu. ins.

Bore and stroke:
3.90 x 3.62 ins.

Horsepower:
425

Body styles:
GT Coupe

No. of seats:
2

Weight (lbs):
2,200 lbs

Price:
c. $200,000

Produced:
On Sale 2002

of the new millennium, maybe. Mosler intends
produce two versions: one "basic" model intende
solely for GT competition, designated R f
Racing, and an S for Street car that will featu
such refinements as power windows, pow
steering, traction control, anti-lock brakes and a
conditioning. The Mosler is a fantastic automobi
with a great pedigree: a brave endeavour th
richly deserves to succeed.

A similar concept has been developed by Stev
Saleen, who has, over the years, produced some c
hottest Mustangs ever to scorch the blacktop. H
S7 roadcar (see page 493) is built on a spacefram
chassis, reinforced with honeycomb composit
material for lightness and strength. The bod
panels are formed from carbon-fiber. The S7
powered by a V8, based, predictably, on a For
design. Despite the use of space-age materials
Saleen has stuck with a tried and trusted, valve-ir
head engine design in the All-American, bulle
proof tradition. Air is introduced via
carbon-fiber induction system, leading t
magnesium inlet manifolds. The aluminur
cylinder heads are tuned on digitally controlle
lathes. The valve seats are are formed fror
Beryllium to assist heat transfer and the valve
themselves are stainless steel with titanium seats
The pistons and rods are forged from billet steel. A
dry-sump lubrication system ensured improve
lubrication whilst assisting in engine ground
clearance. The G-forces generated in an autom

*Right: The Mosler
MT900 is the first
supercar to have been
been designed in
cyberspace without the
use of models or
drawings. So accurate was
the computer's data that
the glass for the car was
molded before the body
was completed and every
piece fitted precisely.*

Above: The fluid lines of the Mosler are strikingly successful - a perfect melding of form and function to rival anything from the great Italian style houses.

Below: The forward and upward - opening "butterfly" doors of the Mosler appear to have been inspired by the amborghini Countache.

bile like this can be enormous and this ubrication system prevents oil starvaion under hard cornering and braking. he 7 liter S7 engine produces 550 bhp nd the car can accelerate to 60 mph rom rest in under 4 seconds. Top speed s in excess of 200 mph. Handling is eutral under all conditions due to a ear-perfect weight-distribution and alance. Unlike many cars in this ategory, the Saleen doesn't stint on river comfort. The car is air-condi-

tioned, trimmed in the finest Connolly leathers, equipped with a CD player, power window lifts and adjustable pedals. Rear vision is by way of a video camera discreetly mounted on the rear of the car. To assist entry and exit, the steering wheel can be instantly released, just like in a Formula 1 car. People like Steve Saleen and Warren Mosler are putting American automobile right at the cutting edge of performance technology.

SPECIFICATIONS

CHRYSLER PACIFICA

Engine:
V6 - All aluminum

Displacement:
215 cu. ins.

Bore and stroke:
3.78 x 3.19

Horsepower:
250+

Body styles:
4 door sedan

No. of seats:
5

Weight (lbs):
c. 3,500 lbs

Price:
To be announced

Produced
-

This is the most exciting part, hopefully. Wh next? Will the current fashion for "retro styling continue? Does the taste for cars that loo like the cars that their designers thought were co when they were kids, demonstrate and unhealth inability to grow up and face up to curre challenges like pollution and diminishing reserve of fossil fuels, and our dependency on states th might prove, any minute, not to be dependable?

In the new and uncomfortable and unpre dictable world of the third millennium, t accepted safeguards and certainties of the way life of the United States - of the entire free world have been called into question. Even so, it would sad to think that insecurity regarding the futu could blunt the creativity of that most imaginativ of institutions: The American Automobile Indu stry. It's easy to read too much into trends fashion and design; in fact you can make a case fo whatever interpretation of the facts takes you fancy. It could be argued that the recent explosio of enthusiasm for Recreational Vehicles in gener and four-by-fours in particular is a manifestatio of some kind of yuppie insecurity: middle-clas moms using semi-armored personnel carriers - a bull-bars and off-road capability - to pick up the kids from school. It could be argued that the rece explosion of enthusiasm for Recreational Vehicle in general and four-by-fours in particular is manifestation of a new sense of freedom an confidence: a rediscovery of the pioneering spir

Right: *Like the PT Cruiser and the Plymouth Prowler, Chrysler's Pacifica is another Concept Car carried forward into production as is scheduled to be in the showrooms in the spring of 2003.*

d a yearning to experience the Great
utdoors. So either we're scared to go
t or we can't bear to be kept in...

Will looking back over all the
onderful - and not so wonderful -
itomobiles that fill the pages of this
ook give us any insight into what the
rs of next year will look like?
robably. Will we be able to make an
curate prediction of what cars will
ok like in ten years? Maybe. How
out twenty years? Look back at, say,
e 1919 Ford Model T and then look at
e 1928 Model A. Nearly a decade
tween them but not a whole lot of
fference, right? Now try the '39
lercury; could you have seen that
oming, sitting in a Model T? Look at
at fabulous '59 Cadillac and then turn
the 1980 model, then try the same
ith the Corvette! We can see that there
e "generational" shifts in auto design,
with most other things. Cars look
Fifties" in the same way that clothes or
ectrical appliances of the period do.
ometimes styling details from an earlier
eriod are picked up on by a new
eneration and recycled. In recent years
hrysler have produced Concept Cars
at hark back to the 'thirties. Who's to
iy that Cadillac may not revive the fin

one day, or Buick the Ventiport?

For many years - many more years
than most people imagine - the styling of
automobiles was separate and distinct
from their design in engineering terms. It
was in the early 1920's that the
indomitable Alfred P. Sloan circulated a
memorandum to senior staff at General
Motors to the effect that the basic design
of the automobile - in engineering terms
- had been established and was unlikely
to change radically. He was right - in
many ways, it hasn't! The only way to
encourage people to keep buying new
cars, therefore, he opined, was to make
them appear different, even if, underneath, they were pretty much the same.
The idea, basically, was to move the
automobile from being a consumer
durable, like a stove or a refrigerator, to
being a "disposable" item, insofar as its
styling would automatically become
outdated by the introduction of a "new"
model - every year. Cars, like clothes,
would become subject to the whims of
fashion. So, in 1926, GM's legendary
"Art and Colour Section" was
established and Harley Earl elected to
head it, and the annual model range was
introduced throughout every division in
the corporation. Henry Ford's vision of
the simple, sound design, ceaselessly
refined and improved, was destined for
the glue factory. Whether that was a
good thing or a bad thing is debatable.
The fact is that the Great American
Public fell in love with the idea of
novelty and innovation, even when it
was innovation for innovation's sake,
and they didn't care what anybody else
thought about it and, by and large, they
still don't.

I have to say that, in my humble
opinion, without the creations of men
like Earl, and Bill Mitchell, and Virgil
Exner, and Alex Tremulis and Raymond
Loewy and Frank Spring and "Dutch"
Darrin and Gordon Beuhrig and Elwood
Engel and David North, the world
would be a far, far less colorful and
exciting place. So a lot of the things they

SPECIFICATIONS

CHEVROLET CORVETTE

Bore & Stroke:
3.90 ins. x 3.62 ins.

Horsepower:
350 bhp

Engine:
LS1 350 V8

Displacement:
346 cu. ins.

Body Styles:
convertible, coupe, hardtop

No. of seats:
2

Weight:
3,245 lbs

Price:
$40,000

Produced:
launched 2003

designed were impractical and excessive; the same could be said of baroque architecture, and - let's face it - of the pyramids of Egypt and the movies of C.B.deMille. People like spectacular things and the American automobile industry has produced plenty in the past hundred years.

It's tempting to try to pick a favorite, or to try to decide which was the Greatest American Automobile ever made - or not made. Discussion of this topic can provide hours of enjoyment, but be warned, debate can get pretty heated. Try it: if you could have any U.S. auto ever produced, regardless of price or rarity, which one would it be? A J-Series Duesenberg? An 812 Cord? A V16 Cadillac? A Chrysler 300C? A '63 Corvette? A Viper? Just flipping through these pages demonstrates the truly remarkable range of machinery that has been produced in the United States over little more than a century. We can see changing fashions and fortunes reflected at every turn; technological advances, the influence of legislation on safety and emissions; consumer confidence waxing and waning... The whole history of the American people has been recorded in steel. Will this continue to be true now that

nerica is part of a truly globalized
arket? Who could have imagined, in
e early 'fifties, that by the end of the
ntury many Americans would aspire
 the ownership of automobiles from
ermany and Japan? Now that all our
anufacturers have agreements with
reign concerns, it is possible that the
merican automobile could lose its
imistakable identity - but somehow, I
n't think that that's likely. For one
ing, it is possible that more and more
reign buyers may want to own an
nerican car - and they'll expect it to
ok and drive like one.

What has been noticeable over the
st couple of decades of the twentieth
ntury is that that cars have got
bunger, sort of. It's remarkable to

elow: Despite its awesome complexity,
e 2003 Corvette shares its GRP body
anels and front-engine/rear-drive
yout with the '53 model. Some things
e simply unimprovable.

remember that those finned, two-tone,
chrome-laden rocketships of the ninet-
een-fifties, the Eldorados and the Roadmasters, were bought and driven by
sober businessmen. We associate many
of those cars with the Rock & Roll years
but the kids who were doing the rocking
and the rolling weren't in the market for
new cars. Elvis had a Cadillac but the
millions who bought his records managed without. Nowadays, auto makers
have to appeal to a much youn-ger
market and it seems that many of them
are a lot more practically- minded than
their parents and grandparents.

So what's going to happen in the
coming years? It could well be that our
method of buying cars could change,
with virtual showrooms replacing expensive real-estate. New technologies will
surely give us cleaner and more efficient
power plants and a more environment-
ally-aware generation will be starting to
favor low-emission or even no-emission
fuels. The ever-increasing volume of
traffic coupled with the limitless possibilities of computer-based communication
and navigation systems may well result in
automated traffic-flow management,
particularly in congested city centers. The
day may not be far away when, in
downtown New York or Los Angeles, the
car will be driven by the city's road-traffic
control system. The driver will simply
announce the required destination, sit
back and watch TV on the way to work.
Everybody will be chauffeur-driven.

Whatever happens, it is likely that the
automobile will remain a "personal
choice" item rather than a purely utility
purchase. There are already examples of
cars that can be customized on an
almost daily basis, allowing different
configurations of seats, even interchangeable body panels, to suit the owner's
changing needs or just their whims.

The American people will still want to
travel, whatever happens, and on the
evidence of the last century, their auto
industry will make sure that they can do
it in style.

PICTURE CREDITS